Restorative Justice

Healing the Effects of Crime

Jim Consedine

In honour of

JEAN STEWART

prophet, activist, Christian woman,
founder and president of the
Movement for Alternatives to Prison

and

In memory of my niece

SUZANNE ELIZABETH CONSEDINE

a bright, beautiful, compassionate, loving, wise and generous spirit who
brought an enormous amount of laughter, joy and tears to us all,
accidentally killed at Anakiwa,
3 August 1993

First published 1995, reprinted 1997.
This revised edition published 1999.
This book is copyright. Except for the purposes of fair reviewing, no part of this publication may be
reproduced or transmitted in any form, by any means, electronic or mechanical, including photocopying, recording,
or any information storage and retrieval system, without permission in writing from the publisher.

ISBN 0-473-05656-9
Copyright © 1995, 1999 Jim Consedine

Published by Ploughshares Publications, PO Box 173, Lyttelton, New Zealand.
Ploughshares Publications is a branch of Te Wairua Maranga Trust, Otautahi/Christchurch, New Zealand.

Production and design by Orca Publishing Services, Christchurch, New Zealand. Printed in Australia.

Contents

Acknowledgments

Many people have shared ideas and energy to help bring this book to fruition. The most vital role has been filled by Sue McNabb, at whose word processor I have sat for hundreds of hours mulling over the text, getting the sequence muddled and jamming the printer. Sue has not only unveiled the intricacies of computers to me, but unravelled the mess I've occasionally created, and offered critical comment on structure. Her commitment to the book has been unwavering, her kindness, generosity and support integral to its publication. I thank her sincerely.

Special thanks too must go to Cynthia Brooks for her editing. Her generous response to my invitation to edit reflects her kind and expansive spirit. Needless to say, any brickbats regarding the quality of the final copy should come my way, not hers – her job was simply to supply the spit and polish to my rather garrulous original text.

A special word of thanks also to Judge Michael Brown of Nga Puhi and Ngati Kahu, who humbled me with the content of his foreword. If ever history bestows an honour on the single most influential figure in the modern-day development of restorative justice in Aotearoa, it should go to Mick Brown. His pioneering work on youth justice set the scene for later developments both in the formulation of the Children, Young Persons and Their Families Act, and in the field of adult restorative processes.

Thanks too to various people for insights into differing chapters. Thanks to Waha Stirling of Ngai Tahu and Ngati Porou, who said this book 'had to be written', and to Judge Fred McElrea, who shares a passion for restorative justice and has the mind and courage to match his ideas. Thanks also to that prophetic figure Moana Jackson of Ngati Porou and Ngati Kohungunu for his research, encouragement and insights, which helped me understand a different but equally important vision of criminal justice for Aotearoa.

I am extremely grateful to Malama Meleisea for his guidance with the Samoan chapter, to Peter Norden S.J., of Melbourne, and Dr Bob Bellear, of Sydney, for hospitality offered and encouragement given while I researched the Australian and Aboriginal chapters, and to Howard Zehr, whose inspired writings and vision first set me alight with the possibilities for restorative justice in this country.

Thanks to Barbara Corcoran for all her help in producing this revised edition. Thanks too to Lesley Knight, who designed the cover; Marge Pollock for the logo; Martin Woodhall for the photo; and Lesley and Peter Croucher for their ideas. Thanks also to Quentin Wilson and Rachel Scott of Orca Publishing Services for their advice and encouragement.

Finally, thanks must go to my basic family groupings: my own immediate family, with whom I share a vision of justice implanted in us by our parents; the Christchurch Prison Chaplains team, who have nourished me spiritually and sustained me week in week out for many years; the members of St Joseph the Worker Parish in Lyttelton and Diamond Harbour, with whom it is a privilege to live and worship; and the extended Catholic Worker community, who offer daily friendship and support in the work of building a more just and caring society.

We are all interconnected, woven together by the grace of God and the love we share. This book is a fruit of that process in which my role, though pivotal, owes much to countless others.

Foreword

I have been involved as a practitioner in the criminal justice field for about 30 years, the last 15 of which have been as a District Court judge. For a great deal of that time I have been invaded by reservations as to our present punitive practices, which in turn have led me from time to time to question my own participation in such a system. The rationalisation that perhaps it can be better changed from within has subdued and dulled that dilemma but never laid it to rest.

For almost a decade, between 1980 and the end of 1989, I was a District Court judge in West Auckland, where I had the opportunity of observing and working with such enlightened people as Dr Peter Sharples and his team at Hoani Waititi Marae. Of particular interest was their work with Maori committees involving Maori youth who had offended. By taking matters out of the courtroom and using other venues such as marae or even school grounds, a much more egalitarian environment, I began to sense that there may be alternative ways of handling these matters.

By changing the emphasis from a punitive condemnatory stance to one where the group sought to repair the emotional and material damage of crime, I glimpsed the potential for a wider applicability of such a process and the capacity for far more creative resolution of problems.

With the advent of the Children, Young Persons and Their Families Act in 1989, particularly with the provisions for family group conferences, my enthusiasm blossomed. The undeniable success of that process with its exciting and limitless potential, particularly for victim involvement and input, has been a wonderful experience. The robustness of the exercise and the enthusiastic involvement of the police Youth Aid Section made this a most satisfying and encouraging area within which to work.

As a result various questions have presented themselves. Could we place this technique in some historical context? Is this a procedure amenable only to the Maori mind? Is this process limited only to the New Zealand situation? Does it work for other young offenders?

Subsequent interest from most of the Australian states, Britain, the United States, Sweden and South Africa has provided stimulating exchanges. In particular, the approval and support from such distinguished international scholars as Dr John Braithwaite and Professor D. L. Nathanson, as well as constructive discussion from such New Zealand scholars as Dr Gabrielle Maxwell and Dr Allison Morris, have provided an exciting stimulus to this work.

In New Zealand the research work done by my brother judge F. W. M. McElrea after study leave at Cambridge University has added a further intellectual rigidity to the concept of a restorative model. Similarly, a recent visit by Dr Howard Zehr enabled us to compare notes on work being done independently in the United States.

Now we have this significant contribution from Father Jim Consedine. In his first section on retributive justice he articulates those flaws that I and others had sensed in our present system and, in taking a comparative view from other jurisdictions, exposes the pointlessness and waste, both in fiscal terms and, more importantly, in terms of human destruction and degradation, serving only to compound the problem rather than find the solution.

This is aptly captured in the book's introduction, where he says:

> The millions of dollars we waste on building new prisons and maintaining our old ones is, generally speaking, money wasted. In no other area of public tax funds expenditure do public monies get less scrutiny in terms of positive effectiveness than in the area of penal policy.

This book is not just another diatribe against penal policy. Rather I see it as a powerful polemic, carefully sourced and widely researched, which offers a closely argued possible alternative solution.

By drawing together the universality of the restorative process with its biblical roots and even wider derivation with other cultures, the book and its message could be a blueprint for a vision that is so badly needed in contemporary Western society.

Jim Consedine's unique experience and contact with prisoners over a long period must lend to this volume a special credibility.

Apart from those marvellous insights, after so long an exposure to the raw side of humanity, it is the essential essence of Christian humanity pervading the book that makes the reader so conscious of the potential of the human spirit.

Michael J. A. Brown
Principal Youth Court Judge
Auckland, New Zealand
6 October 1994

Preface by Archbishop Desmond Tutu

Problems relating to crime and law and order are endemic throughout the world. The traditional methods of dealing with them are by focusing on retribution and punishment, with imprisonment the crown in 20th-century penal policy.

That this policy has been a proven failure stares out from every statistic from every country and jurisdiction. Crime rates continue to rise, imprisonment numbers mount endlessly, costs become astronomical.

Crime is everyone's problem. It reflects an inability of people to be just and fair in their dealings with one another. It panders to the shadow side of human nature where greed, violence and injustice lurk in each of us. Crime is a complex issue involving family background, employment opportunities, education levels, economic and social positions, as well as individual personal choice. How much crime is committed by people who themselves are the victims of fundamental injustice? Or by people whose basic human rights have never been respected?

In South Africa, street crime has escalated with the advent of liberation. While the structural crime of apartheid is now dead, its legacy lives on in the social injustice it spawned.

The solutions are complex. Imprisonment is not an answer. It should be restricted and used only for the small minority too dangerous to live in the community. New and constructive non-violent options must be pursued to enable law-breakers to take responsibility for what they have done and encourage their attempts to repair the damage. Victims too need a better deal.

The Truth Commission is a radical effort to find new non-violent ways of confronting the enormity and brutality of injustice by seeking acceptance of personal responsibility, healing, forgiveness and reconciliation as primary objects.

So too do restorative justice processes. Rooted as they are in all indigenous cultures, including those of Africa, they offer to provide a better form of criminal justice than that which currently exists. They focus on repairing the damage done through crime, on victims' needs, and on the part God's great gifts of healing, mercy and reconciliation can also play. Restorative justice is a challenge to all caring people to create a more positive, fruitful criminal justice process to carry us into and through the next millennium.

Jim Consedine's book requires us to be creative, and to see things through God's eyes as brothers and sisters of one another. Each of us has the capacity to grow through the pain and distress crime creates. Broken though many may be by horrendous offences against themselves or their loved ones, all are capable through God's healing grace of forgiveness and mercy. This is the only road that leads to reconciliation and peace.

This very ancient yet desperately needed truth lies at the heart of this book and presents a challenge to us all. It is one we ignore at our peril.

Desmond Tutu
President – Truth and Reconciliation Commission
Cape Town
South Africa

Introduction

The families of two South Auckland boys killed by a car welcomed the accused driver yesterday with open arms and forgiveness. The young man, who gave himself up to the police yesterday morning, apologised to the families and was ceremonially reunited with the Tongan and Samoan communities at a special church service last night.

The 20-year-old Samoan visited the Tongan families after his court appearance yesterday to apologise for the deaths of the two children in Mangere last Tuesday. The Tongan and Samoan communities of Mangere later gathered at the Tongan Methodist Church in a service of reconciliation. The young man sat at the feast table flanked by the mothers of the dead boys.

NZPA, 21 December 1993

One of the most lasting television images of 1993 had to be that of the families of two South Auckland boys killed by a car welcoming, with open arms and forgiveness, the accused driver and his family.

Both Tongan and Samoan communities have a tradition of restorative justice when it comes to offending in the community. This means that the wellbeing of the community and its restoration to peace and harmony are the primary values sought in the justice process.

So restoring the young man to his family and restoring the good bonds between the two communities were the primary objects. The offer of a sincere apology and its acceptance through forgiveness and mercy form the natural flow-on from such a tradition. Sanction forms a less important part of the proceedings.

The alternative response happens in mainstream society every day. We rely too often on the law, by itself a soulless set of rules, to attempt to see justice achieved. In effect, there are no mechanisms in mainstream society for reconciliation to be achieved from such a tragedy. Within the confines of the social structures of mainstream law, apology and sorrow cannot meet mercy, forgiveness and reconciliation. Instead the victims and their families are shut out of the processes from day one, and the offender awaits his or her just desserts, often in isolation, always in fear and trepidation. This usually happens in a prison cell, cut off from grieving families on both sides of the tragedy.

The consequence of this situation is an almost total lack of healing for the offender and the victim, resulting in a residue of deep bitterness and anger that can last for years.

Would that our wider society could learn from the wisdom and traditions of Polynesian New Zealanders and other indigenous peoples. Maori have a tradition of restorative justice, still in effect in many rural areas, whereby the restoration of all concerned – the victims, the offenders, the whanau, the iwi – is the principal objective.

Such a process allows a human face to be put on offending, and allows healing to occur in place of bitterness, mercy to be effected in place of retribution, and constructive sanctions to be put in place instead of useless ones such as imprisonment.

The millions of dollars we spend on building new prisons and maintaining our old ones, generally speaking, is money wasted. In no other area of state expenditure do public monies get less scrutiny in terms of positive effectiveness than in the area of penal policy.

Restorative Justice

We need to discover a philosophy that moves from punishment to reconciliation, from vengeance against offenders to healing for victims, from alienation and harshness to community and wholeness, from negativity and destructiveness to healing, forgiveness and mercy. That philosophical base is restorative justice.

A positive philosophy that embraces a wide range of human emotions, including healing, forgiveness, mercy and reconciliation, as well as sanction where appropriate, has much to offer. In New Zealand the Children, Young Persons and Their Families Act 1989 has shown that a restorative rather than a retributive philosophy bears far better fruit, but such a process is a relatively new development for modern times. Howard Zehr, an international expert in the field of criminal justice, writes:

> Throughout most of Western history, crime has been understood as an offence of one person against another person, much like other conflicts and wrongs which are treated as 'civil'. Throughout most of this history, people have assumed that the central response must be to somehow make things right; restitution and compensation were very common, perhaps normative. Crime created obligations, liabilities, that needed to be taken care of, usually through a process of negotiation. Acts of vengeance could occur, but not, it appears, as frequently as is usually assumed and the functions of vengeance may have been different to what we expect. Both victim and offender had a responsibility in this process, as did the community. The state had a role as well, but it was limited and was by necessity responsive to the wishes of victims.

This is a gross simplification, of course, but to some extent our history has been a dialectic between two modes of justice: state justice and community justice. State justice was imposed justice, punitive justice, hierarchical justice. Community justice was negotiated justice, restorative justice.

State justice has operated in some form during most of Western history. However, community justice predominated until fairly recently. Only in the past few centuries did state justice win out. The state won a monopoly on justice, but only with a great fight. The victory of state justice constituted a legal revolution of tremendous import, but a revolution which has been recognised and studied too infrequently. It is no accident that the birth of prisons – a new technology for delivering doses of pain – coincided with this legal revolution.[1]

Restorative justice is really not new. Biblical justice was restorative. So too was justice in most indigenous cultures. In pre-colonial New Zealand, Maori had a fully integrated system of restorative justice that used Maori legal processes. Many argue that the Treaty of Waitangi guaranteed its continuance. It was the traditional philosophy of Pacific nations such as Tonga, Fiji and Samoa: restorative justice was 'the Pacific way'.

Corporate Crime

We also need to reassess our understanding of crime and ask why it is that corporate crime advances virtually unhindered, while localised 'street crime' has become such an obsession for so many. The answer lies somewhere in the mixed realm of our own hidden fears and our sense of powerlessness in the face of crime, and the immense power of vested interests who gain so much from the current situation.

The *Oxford English Dictionary* gives a three-part definition for the word 'crime'. *It is an act (1) punishable by law, (2) as being forbidden by statute, or (3) injurious to the public welfare.*

As a society we focus almost exclusively on the first and second definitions, neglecting the third. Crimes are written into law at any given point in time by governments through parliaments, assemblies, decrees or proclamations. Certain actions (for example traffic offences) are made unlawful in order to protect what politicians perceive to be the interests of the common good, or else to protect and advance their own interests and those of their supporters. Thus, what may be a crime in one country, for example prostitution or cannabis smoking, may not be a crime in another.

The first two definitions do not demand a moral underpinning, though many laws and statutes obviously have a moral dimension. It is the third definition of crime as being *'an act injurious to the public welfare'* that implies a moral basis. The words demand a moral evaluation as to what constitutes public welfare or common good. This is precisely the point at issue in many areas involving corporate crime.

11

Corporate crime is endemic the world over. Very few are ever held responsible for its devastating effects. It reaches into virtually every aspect of our lives, yet so widespread is its influence, we are often unaware of its presence. It hits us in so many ways: from the added-on costs in our supermarkets to the pollutants in the air we breathe, from the hidden costs of our banking and financial systems to the costs of medicines we take for our illnesses. The tentacles of corporate crime touch all these areas and many more.

Yet we rarely speak of it, read of it, or hear of it for any sustained period. We have become totally preoccupied with individual 'street crime', although corporate violence and crime inflict far more damage on society than all the street crime combined. Just one major tobacco company, for example, arguably kills and injures more people than all the street thugs put together. Public corruption, pollution, procurement fraud, financial fraud and occupational homicide inflict incredibly serious damage on workers, consumers, citizens and the environment. [2] Ruth Morris, a world authority on corporate crime, asks the question: 'Why on earth is a criminal justice system geared to sifting the poor and minor offenders, pretending it is dealing with crime and social harm, when all the major harm is being done by the hidden rulers of our world, the multinational corporations?'[3]

A major reason for this is the consistent presentation by the media of crime as being primarily personal. Through newspapers, radio and especially talkbacks, and in news and entertainment on television, crime is deliberately portrayed in manageable portions of murder, muggings, burglaries and theft, allowing the age-old notion of scapegoat full rein. We all sit back in our chairs and like to see the 'baddies' caught.

The public perception of crime is largely shaped by corporate media and tabloid television, which focus overwhelmingly on street crime, illegal drug use, robberies and theft. If these media devoted proportionate time to the corporate muggings and homicides that are carried out through fraud, unsafe products, usurious lending policies, pollution, occupational accidents and starvation wages, public perceptions would shift to reflect reality more accurately. This will never happen. The same big business people who perpetrate corporate crime control the media through colossal advertising budgets, cross-directorships and ownership.

Yet all over the world the politicians and this same media have foisted upon the public the notion that major welfare payments to the unemployed, the sick, the hungry and the homeless are unaffordable because they cost too much. Beneficiaries are often presented as parasites preying off the common purse. Benefit fraud is almost a *cause celebre*. People everywhere are being made to work for their dole money as if they were responsible for their own plight. Yet, for example, in the United States, tax breaks and handouts for the rich ($448 billion) consume four times the amount that is spent on the poor through benefits ($130 billion).[4] Legal it may well be, but morally, this is big crime.

We are left with the question: what is real crime and who are the biggest criminals? Until we start to focus on crime in its global corporate context and not restrict ourselves merely to the localised street version, we will never learn to identify and grapple with some of the biggest criminals in our society. And we will never create a society where the common good is achieved, where people are truly respected for who they are, where true justice prevails.

The early chapters in this book will look specifically at the abysmal failure of the retributive system to administer justice fairly. The latter chapters provide insights as to how other cultures and traditions have fared under a restorative system.

The law imposed by the English, wherever they colonised, was the law always of a conquering empire. The English did to others what the Roman Empire had attempted with them – imposed their own form of imperial law. In essence it was hierarchical and centralised. In criminal matters it was retributive in nature, vengeful and punishing in effect. The restorative indigenous law of Ireland, Africa, Asia, the Pacific and the Caribbean was crushed and replaced by the imperial law of empire.

This book poses a question to nations seeking freedom and independence from former colonial masters: should not the philosophy underpinning criminal law also be reviewed? If, as this book alleges, the retributive system of criminal justice imported with colonisation is proving to be as disastrous as the statistics demonstrate, should not a free and independent nation shrug off the worst of its features, particularly if a local indigenous model promised to work better?

This book argues that the very ancient but very modern system of restorative justice would produce much more benefit for victims, offenders and society generally. Our resources and energies would be much better spent following such a philosophy. Do we really want to live in fear of criminals and violence? Many do already. Insecurity and fear are the dominant factors in their lives.

But that need not be. There are other ways: better ways, more positive and constructive ways, ways that will heal the hurt and pain of victims of crime using holistic and creative means. Why carry all that pain for a lifetime when, if the opportunity were provided, it could be dealt to and integrated into our lives? The results would lead to healing and peace of mind and a resumption of normal life.

It cannot happen under the present retributive criminal justice system. It could happen for many under a restorative one.

Footnotes
1. Howard Zehr, *Justice: the Restorative Vision,* Mennonite Central Committee, US Office of Criminal Justice, 1989
2. Russel Mokhiber, *Multinational Monitor*, December 1993
3. Ruth Morris, *From Misery Justice to Transformative Justice*, paper delivered at ICOPA Conference, Auckland, March 1997
4. Mark Zepezauer and Arthur Neiman, *Take the Rich Off Welfare*, Odionian Press, Tucson, Arizona, 1996

SECTION ONE

Retributive Justice

Each year jails take large numbers of hopeless people
and turn them into bitter hopeless people.

Time, 28 June 1993

CHAPTER ONE

Retribution: A Dead-End Street

Wayne, one of four children, was only five years old when he first got into trouble. He ran away from home and hid in a vacant house from which he stole some food. His drug-addicted mother had already had a child die at birth and another from a preventable disease at three years of age. His father, also an alcoholic drug addict, had recently returned from yet another term of imprisonment for violent assault, burglary and assorted drug offences.

When I was called to the house, Wayne was in his bedroom crying from the hiding his father had given him. His parents were anxious about how to keep him at home in the future. His thrashing wasn't an issue with them – that was the way they usually dealt with the children when they were naughty. In their own way they really did care for him and realised that their own dysfunctional behaviour was largely responsible for his plight. They didn't really know where to turn for lasting help.

The family was caught in a vicious cycle of deprivation, violence and hardship, alleviated by drugs and alcohol when money allowed. The parents' solution to their own relationship problems was usually violent, either verbally or physically. Social Welfare's options were limited. They were, on occasion, appalled at the standard of lifestyle of the family, but rightly recognised the love, tenderness and bonding that was present when things were 'going right'.

At four years of age, Wayne's chances of a drug-free or jail-free life were already minimal. His models of adult behaviour all involved violence, drugs, alcohol, unemployment and struggle. While there were brief periods of real stability and joy in his childhood, they were few and far between.

There was no possibility of his mother becoming and remaining drug-free because there was no programme within 800 kilometres that could provide the means of her coming to terms with her addiction while remaining bonded to her children. The resources were simply not there. There were no social or community workers equipped to help her learn good parenting or support her on her 'bad days'. The only option she felt she had was to call social workers at the centralised

Social Welfare office where, because of their stress-filled caseloads and her frustrations, there was often conflict. There were no jobs for her husband, who could be an excellent and willing worker but was always perceived as an ex-convict – obvious from the tattoos – and a drug addict as well. Rarely can such people find employment.

Wayne drifted through school, became bored by the age of 10, was caught stealing at the age of 11, and ended up in Social Welfare custody at 13 years of age. Now in his early twenties, he is a drug addict, has become an expert burglar, and is currently serving six years' imprisonment for the aggravated robbery of a service station. He went to jail on this sentence at the age of 17.

In order to survive he has grown devious and cunning. He is liable to emerge from prison a skilled safe-cracker, car thief and drug dealer, with a network of contacts that equals that of the 'old school tie' brigade. The taxpayers have already spent $400,000 on his tertiary 'education'. If he doesn't die violently by the time he is 30 years old – and there is a good chance he will – the government will probably have spent another $500,000 on incarceration fees. By that stage imprisonment will have harmed him almost beyond repair.

Because of stories like this, the New Zealand Catholic Bishops' Conference in 1987 described imprisonment as 'a poison in the bloodstream of the nation'. They called it an affront to human dignity, responsible for destroying, partially or totally, temporarily or permanently, those confined. They found it hard to imagine a more destructive or wasteful method of spending public funds.

The bishops were being cautious in their assessment. It is more than that. It is a deadly virus that contaminates all those associated with it. Despite the best efforts of some good staff and the positiveness of a percentage of inmates, the boredom, tedium, violence, waste, oppressive structures – the sheer inhumanity of the prison system – leaves its mark on all.

The system creates, and then exists within, a sub-culture all of its own. Few who spend any time in it ever fully recover from its negative effects on their lives. It changes people forever, and usually for the worse. Despite being well primed for it by his home life, Wayne is yet another victim of its voracious appetite.

The slim hope that he has is that the grace of God will yet intervene in his life and help him turn it around. That intervention could come in the form of a suitable habilitation programme with components that will help him face life drug- and alcohol-free, and help provide work-skill attributes that can lead him to paid employment as well.

Maybe the love of a good sensible partner will aid him in the process. It would certainly mean a tough transformation for him from the almost total self-centredness that survival and addiction have demanded to an appreciation of others. To love appropriately will be a learning process for Wayne and will not come easily, but it is still clearly possible. He will have to learn that love involves a lot more than sex.

For all that, Wayne's future appears bleak. It has been bleak right from the time he was a baby. He didn't seek drug-addicted, alcoholic, violent, unemployed parents. But to these he was born, and it is from that starting point that he must advance in life. However, the unevenness of this playing field makes it extremely difficult for him to ever catch up. He has a bigger handicap than a horse trying to win a Melbourne Cup carrying 100kg, or a New Zealand Cup starting off with a handicap of 150m. Even Cardigan Bay would not have been able to do it. The very best that Wayne can hope for is to keep touch with the pace and not get too far behind. The glittering prizes our culture holds before us as the rewards of success will never fall his way.

Any debate on social justice, law and order, crime and punishment, prisons and their effects, must always be placed in the wider social context of the society in which the debate occurs. There are cultural, economic and social influences abroad that markedly influence the type of crime committed, the levels of order and social control, the type of criminal justice system a nation has, and the role of imprisonment within that society.

For example, for widespread fraud you could be executed, or receive a heavy fine or a community-based sentence. The penalty handed down would depend on whether you lived in China or a modern capitalist Western nation. The difference in treatment flows from the culture of the people, and the ideology and rule of law imposed by its governing powers.

Most law is determined by culture and ideology. The ideology of the governing powers in Aotearoa/New Zealand is that of corporate capitalism, dominated by a particular type of monetarist capitalist ethic called the New Right. This ideology flows from a narrow consumer model of economics that allows 'market forces' to determine the various levels at which people may participate in society, contribute to it, and benefit from it.

In 1987 the Ministerial Committee of Inquiry into Violence in New Zealand produced a frightening indictment of our consumer culture. The report concluded that:

> We have the sort of society we deserve. For the past two or three decades permissiveness has gone unchecked, domestic violence is rampant, the macho image has been encouraged by advertising for commercial gain to the detriment of women, and aggressive behaviour and violence in sport have become accepted.[1]

The same violence that was analysed and condemned in 1987 is still found every day in our homes, on our streets, in our communities. It flows from a culture dedicated to the acquisition of material goods and money at the expense of practically everything else. Wayne, and a majority of imprisoned people like him,

17

never receive the rewards that society offers achievers because too often they are handicapped out of the race by the social structures in which they live.

Penal Policy

Where does crime fit into this scenario? Sarah Van Gelder, an American sociologist, suggests root causes that lead to much criminal offending:

> Crime comes about when the underpinnings of our culture fail, when the ties that hold us together, socialise our children, and satisfy our needs are broken. Just as the environmental crisis reflects our failure to act in mindfulness of the interdependence of the human species and the other living creatures of the Earth, crime reflects our blindness to the fundamental interconnectedness of people.
>
> The result of this uprooting and neglect is that the solid core of contributing adult members crumbles, and the institutions that provide the foundations of community fall apart. The community safety net is left tattered. Parents, exhausted by long hours required to make ends meet or demoralised by their inability to cope with the hardships of poverty, may turn to drugs and alcohol. Kids are left on their own in what Elliot Currie calls 'adultless communities'.[2]

The end result of breeding generations of socially dysfunctional children is the breakdown of acceptable social mores and patterns of behaviour. Crime and violence result. At the heart of our means of control of such violence we have a philosophy of retribution, vengeance and punishment. These people will all be punished more. We are a punitive people and we are now being forced to live with the fruits of our desire for revenge. At the centre of our punitive obsession is the prison system upon which we spend hundreds of millions in a single year.

In the current system all power is given over to the state – judges, police, prison wardens. Victims and offenders are left feeling powerless; victims because they are shut out of the 'justice process' right from the beginning, and offenders because they are not offered the opportunity to take any real responsibility for their behaviour and actions. Instead, the orientation is merely to punish and the twin notions of taking responsibility and making things right again are ignored. Victims and offenders are denied power and accountability.

Punishment

The aim of good law is to build a strong, safe, healthy and just society. In dealing with crime, punishment or 'just desserts' must be in proportion, must contain a message of denunciation or moral censure, and must provide protection to the community and reparation to the victims.

This book argues that, for two reasons, none of these ideals is being achieved in the current retributive system. One reason is that our social structures are so inherently unjust that achieving such ideals is impossible without social transformation. The other is that the current criminal justice system focuses primarily on punishment.

The basic assumption about the relationship between criminal justice and punishment needs to be re-examined. Punishment is the deliberate infliction of suffering: it is legal violence. This book claims that punishment is counter-productive and needs fresh examination, as does the system that perpetuates it. This system is revealed as an emperor with no clothes. The idea that it can be reformed is a myth. That it is the only or best way of dealing with offenders is not true.

Let's take an illustration. Most big white-collar fraudsters are on bail until sentencing date, are given almost automatic minimum-security status within the prison system, and are released at the earliest possible date – usually after one-third of their sentence. On the other hand, blue-collar drug-addicted burglars, who usually have done much less social harm, are often remanded in custody until sentence, remain in medium-secure conditions while in jail (fewer privileges, worse prison conditions), and serve two-thirds of the sentence imposed.

In both cases, the punishment inflicted not only fails to achieve positive change in the offenders but guarantees a high chance of re-offending. It does not treat people fairly, gives a muddied message of moral censure (gross white-collar crime can be very profitable), provides no reparation to the victims, and only partially protects the community. Repeat offending upon release will be inevitable and will encompass fresh victims.

Punishment has become something the dominant group in society imposes on those of little status and power who are not in a position to challenge its fairness or its usefulness. The political authorities are seen to be doing something about crime, but because what they are doing is counter-productive and actually a cause of more offending, crime rates continue to climb and more and more disempowered people get caught in its net.

The adversarial legal system spawned by the logic of punishment, as Canadian criminal justice consultant Lorraine Berzins says:

> ...is actually destructive of some of justice's most cherished objectives: the shared sense of what is right and wrong, the holding to account for wrongdoing, the affirming of the importance of the rights of the person injured, the sense of proportionality to the gravity of the misconduct, and the prevention of further harm.

Today, the legal industry turns the search for justice into a game of technicalities played between lawyers in court. The central focus is that a law has been broken. This message overrides the victim's priorities and considerations, as well as any other rational concern for protection, rehabilitation and ultimate healing of the relationship with the victim or the community. The entire symbolic message of denunciation must be carried by the length of prison sentence that is broadcast in headlines to the rest of the community.[3]

Imprisonment breaks down social personality and disempowers people. The vast majority of prison inmates become more self-centred and dependent on others during their time in prison. When one's world is reduced to a 3m by 2m cell and survival becomes the driving instinct, self-interest and self-centredness become major preoccupations.

Food becomes a primary concern and mealtimes become the focal point of waking hours. Life is trivialised. Mortgages, the kids, employment, your relationship with your spouse or partner, the depleting ozone layer and the nuclear threat are replaced as the major issues by the quality of the food, the amount of television viewing allowed, and the body odour of your cell-mate.

Imprisonment distorts and twists the psyche and the spirit of the imprisoned. For those already disturbed when they arrive, it aggravates their condition. Imagine a rapist sent to prison for 10 years lying day after day, night after night in a cell, dwelling on sexual fantasy and distorted visions. Imprisonment simply reinforces twisted thinking and unreal expectations of life. For many it guarantees more serious re-offending, which means more victims, more hurt, more pain and, for some, more terror.

It also has a destructive impact on innocent family members. Can anyone who has not experienced it have any idea of the horrific effect imprisonment has on family life? The impact is often horrendous when a principal adult figure is removed from the family. Children may lose a father or mother, parents a son or daughter. They are often then farmed out to relatives or the state for the duration of the sentence.

Alternatively, a spouse is left to survive as a single parent. Whatever strains existed in the relationship before the sentence are exacerbated by it, often to breaking point. The family is thrown onto a state benefit, which these days is often not enough to survive upon adequately. The model of adulthood placed before growing impressionable children is that of dad or mum who is a prisoner, a bad person, a jailbird, a convict.

Even visiting your loved one in prison is impossible for some. Most prisons in New Zealand are situated in the country and transport services are infrequent, if they exist at all. It's not hard to imagine the struggle some spouses must go through to bring themselves and their children out to see mum or dad between certain limited hours on a Saturday. This occurs week after week, often with little or no spare money or wider family support. Then there are the children at school – who is there to help the young people cope with the ignominy of having a parent in jail?

Former prison inmate Mike Martin writes:

> Prison may change people, it may cause some to be more crafty, but because of its punitive nature it is incapable of turning them into anything other than a lifetime liability to society.
>
> It is the very structure of penal policy that reinforces the inadequacies that lead to a criminal lifestyle in the first place. The more we elect to hide our small social problems behind high walls, the more deeply entrenched will be the problems that led people there. Worse than that is the fact that the offspring of our current jail population will soon follow in their parents' footsteps.
>
> Prisons cater to a public need: a need based on fear and ignorance; a desire to punish through retribution. It doesn't have to be that way, in fact such an attitude is little more than a mass cop-out. What we have developed after 100 years of penal policy is a vast and costly delaying mechanism. Imprisonment is used to delay confronting the real problems facing the community: it stops (for a while) an offender indulging in more crime; it delays social progress. It offers a breather and gives us a chance not to think about how to deal with the additional problems that will face the inmate on release.
>
> For 'justice' to mean anything, it must extend beyond a punitive reaction to an unacceptable action. Justice must mean much more than simply transferring a criminal from general society to a hidden society. The present method of justice is compounding the alienation of each individual. It is bonding people together within the source of their alienation.[4]

The great majority of prisoners are not murderers, rapists or desperate villains. They are ignorant young men under 30 who have failed at school or have been failed by school, and have no strong family or community links with anybody of sense. Their offences relate mainly to drink, drugs and cars. They are limited in their understanding of the difference between right and wrong and are in urgent need of education in every way. We, for our own future protection, are in urgent need that they should be educated.[5]

Many would argue that we have lost sight of the moral base underpinning both the law and our criminal justice system. As a result the aims of both are no longer clear to all. It is appropriate then to reflect on both law and morality if we are to ever recover or develop a social system that is clear in its objectives and fair to all.

Law and Morality

We are a nation with Western Judaeo-Christian traditions. This has had enormous impact on our social institutions, none more so than the law. Interpretations of scripture and the teachings of the Church from the 13th century on have helped shape the body of law we have inherited and our understanding of it.

Law has two dimensions, moral and legal. It is built on morality and is never neutral, always reflecting a system of values. Justice, truth, honesty, compassion and respect for people are the basic tenets of an acceptable morality that should seek to protect and enhance the common good.

Law and justice then are, regrettably, not synonymous terms. The law is not sacrosanct and never should be. What is sacrosanct is true justice, the dignity and equality of people, and respect for the human person over and above every other consideration.

In a secular society, good law and justice have to have the protection and enhancement of the common good as their starting point. Problems arise when the law is written by powerful interest groups with little feeling for the common good. This is the basis for unjust law, and the laws of apartheid were a stark illustration of this. It is worth noting that in countries such as the United States, Australia, Britain and New Zealand strong sectional interests have also had a major input into legislation; sometimes, it would seem, with scant regard for the common good. Good government should define, defend and protect the common good, particularly when there is a conflict of interest. This is precisely what Parliament in a true democracy should be about.

The promotion of the common good – that is, the good of the many as it is appreciated and understood by the majority – is at the heart of a fair and just moral code and central to the creation of good law. If the common good is to be achieved, our Judaeo-Christian heritage still has a special contribution to make. This religious tradition demands that the poor, the sick, the dispossessed and vulnerable minorities be especially protected. International covenants such as the United Nations Declaration of Human Rights and, in Aotearoa, the Treaty of Waitangi, seek to provide the same protection.

In our society this provision has clearly been eroded and massive injustice has resulted. The fruits of that injustice are everywhere. Poverty, racism and street kids are just three of many symptoms. The very fabric of our society is being strained and nowhere are its effects being felt more than in the criminal justice system.

I no longer believe that the retributive philosophy underpinning our criminal justice system can always offer a fair and just way of practising law. It no longer gives people justice in anything like the sense outlined above. Too often it fails to protect the common good. Certainly the poor more than anyone else get hammered by it. An adversarial court system that seeks to win regardless of the facts is just one blind spot in it. Its enormous costs in both human and financial terms are others. The elimination of victims from its central equation is another.

A philosophy primarily based on negative features such as punishment and vengeance is creating throughout the world a monster the likes of which will make the next century a living hell of fear of crime for a large portion of the world's people. It already is for many people in large cities.

As Howard Zehr says:

> Retributive justice defines justice the Roman way, as right rules, measuring justice by the intention and the process... All action is hierarchical, from the top down. The state acts on the offender, with the victim on the sidelines. Retributive justice as we know it views everything in purely legal terms. As Nils Christie has said, legal training is trained tunnel vision. In law school you are taught that only legally defined issues are relevant.[6]

We have failed to address the shortcomings of the retributive system and accept why it has proved to be such an abject failure in terms of addressing rising crime rates, the rights of victims, and the health and wellbeing of the community. A philosophy built on negativity can only produce negative results.

We should have learnt from the German experience. Professor Christian Pfeiffer, speaking at a conference in Perth, reported that 20 years ago West Germany had a sharp 50 percent increase in the use of imprisonment, with the inmate level rising to nearly 50,000 in 1983. From then on there was a sharp decline. Why did this happen?

The nation at the time was indulging in prison reform. The Social Democratic government, which came to power in 1972, had as one of its goals the reform of the prison system. They sought to make the system rehabilitative – really useful to society – and to educate young offenders in the institutions so as to make them better people afterwards. They passed legislation, built more prisons and invested a lot of effort in employing more social workers and psychologists.

This approach completely failed. Despite all the effort there was no change in the re-offending rate. Research on young offenders found 44 percent were unemployed when they entered prison and 66 percent were unemployed half a year after release, despite a lot of job training and meaningful activities while they were in prison.

Why did it happen? Because society does not accept ex-prisoners, and the inmates were insecure knowing that. They were theoretically prepared for the job market, but ill-prepared for the negative response they received from society. The recidivism rate remained at around 90 percent both before and after the new approach.

So the Germans changed tack: mediation within the community became the new approach. They used the insights of modern criminology to create varying non-custodial sentencing options. A wide range of community justice programmes were introduced, which, rather than seeking to punish offenders, sought to develop their life skills, self-esteem and sense of responsibility. Judges were urged to use fewer remands in custody and sentences of imprisonment. Research into judges' sentencing patterns revealed that 20 percent of judges were responsible for 50 percent of the jail sentences, so these judges were encouraged to change.

Prosecutors were urged to use their discretion and dismiss more cases where diversion was applicable or prosecution less warranted. New prison construction was halted, and widespread reparation was introduced.

Within a few years imprisonment numbers had been reduced by 20 percent throughout Germany, and in some cities, such as Berlin, by more than 50 percent. In the same period crime rates dropped significantly and the re-offending rate was reduced substantially.[7]

It is interesting to note that in Japan police, prosecutors and judges share an overriding mission to correct rather than punish, incapacitate or rehabilitate. American law professor John Haley, whose special expertise is Japanese law, reports that from the initial police interrogation to the final judicial hearing or sentencing, the vast majority of those accused of criminal offences confess, display repentance, negotiate for their victim's forgiveness and submit to the mercy of the authorities.

In return they are treated with extraordinary leniency, gaining at the very least the prospect of having their case dropped from the formal process altogether. To justify such leniency, law-enforcement officials must be satisfied the offender and the community are working together to compensate the victim and restore peace. Offenders' families become involved and, with the community, accept responsibility to ensure that steps will be taken to prevent further misconduct and provide some means of control. In addition, the victim must express forgiveness.[8]

The Japanese statistics are compelling. It is estimated the police do not report up to 40 percent of all apprehended offenders. Of those reported, prosecutors suspend up to one-third of all cases. For those who get to court, judges suspend sentences in nearly 60 percent of adjudicated cases. Only a fraction of offenders go to prison. Japan's imprisonment rate is 37 per 100,000 population, or about one-quarter the New Zealand rate. The most recent studies of recidivism indicate that the more lenient the treatment of offenders, the less likely the offender is to commit another offence within three years.

Perception versus Reality
If this is the case, then there is obviously a massive gap between public perception of how to deal with crime and the reality. There is also a huge gap between what people perceive to be the level of crime in the community and the real level. Here the media play a crucial role.

In October 1994 a young woman in South Carolina named Susan Smith spoke tearfully of the anguish she was enduring as a result of her two children being abducted. On nationwide television she begged for their return, claiming that a masked black man had been responsible. In South Carolina, a former slave state, that claim touched a deep nerve among white residents. The nation was stunned at the callousness of the act. Yellow ribbons, signs of hope and a safe return, were wrapped around trees. Candle-lit prayer vigils were held throughout the land. Mass media carried her story around the world, and President Clinton made a special statement. Dozens interviewed on television spoke of their insecurity regarding their children, and wondered out loud what was happening to America. It was no longer a safe place to bring up kids. Who would be next?

Then the facts emerged. The children were dead and their mother had killed them. After nine days, Susan Smith was arrested and charged with double murder. But the perception portrayed by the media of an unsafe, insecure environment for children will long remain etched into the scarred emotional tissue of the nation.

People in the United States should feel the safest in the world. In 25 years, since 1968, in order to make themselves safer and feel more secure, they have increased their prison population by a whopping 700 percent. Yet do Americans feel any more secure as a result? No way, it seems. In 1994 they voted to double that rate again within the next decade. Will they feel safer and more secure then? I fear the answer will still be no.

The same policy has been followed in New South Wales. There, the upping of the hype by politicians calling for harsher penalties in the early part of this decade resulted in a massive 60 percent increase in imprisonment and the construction of five new prisons. Next door in the state of Victoria, where the crime rate is virtually the same but where there was no political hype, the imprisonment rate remained constant at about half the NSW rate.

This trend is all about public perception and has little, if anything, to do with reality. To tackle the causes of crime and deal with the causes of criminal offending requires a much more mature, informed response. But public fear sells newspapers, raises TV ratings and gets politicians elected. It leaves the rest of us with a legacy of a continued high crime rate, insecurity and financial indebtedness.

The media, especially television, must take some responsibility for the distorted perception they present of crime in the community. It fuels public fear and insecurity, which in turn tend to influence politicians in their legislative role and judges in their sentencing. How often does the television news start its presentation with two or three crime stories, one after the other? An armed hold-up here, a sex offender sentenced there, and a shoot-out in Miami or Rome to bring an international dimension. This type of 'news' has become part of the daily television diet, beamed into family home across the country.

Who gains from such coverage? Only the television companies, the advertisers and the titillated. Often the police have had to remind us, after saturation coverage of a particularly nasty crime, that this is still a safe country to live in.

It's not that the stories are necessarily inaccurate, (though it is difficult to see how much balance one can get in a 15-second 'bite'). It's the portrayal of society that is the most distorted. Listening to talkback radio shows how distorted the public perception of crime is. Seeing crime stories every day leads people to feel that the community is full of criminals waiting to attack. That is simply not true.

Conclusion

Retributive justice is a philosophy that is bankrupt. Just how bankrupt it is will be clearly seen in the following four chapters, which look at its effect in New Zealand, Britain, Australia and the United States. It no longer offers any positive contribution to the wellbeing of communities or the development of a just social fabric for society. As Christchurch lawyer Wolfgang Rosenberg says, '… The public cry for retribution shows that we are still close to barbarism. Civilisation begins when vendetta ends.'

Its deformed stepchild, the prison system, is an even bigger evil. Prison is a dead-end street. Socially, morally, financially and spiritually, it is a cancer eating away at the heart of the human community. It is as evil and obsolete as slavery. While most acknowledge the need for a few dangerous offenders to be kept locked away from society, such offenders need to be kept in a positive, constructive, secure environment where they are still treated with respect.

For the rest there are creative, community-based alternatives, including a wide range of city, urban and marae-based habilitation centres. The 1989 Prison Systems Review headed by a former High Court judge, the late Sir Clinton Roper, recommended more community work options and employment schemes. These, the review said, should be coupled with genuine preventative programmes such as parenting groups, co-operative neighbourhood work schemes, more free adult education courses, and the development of good local health-care programmes.

The millions of dollars wasted so sinfully on the prison system could be freed up to provide the resources necessary to attack crime at its very roots, thus preventing its development and escalation.

Footnotes

1. Report, Ministerial Committee of Inquiry into Violence, Government Print, Wellington, 1987
2. Sarah Van Gelder, 'The Ecology of Justice', *In Context* No 38
3. Lorraine Berzins, article in the *National Prison Project Journal*, Spring 1993
4. Mike Martin, *NZ Listener*, 22 June 1985
5. *Sunday Times* (UK), 1 May 1994
6. Howard Zehr, *IARCA Journal*, International Association of Residential and Community Alternatives, March 1991
7. Professor Christian Pfeiffer, paper, 'Criminal Justice: An Alternative View', from the conference 'Prison, the Last Option', 18-19 October 1991, published by the Anglican, Catholic, and Uniting Church of Australia
8. John Haley, *Crime and Justice Network Newsletter*, Mennonite Central Committee, Pennsylvania, September 1991

CHAPTER TWO

New Zealand Criminal Justice:
A Punitive Obsession

> The evil of our prison system is that not only are our prisons generating more criminal activity, but they are promoting crime.
>
> *Peter Williams Q.C.*

In May 1993 an 80-year-old Auckland man was sentenced in the Auckland District Court to six months' imprisonment for benefit fraud. The sentence for this World War II veteran was confirmed by a High Court judge on appeal.

The sentence came in a week that saw the Minister of Justice, Doug Graham, and the head of the Justice Department's criminal justice section, Mel Smith, calling for imprisonment to be used only as last resort.[1] It was a sentence that highlighted the punitive nature of New Zealand society and the inability of the judiciary and courts to look beyond their tunnel vision to see what is appropriate and what is not in sentencing options.

That New Zealand is a punitive society can become very clear to anyone listening to a radio talkback session any day of the week. Mel Smith says that as a society we are more puritanical than, for example, Australians, and we prosecute people for a wide range of behaviour ignored overseas. He says there is more reporting of crime in New Zealand and our police force is better at catching offenders. Criminals who a few years ago attracted fines are now being sent to periodic detention, often because they cannot pay. The next time they offend, they end up in prison. They can, and should be, dealt with outside the prison system.[2]

Doug Graham agrees. He says our imprisonment rates are higher because we live in a society that exacts revenge. People are more interested in revenge than in some other elements of criminal justice.[3]

We should have recognised the opportunities offered by the 1989 Prison System Review of Sir Clinton Roper and his team and created a parallel system of sanction that dealt to the causes of offending. A nationwide series of habilitation centres would already have been producing the fruits of their endeavours and, if Justice Department figures are anything to go by, would have been reducing re-offending.

> The evidence suggests that well-run treatment programmes for some types of criminal offenders can reduce the incidence of re-offending substantially. Given good conditions, reductions in reconvictions of 15-20 percent can be expected.[4]

Three pilot programmes initiated in 1993 have commenced. Unfortunately, instead of following the suggestions of the Roper Report, the government decided that the programmes would be run post-early release and for a strictly limited number. This undermined the concept. Partially strangling the proposal at birth has meant positive results have been slow in coming.

All the indications are that there is very little political will to grapple realistically with crime and its consequences. Instead, a 19th-century rationale and process remain at the heart of the nation's response.

New Zealand politicians simply do not take crime seriously. For too many their tub-thumping, emotive, vote-catching spiels reflect ignorance and prejudice rather than intelligent comment. If the politicians did take crime seriously, they would have developed a pan-party national strategy to hit the causes of so much offending – male violence, drug and alcohol addiction, unemployment, sexual aberration, spiritual and cultural alienation, motor-car addiction.

In 1995 we imprisoned at a rate of 130 per 100,000 population. Queensland jailed at a rate of 71, Victoria 51, Ireland 44, Holland 39, the Philippines 22. By September 1998, the New Zealand rate was 165 per 100,000. In 1981 we jailed 3531 adults. This figure had grown to 5500 by 1999 and the projected figure for 2005 is 6700.[5]

When it comes to numbers within the wider corrections system, including periodic detention and community services, New Zealand is way ahead of any Australian state and all of the above-mentioned countries with a whopping 756 people per 100,000 of population. This is despite the fact that the rate of offending in Aotearoa has been similar to and sometimes lower than that in these other states and countries.

The imprisonment rate increased by 58 percent in the decade from 1987-96. Sentences got longer, with 75 percent of inmates serving a sentence of more than 12 months. Almost 60 percent of inmates have committed some type of violent offence. Despite more punitive legislation and harsher penalties, number of convictions for violence has increased by 89 percent since 1987. In 1998, 18 percent of the total inmate population was under 20 years of age.

> Furthermore, analysis in modelling undertaken by the Ministry of Justice suggests that the steady rise in the prison population is, under current policies, likely to

continue in the foreseeable future with the population projected to grow 190 per 100,000 by the year 2005. Some of this growth is undoubtedly attributable to an increase in the number and seriousness of cases coming before the courts. But it is undeniable that there has also been an increase in severity of sanctions. This is demonstrated, for example, by the fact that between 1987 and 1996 the average sentence length for rape increased by 21%, injuring or wounding by 32%, robbery by 44%, burglary by 31% and fraud by 22%. In short, recent social changes tend to be producing a more and more draconian penal culture, and under the conventional model we seem to be powerless to halt or reverse that trend.[6]

We imprison far more and it is costing us heaps: around $350 million annually. Some 3000 staff are needed to provide round-the-clock surveillance. The average annual cost of holding an inmate in 1997-98 was $51,000.[7]

The truth of the matter is that many offenders who in New Zealand go to jail, would receive community-based sentences elsewhere. And many offenders who receive community-based sentences here, especially periodic detention, would receive fines or a non-supervisory sentence elsewhere.

The New Zealand criminal justice system has close to the largest number of people per capita under its control of any Western nation. As Minister of Justice Doug Graham said in a speech in 1991:

> The probability is that if prison sentences in the vast majority of cases were halved, the crime rate would not increase and the public would be no less safe.[8]

All the evidence is that long prison sentences and increased prison numbers do not lower crime rates. The number of New Zealanders in prison has increased every year since 1980, the population level has remained reasonably static at 3.3 million people, yet the crime rate has soared.

The Justice Department report to Parliament in 1993 said that despite the prison muster rise and harsher mandatory sentences, imprisonment numbers and crime continued to increase. The report also said the department was convinced that the continued use of prison sentences was not succeeding in reducing crime.

This confirms all the overseas research, which shows exactly the same pattern. For example, in Texas, Nevada and Florida, where the imprisonment rate is higher and sentences longer than anywhere else in the United States, the crime rate is approximately the same as in states such as Minnesota and Hawaii, where the imprisonment rate is one-fifth to one-quarter the size.[9]

Sociologist Greg Newbold believes that tough prisons produce tough citizens who are dangerous inside or outside prison. He quotes figures from the United States to show that harsher penalties and tighter security in jails lead to higher crime rates. In 1986 the average sentence for robbers was four years' imprisonment. By 1991 it had risen to seven and a half years. Yet there was no real sign of a reduction in the number of robberies being committed.

Since 1976, when capital punishment was re-introduced, largely as a deterrent, homicides have increased from 16,600 per year to more than 20,000, and death rows in most states are bulging. The implication is that the tougher we make prisons and the longer we make sentences, the greater will be the crime rate and the more horrendous the nature of some of the crimes committed.[10]

During 1997, 428 additional cells were built and a further 348 in 1998. A new 180-bed remand facility replacing the antiquated Addington Prison was opened in 1999. In addition, the government has let contracts for its first private prisons in Auckland. This includes a new remand facility at Mt Eden.[11]

Imprisonment: The Facts

There are several facts that need to be noted about imprisonment.

1. The Poor Go to Prison

The 1981 Penal Policy Review of Mr Justice Casey put it starkly:

> Most offenders are disadvantaged, handicapped emotionally or spiritually, immature or merely stupid. Very few are motivated by what moralists of the older generation would call 'the forces of evil'.[12]

According to the Justice Department a pen portrait of the average inmate goes like this:

> Aged 27, three-quarters are single, divorced, separated or widowed. About two-thirds are beneficiaries, three-quarters unemployed, half have severe alcohol and/or drug problems (two-thirds of women inmates), half have had psychiatric assessment, half come from broken homes, nine out of 10 have no formal qualifications, and only a handful own their own homes or have significant assets. A little fewer than half are Pakeha, the rest Polynesian.[13]

This picture is the same in every similar country in the world. The poor, the dispossessed, the vulnerable, the sick and the addicted are those who fill our prisons.

Interestingly, even having a job with poverty-line wages is no guarantee that one can avoid imprisonment. A study undertaken in 1993 by Tony Short, senior law lecturer at the University of South Australia, showed that the employment contracts system had been a large contributor to New Zealand's having the worst crime rate in the industrialised world.

His report compared his research with a Dutch Justice Ministry study based on surveys in 1989 and 1992 among 55,000 people in 20 countries.[14] He concluded that the act was a significant cause of poverty and misery. It had succeeded in driving down wages in low-skill industries, which in turn had led to increased poverty and crime. Both reports found that the two were clearly linked.[15]

2. Imprisonment Increases Crime Rates

Prisons, long known as 'universities of crime', are a primary place to recruit new friends and new gang members, learn new criminal skills, plan new crimes. Much of the daily conversation among inmates involves bragging about what has been done in the past and what might be possible in the future. Many major crimes are performed by groups of ex-prison inmates who combine their various skills to perform the crime. Often they have been colleagues in prison. Fellow graduates.

Most of the horrific crimes of rape and murder committed in recent years have been carried out by ex-inmates. All prison did for them was harden them in their attitudes, make them more bitter, and set them up emotionally and socially to perform some horrendous act of violence. Upon release they became walking time-bombs.

Yet where is the public outcry at the abysmal failure rate of our prison system? Why are we not demanding some positive results? If the education or health system failed as regularly and made people less literate and more sick, the streets would be packed with demonstrators demanding value for their tax dollar. Why doesn't it happen for the criminal justice system? It has proven to be a total failure now for decades.

Such failed policies as the increased penalties of the 1980s have guaranteed some of the horrific crime of the 1990s. In 1982 only 18 percent of offenders (excluding traffic cases) were imprisoned or received periodic detention. By 1991 that figure had reached 39 percent. The number of convictions had not risen – what had risen was the rate of imprisonment and periodic detention as the means of sanction.[16]

Statistics show that most prison inmates are affected by one or other or all of the following problems: drug addiction, illiteracy, dyslexia, alcohol addiction, a propensity for violence, unemployment, poverty, the absence of a meaningful spirituality and the ethics and values that flow from it, self-hatred, sexual aberration. A high proportion of crime flows from the inability of the person to deal adequately with life because of the effects of one or other of these deficiencies.

For example, it has been estimated that up to 75 percent in some prisons cannot read and write well enough to cope with everyday aspects of life such as filling out forms or reading a newspaper. Yet there is growing evidence that when dyslexia, hearing problems and illiteracy are tackled, a dramatic change in the outlook on life results for the newly literate. Their self-esteem mushrooms, their confidence expands and there is a flow-on effect into other areas of life.[17]

More than 75 percent of inmates have a problem with alcohol or drugs or both. It stands to reason that if such cases were dealt with by adequate programmes backed by the substantial resources required, re-offending would drop. The fact that a parallel system of habilitation centres, some of which could have focused on drug and alcohol addictions, has yet to become a reality while an extra $180 million has been spent since 1989 on new prisons and upgrading old ones is indicative of where the Justice Department's priorities lie.

3. Imprisonment Brutalises People

It is difficult to assess just how damaged people can be by a prison sentence. For those who go immediately to new minimum-security facilities, the damage may be minimal. But for the majority who have to spend time in our larger institutions, prison life can brutalise. There are many ways this can happen.

Any notion of self-responsibility is abolished upon entry. You are there to do as you are told, when you are told. You lose most of the control of your life and its direction. Decisions are made, orders given, and a paramilitary-type structure implements the orders.

Your senses are under attack – by noise, by yelling from guards and inmates, by televisions and radios going at all hours of the day and into the night. You adapt and cope but are desensitised in so doing. Then there is the tedium and boredom, the real killers in our prison system. As Phil Berrigan says, it is a deadly abrasive that works upon a person's spirit like wind and water on loose soil. The erosion that results is very nearly inevitable. How depressing, he says, to see men of intelligence and accomplishment licking their wounds like punished children, feasting on distractions, and longing uncritically for a society that has misused them. Tedium feeds on drabness and routine. As such it is a real form of structural violence.[18]

Then there is the physical violence. One in six inmates is kept in a special wing away from others for fear of physical violence. The macho culture of the prison sees to it that few people escape its all-embracing effects. 'Control squads' of prison officers are designated in all major prisons to quell disturbances and violence. That we need them as part of a national policy is merely indicative of how violent prison can be.[19]

In February 1991 inmates smuggled reports out of Mt Eden Prison in Auckland that gave a picture of conditions among the worst in the country. For example, in East Block, a wing of the prison, they claimed the following constituted their daily routine and living conditions.

> Unlocked at 6am for 10 minutes to collect breakfast. Locked in cell until 8am. Spend time in the exercise yard. At 10am returned to the wing for showers, and lunch is served between 10.30 and 11am. Locked in the cell from 11am until 1pm. Locked in the yard from 1pm until 3.30pm, then returned to the wing and served dinner. Locked away until the next day to start the routine again. The total hours of lock-up are 18 out of 24 hours. All meals are eaten in the cell.
>
> The cells are grim, grimy concrete caves with two steel beds and a toilet.

Poor natural lighting comes from a 50cm by 25cm barred window. Even during daylight on a sunny day the light has to be turned on to enable you to read. The floor of the cell is bitumen, a breeding ground for germs. The walls in most cells are filthy and the wiring in some of the cells is exposed and in a dangerous condition.

A cell is about the size of an average bathroom, and if you can imagine spending 18 hours a day in your bathroom, eating, sleeping and relieving yourself in the company of your cell-mate, you start to have an idea of what it is like. The difference is that the average bathroom is clean.

The exercise yard is a concrete compound with a lean-to at one end. In the corner of the lean-to is a toilet, urinal and cold-water shower, all open to the view not only of other inmates but of the officers who overlook the yards. Many of the officers are women. The other half of the structure has wooden benches and a TV set, where men huddle when it is windy or raining. Often it is standing room only. The only exercise equipment provided by the Justice Department is a plastic football.

At the moment the muster is 59 men. When we are let in for a shower at 10am, the water remains hot for about 10 minutes. There are six shower heads for the whole wing. On Mondays we have a change of underwear, and on Thursdays a full kit change. During kit change there always seem to be female officers present even if they have not been on duty in the wing during the day. The whole system is dehumanising and demoralising.[20]

The taxpayer invests over $50,000 a year on average per prisoner to keep this iniquitous situation in force.

4. Imprisonment Wrecks Relationships

Thousands of families have a partner torn from their midst and imprisoned every year in New Zealand. For the one imprisoned this means the heart-wrenching effects of being isolated from spouse and children, and the fear of never quite knowing what they are doing at any given time. For some there is a constant worry as to whether a partner is remaining faithful on the outside. 'Dear John' letters are not uncommon in prison. There is also the loss of employment for many upon their imprisonment.

As noted earlier, for the families the break can be even harder. There is the stigma of having a spouse, a son or daughter, a brother, a partner, a sister in prison. There is the ignominy for some of having to be supported on state benefits. Being dependent on welfare is not everybody's cup of tea. There is the added stress of trying to maintain a relationship when contact is limited to one hour a week. For many, even getting to the prison is a difficulty since they have no transport and some of the larger prisons (Paremoremo, Rolleston, Paparua, Waikeria) are in rural areas. It is often the family who do the hardest part of the sentence.

5. Drugs in Prison

A drug-addicted veteran of the New Zealand prison system, writing in the magazine *Wide Appeal* (Issue Zero, February 1994), spoke of having used most drugs while doing time over 12 years, including everything from cannabis to morphine:

> I believe people use drugs in jail mainly to escape the reality of confinement. It is a mental state of escaping. When you are stoned on drugs in jail, you are in another reality that is not prison (hopefully!). A group of blokes that use drugs is often called 'the crew'. Getting stoned within the crew is an everyday thing. The crew live and breathe drugs. Drugs are their existence, their reality, their life. Without the use of drugs these inmates can become very depressed and angry. Hanging out for days is possibly more damaging than using. I have seen men nearly kill for drugs, and escape 'over the wall' in order to 'escape' again when they score.
>
> I have seen many dangerous situations where the inmate is too stoned to know what he is doing, where one crew is fighting another crew because one group has more dope than the other. To be part of a 'drug crew' may even be something other inmates look up to. Using syringes is common, yet there are very few syringes available. They are hard to obtain and have to be smuggled in. Sharing the 'gun' or the syringe becomes par for the course, so the Hepatitis C virus moves on and on and on!
>
> I have noticed over the years the number of inmates using drugs has risen alarmingly. Compared to 10 years ago, when there would be 35 percent using, now it's 90 percent using one form of drug or another. There is no way the Justice Department can stop drugs being brought into prison. If an inmate wants drugs then he will think of a way to get them. Due to cost-cutting in prisons there is very little treatment for drug users. If an inmate is released from prison with a drug habit, what start has he or she in society? They will only link up with their drug peers and the circle of offending will only continue.

One of the anomalies of imprisonment is that prison is the place where some inmates first get introduced to drugs. They go in clean and can come out drug addicts. That drugs are readily available in prisons is known by all who live and work in them. In January 1994, the MP for Wellington-Karori, Mrs Pauline Gardiner, herself a former drug counsellor, told of a former Christchurch inmate who ran up a $6000 drug debt while in prison.[21]

A 1992 Justice Department report found that over two-thirds of female inmates and roughly half of men in prison were identified as having some sort of problem with substance abuse. Drugs used most frequently were marijuana, tranquillisers and opiates. Just over two-thirds of the men and just over half of the women indicated they had not discussed or received any help for their substance abuse while in prison.

Fleur Grenfell, general manager of Arohata Prison, says it is not unusual for inmates to be introduced to drugs in prison.

> I hate to see glue sniffers turning into needle users. But you put druggies together and that is what you are going to get.[22]

As for getting off drugs while in prison, for most it is impossible. Timaru-based alcohol and drug centre worker Debbie Martin pointed out to a Christchurch conference the difficulty of coming off drugs in jail.

> Intravenous drug users who have a habit find they are unable to stop it if they go to jail and there is not always effective treatment for them. So they have continued to use drugs.[23]

The co-ordinator of Christchurch PARS, the Prisoners Aid and Rehabilitation Society, Kathy Dunstall, disclosed that PARS officers regularly see inmates and former inmates with debts of $200-300 for drugs brought in prison. Pressure could be exerted on inmates while they were in prison and after their release.

Inmates take drugs to escape the boredom of prison life, and some acquire their addictions while serving their sentence.[24]

The problem does not stop there. Pressure is often brought to bear on vulnerable partners and spouses of inmates by outside contacts of drug-selling prisoners to pay for jail drug debts. Threats and intimidation are not uncommon in securing such payment.

New harsher surveillance of drugs in prison during 1998-99 has resulted in some curtailment of the flow of drugs into prisons. Visitors entering prisons can now be searched at random. Drug tests of inmates can be conducted at any time, and have resulted in harsher conditions and additional punishments for those caught with drugs.

6. Prisons Are Recruitment Grounds

There is no better recruitment area for criminal behaviour and gang and club membership than prisons. This is not necessarily always a negative thing. If a person is recruited by one of the more progressive and mature gangs or motorcycle clubs, then for the first time a young offender might find a sense of identity and self-esteem. More often, though, it is the heavy gangs, well into criminal activity, who do the most recruiting. The rise of 'white power' gangs in the community and of some of the more disreputable Maori and Polynesian groupings can be directly attributed in part to the time spent in prison by members.

For a person wishing to break his or her gang affiliations, prison can prove to be an impossible place to be. Many young men and women recruited as teenagers into gangs wish to break off their association as they mature, raise families and seek a different lifestyle. Prison reinforces gang affiliations and makes it extremely difficult for members wishing to make the break to do so.

7. Deterrence is a Myth

One of the most frequent phrases heard from sentencing judges is that the sentence to be imposed will help deter other offenders. Every person working with offenders knows that to be simply a myth. It is a concept promoted by middle-class educated people about themselves. They are saying that the threat of imprisonment and exposure would deter others like them from offending.

Recently the rape sentence maximum was raised from 14 to 20 years. The change attracted a lot of publicity and most adults probably heard mention of it. Has this move slowed the pattern of rapes and attacks on women? Not if reports in the media give any indication. Such violence is as prevalent as ever.

In the period 1985-92 incidents of violent crime rose by 41 percent, despite a nearly two-thirds increase in the length of prison terms for such offences. Statistics in New Zealand also revealed a 3 percent decrease in overall crime figures in the year ended 30 June 1994. Many areas of criminal offending – traffic, fraud, burglaries, thefts – showed a marked drop in offending rates. The two areas where offending rose substantially against this national trend, violent crime and drug offending, were the two areas where penalties had increased most in the previous 10 years. The rationale behind increasing the penalties at the time was one of deterrence.[25]

Mike Martin, a man who has spent most of his adulthood in prison, writes:

> We must stop imposing sanctions on criminals simply because we think a particular form of punishment would deter us. We, that is you and those who represent you, are not the offender, so it is time you stopped believing the punishment that would deter you would also deter the average criminal. If anything the opposite is true.[26]

The recidivism rates tell it all. Nearly two-thirds come back to prison within two years of a sentence. Does the burglar think of prison when he or she goes out to burgle? Does the car thief? The rapist? The molester? The fraudster? The conman? Not if you listen to their stories. Being caught does not enter their calculations.

8. Prisons Are Expensive

Prisons are very expensive to run. There is real irony in the fact that after little enough is spent on some youngsters by way of education, health, clothing and shelter during their formative years, when they hit prison the state becomes extremely generous. The state will spend nearly $70,000 a year for a maximum-security prisoner, and between $24,000 and $35,000 for a minimum-security inmate. This breaks down to $1500 a week spent on each prisoner's care and upkeep for the length of a prison term, or about $200 a day.

Of course it will not all be spent on the inmate. In fact very little will be. From that sum, $1375 will be spent on the administration of the prison, mainly in the form of prison officer wages. The prisoner's food costs only $5-6 per day.[27]

Yet all over the country, the internal costs of running prisons are being cut back. While more and more cells and prisons are being built, the budgets to keep the current ones up and running are being slashed. The first things to go in prison budget-cutting are the food costs and programmes for prison inmates. For example, at Christchurch Women's Prison in 1993 all outside-supplied drug, alcohol and education programmes were cut because of 'severe financial constraints' imposed by government funding cuts.[28]

Alcohol and drug addiction therapy provided by Odyssey House, the Community Alcohol and Drug Service and Te Rito Arahi, a Maori drug programme, were cut. This left the inmates without professional drug and alcohol therapists despite the fact that 85 percent of the women have drug- and alcohol-related problems.

Ironically the same week these cuts were announced, Dr Julie Leibrich, the Justice Department Centennial Research Fellow, released a report that showed that criminals stop offending when they have something of value they do not want to risk. They change when they come to a personal decision that offending is no longer worthwhile.[29]

Recent Corrections Department policy has sought to change this trend. But things can't be done in isolation. New tough security measures have meant less access by the public to help with prisoner programmes. Despite an attempt to develop some positive initiatives, Integrated Offender Management programmes will do little to stem the tide of recidivism unless a much broader approach is taken to dealing with crime in the community. 'Straight Thinking' programmes and others like them will have little application if the environment inmates return to remains unchanged.

9. The Link between Crime and Unemployment

It is one of the most difficult things to prove, yet one of the most obvious facts of life, that high unemployment breeds an increase in crime rates. In 1972, 12 percent of people sentenced to prison, borstal or put on probation/parole were classed as unemployed. By 1987, along with the vast increase in crime and prison rates, that proportion had risen to 66 percent.[30]

Taken alone, these statistics tell us very little because of other mitigating circumstances. But placed alongside overseas research, they confirm the increased crime/unemployment links. It follows, for example, from Julie Liebrich's research that if a person is unemployed, feeling pretty lousy and not very useful, they are much more likely to offend. If they are employed on a reasonable wage, are treated decently and have something to work for, with a resultant development of self-esteem and confidence, they are less likely to offend.[31]

According to a report published in Britain in 1982, there is a striking relationship between unemployment and imprisonment levels. Researchers found that for every 1000 young people unemployed there are 56 more admissions to penal institutions. Higher unemployment means more crime and more imprisonment.[32]

Researcher M. H. Bremner found in both Britain and the United States that for every 1 percent rise in unemployment there was a 4 percent rise in prison admissions.[33]

A clear corollary follows. A government that stands back and allows market forces to determine unemployment levels becomes a co-respondent in the increase in crime that results. There is a clear link between government policy on unemployment (allowing market forces to prevail) and rising crime rates. One flows from the other. All things are interconnected.[34]

10. The Prison System is Selective

If you are poor, under-educated, Maori or Polynesian, young, unemployed, unskilled or addicted to drugs or alcohol, you stand a very good chance of ending up in prison. According to the Department of Corrections, the number of Maori entering prison in 1997 was eight times greater than for non-Maori. Conversely, if you are educated, skilled, middle-class, Pakeha, employed, well paid and have stable family relationships, there is only a minute chance of it happening. It is not that the second groupings do not break the law on occasion. But the type of offending the former grouping engages in – assaults, minor drug possession and/or dealing, shoplifting, burglaries, thefts, driving offences – is far more highly policed and is the subject of much more media concern that the anti-social actions of their better-off compatriots.

As J. H. Reiman notes in his book *The Rich Get Richer and the Poor Go to Prison*, the criminal justice system does not protect us against the gravest threats to life, limb or possession. Its definitions of crime are not simply a definition of the objective dangers that threaten us. The workplace, the medical profession, the air we breathe and the poverty we refuse to rectify lead to far more human suffering, death and disability, and take far more from our pockets than murders, aggravated assaults and theft. As he says, this type of human suffering is preventable.

So too are unemployment, poverty, racism. And unfair taxation and the opulence of the few at the expense of the many. Yet such inequalities are protected by law in this country. We place individual human rights over and above any other consideration, including that of the common good. The result is that some families can live in packing cases in Auckland carparks while others can have holiday homes and city mansions for their private use. One person can own an island (created 10 million years before he was born) and prevent others from living on it. Another can own 300 homes for rental at any cost, while the law forbids squatting to the homeless family.

Conclusion

We are all responsible for the high crime rates and levels of imprisonment. Naturally offenders must take prime responsibility for their offending. Most make choices that place them outside the law. But successive governments, the Justice Department, and the judiciary are co-responsible with offenders for the high crime rate because of the inept way they have used their power in failing to build a more just society and a fairer criminal justice system.

The media also play a special role in distorting the public perception of the true state of offending in our society.

The Department of Corrections is basically empire-building, protecting its power base and control over the whole correctional field. What other explanation is there for its deliberate subversion of the of the central thrusts of the Roper Report, which recommended a parallel but separately controlled system of sanction? How else to explain their continued belief in the face of so much contradictory evidence that prisons can both punish and habilitate? How else to explain the cynical application of the word 'habilitate' to prison programmes when the report made it very clear that this was a new and fresh way of viewing things and was not a philosophy applicable to traditional prisons? They must be held co-responsible for continued high crime rates and imprisonment numbers.

Successive Ministers of Justice have failed when vision and moral courage was needed. Admittedly, things moved a little under both Geoffrey Palmer in his first term and under Doug Graham. But they have joined other ministers in responding too rapidly with ill-conceived legislation involving harsher penalties whenever the well-orchestrated red-neck element mobilises. Their political parties have failed to think through the implications of continuing with a retributive philosophy of justice. Too many politicians have been happy to accept tired, disreputable arguments about penalties without seeing the ramifications for the wider community and what sort of society we are creating. Doug Graham often brought a balance and a thread of wisdom to some of the emotional debates that rage periodically in the community. He seems to have failed to carry the rest of his party to the same conclusions.

The judiciary must be held to be co-responsible for this situation because of the entrenched harsh views of many judges on sentencing. No-one is suggesting that certain people should not be sentenced to imprisonment for certain offences. But the whole idea of the Criminal Justice Act 1985 was to keep people out of prison by expanding the range of community sentences. This was the will of Parliament. The act lays down clear guidelines to indicate that, apart from special circumstances, only violent offenders should be imprisoned. Yet at the time of the prison census in 1989 only 55 percent of inmates were there because of violent offending. By 1999 it had still not reached 60 percent.[35] As Doug Graham has said, the simple fact is that many people who receive prison sentences in New Zealand would receive community-based sentences in other countries.[36]

Sir Clinton Roper, speaking to Australian and New Zealand judges in 1990, said that in his view:

> ... the act had failed in its purpose, not through any fault in the philosophy behind it but in the failure of the courts to recognise and apply its principles.

Judges, so quick at times to pontificate about the will of Parliament when it comes to increasing prison sentences, have been too often too slow in reflecting the will of Parliament when it comes to alternative sentencing. The Crown has the right to appeal against the insufficiency of sentence and has a very high rate of success in so doing. As a result, a tariff of sentence has been set in many areas of crime by the Court of Appeal, which has severely curtailed the discretion of a sentencing judge.

This means an individual sentencing judge has his judicial discretion to grant a person a non-custodial sentence severely curtailed and this in itself contributes to the abnormally high number of people in New Zealand prisons.[37]

Finally, it has to be pointed out again that the standard of human containment within our prisons in many instances remains diabolical. Is it any wonder so many inmates are hardened and more embittered when they emerge? Is it any wonder so many take drugs while they are inside to beat the pain and boredom? Is it any wonder serious crime is escalating on the outside when we are producing such an array of hardened graduates from the inside?

We need to remind ourselves in all our dealings with the criminal justice system of the need to protect human dignity. If we fail in this, then we return to practising little less than a form of barbarism. Until our society grapples adequately with the shortcomings of a retributive criminal justice philosophy, we will continue to have increasing crime rates, higher imprisonment numbers, less safety in the community, and an extremely expensive ever-expanding prison system.

Footnotes

1. *New Zealand Herald*, 14 May 1993
2. *New Zealand Herald*, 26 February 1994
3. *New Zealand Herald*, 26 February 1994
4. Resource Implications of the Report of the Ministerial Inquiry into the Prison System 1989, Justice Department, October 1989
5. Department of Corrections annual report 1997-1998
6. Allison Morris and Warren Young, *Reforming Criminal Justice*, 29 September 1998
7. Department of Corrections, op cit
8. Hon. Douglas Graham, speech, 22 February 1991
9. UUSC National Moratorium on Prison Construction, Boston, Massachusetts
10. Justice Department report, December 1993
11. Department of Corrections, op cit
12. Penal Policy Review, Government Print, 1981
13. Justice Department report, September 1988

14. *Financial Times*, London, January 1993
15. Tony Short, *Whatever Happened to the Fair Go? New Zealand in the 1990s*, University of South Australia, 1993
16. *The Press*, Christchurch, 30 December 1992
17. *Christchurch Mail*, 30 August 1993
18. Phillip Berrigan, *Widen the Prison Gates*, Simon and Schuster, New York, 1973
19. *The Press*, Christchurch, 23 July 1993
20. *Auckland Star*, 11 February 1991. Full report presented at a public meeting in Auckland on prison violence, 15 February 1991
21. *The Press*, Christchurch, 27 January 1994
22. *Greymouth Evening Star*, 5 April 1988
23. Debbie Martin, paper presented at seminar 'Home Grown '93', 25 November 1993
24. *The Press*, Christchurch, 27 January 1994
25. *The Press*, Christchurch, 30 August 1994
26. Mike Martin, *NZ Listener*, 22 June 1985
27. *The Press*, Christchurch, 30 December 1993
28. *The Press*, Christchurch, 24 September 1993
29. Julie Liebrich, *Straight to the Point – Angles on Giving Up Crime*, Otago University Press, Dunedin, September 1993
30. *Sunday Times*, 9 February 1992
31. Julie Liebrich, op cit
32. Report, 'A Time for Justice', British Catholic Social Welfare Commission, 1982
33. M. H. Bremner, *Mental Illness and the Economy*, Harvard University, 1973
34. Jim Consedine, *A Poison in the Bloodstream*, Cape Catley, Picton, 1990
35. Department of Corrections, op cit
36. Hon. Douglas Graham, speech, 22 February 1991
37. Peter Williams Q.C., speech, Criminal Bar Association, Auckland, 26 May 1989

CHAPTER THREE

Advance Australia Unfair

Politicians and community leaders have used prison to perpetuate the longest-running, biggest social fraud in the history of the modern world... that prisons serve a useful purpose in social control and crime prevention.

Keith Hamburger, Director General, Q.C.S.C.

Poverty – the Breeding Ground for Prison

Social conditions in Australia, as in all socially developed countries, have deteriorated markedly as the effect of monetarist economic policies bites into the economic well being of the lower income groupings. As usual the most severely hit have been the poor and the vulnerable, the elderly without substantial assets, single-parent families, the sick, the mentally ill, the young (especially those poorly skilled), the indigenous population and immigrants. As in all similar societies, it is from these groupings that the prison population is primarily drawn. As a major report on Australian prisons pointed out, prison exists as a powerful emotional and symbolic answer to the crisis of control that exists in society, a guarantee of the state's ability to exercise law and order.[1]

In Australia, poverty is on the increase and the gap between rich and poor is growing. An often-quoted set of conclusions published by Professor John Piggott in 1984 is that the wealthiest 1 percent of adults individually hold 25 percent of private wealth, the top 5 percent hold about 50 percent and the top 10 percent hold about 60 percent.[2] The wealthy often pay very little tax. For example, Kerry Packer, Australia's wealthiest man with an estimated fortune worth $A5 billion, paid only $A30 in tax in the three-year period 1995-97.[3]

Child poverty has increased dramatically since the late 1970s as a result of unemployment, housing costs and marriage breakdowns.[4] According to a study carried out at Macquarie University in Sydney, 25 per cent of Australia's schoolchildren live in poverty. There are now approximately 700,000 children living in poverty in Australia, with a further 500 children being added to the total every day.[5] Poverty brings homelessness. There were at least 25,000 children homeless in 1989, according to the Burdenkin Report. By 1991 the estimate had risen to 50,000: in just two years the number had doubled. Other commentators double or treble that figure. In New South Wales alone, a youth accommodation survey in June 1991 showed there to be up to 30,000 homeless youths.

Poverty is worst among Aborigines. According to the Catholic Aboriginal and Islander Council of Queensland, 48 percent of Aborigines live below the poverty line. Their general rate of unemployment is four times that of others. Their life expectancy is about 20 years less than that of the general population. Twenty years ago, 100 in every 1000 Aboriginal babies died before their first birthday. In April 1994 *Time* magazine reported that the situation remained unchanged.

Similarly, it reported that in 1971, a survey at Royal Darwin Hospital showed that one in five Top End Aboriginal children suffered malnutrition before their second birthday. A 1993 study found no change. In some Aboriginal communities half the children suffer malnutrition. This is a worse rate than in Kurdish or Somali refugee camps.

The report went on to say that more than 30 percent of Aboriginal people are homeless or inadequately housed. Almost all Aboriginal babies have ear infections within the first month of life and few receive treatment, meaning that up to half of them will have some hearing loss. Deafness means problems at school, if there is a school, and if the child attends. Nationally, a quarter of Aboriginal children leave school before the end of their 10th year.

Poverty of this magnitude inevitably leaves its imprint on other sectors of society. According to an Institute of Criminology report in January 1993, of all the people taken into custody in the previous year, a phenomenal 52.1 percent were sent to prison for fines default. This was more than double that of five years earlier.[6] This figure draws a very clear link between poverty and imprisonment. It is of interest to note that New Zealand has, by way of legislation in 1993, virtually abolished imprisonment for fines default.

Inmate Profile

That rising poverty levels lead to more crime is obvious. The more structured the economic gap between those with wealth and those without, the more the prison numbers have reflected this basic inequality of opportunity. There are other factors involved in rising crime rates – unemployment, the break-up of family life and the widespread addiction to drugs being three.

The Australian Institute of Criminology in February 1988 provided this profile of a typical prisoner:

> The prisoner is likely to be a male between 20 and 29 years, Australian-born, in certain states and prisons Aboriginal, a person who has not completed a secondary education, unemployed at the time of the offence.
>
> A relatively large number of persons appearing before the courts suffer some

sort of intellectual disability. About 10 percent of the Australian prison population are intellectually handicapped, and a substantial number are psychologically disturbed. A high percentage of prisoners are affected by alcohol at the time of their offending.[7]

Australia has six state and two territory penal systems and a federal national one. As in the United States, often the rate of incarceration varies from state to state. In 1991 the rate of imprisonment was 69 per 100,000 population in Queensland, 100 in New South Wales, 51 in Victoria, 114 in Western Australia, and the national average was 81 per 100,000. By June 1998 Queensland had a rate of 189, NSW 135.4, Victoria 78.6, South Australia 123.9, Western Australia 171.5, Tasmania 73.9, Northern Territory 451.6 and ACT 49. The national average was up to 133. The total number in prison was 18,692.[8] Imprisonment has become very popular in Australia, but there are wide variations in imprisonment rates. Simply, some states imprison at higher rates than others. For example, New South Wales has twice as many prisoners as Victoria, yet they share an identical crime rate.

Prison Life

Australian prisons in general are just as tough as their American and New Zealand counterparts. Government personnel confirm the harshness of the treatment. A medical officer writes:

> Prisoners get degrading and dictatorial treatment from many prison officers... I have seen the results of the systematic beating of large numbers of prisoners as retribution – no charges are laid. Moreover, prisoners can be denied access to medical treatment at the whim of prison officers.[9]

A prison officer speaks in the report of the frequent tension and sometimes fear where standover tactics and assaults by prisoners on prisoners are the norm.[10]

Prison life has its own unofficial hierarchy and economic system. The problem of drugs in prison needs to be seen in the context of these unofficial structures. Often drugs and the payments used for them form the economic backbone of the black market within the prison. Assaults and beatings are a not uncommon result of dealing to a non-paying debtor. Theft from other inmates is another way of meeting drug debts for the desperate. All such activities form part of the prison culture.

Because inmates are totally shut off from the outside world, they become part of a community, with its own values, language and ways. This is why 'narking' is regarded as such a heinous sin among inmates. It breaks down the tight prisoner community, allowing outside agents to become involved.

The code of prison conduct demands that officers be kept at a certain distance and treated with suspicion and a certain amount of contempt. They are never to be trusted. It also works the other way: prisoners are always treated with some degree of suspicion by officers. Never let your guard down, is a common approach with prison officers.

This negative culture is the principal reason that therapeutic programmes will only ever have limited success within the traditional environment. Negativity breeds cynicism and mistrust. No matter how well a programme may be conducted within the prison during working hours, the 18 hours spent in the wings and cells after each session undo most of the good done. Prisons cannot rehabilitate and punish at the same time.

Deaths in Custody

Prison life also leads to a high rate of suicide. A study published in 1990 by the Australian and New Zealand Association of Psychiatry found that 'prolonged imprisonment and dehumanising conditions' in New South Wales prisons were major contributors to the increase in suicides in custody. The study found that the New South Wales correctional conditions, policies and practices fell far behind the standards and principles adopted as minimum standards by the United Nations in 1980.

The assumption is often made when discussing prison deaths in Australia that it is Aboriginal deaths that is the issue. Aboriginal deaths in custody are certainly a major issue and rightly have taken centre stage. But the number of deaths from all races is also cause for major concern. Australian Institute of Criminology research shows clearly the magnitude of the problem.

> During an 18-year period, 1980-97, 719 people have died in Australian prisons. The largest increase in the number of deaths per year was between 1996 and 1997, when prison deaths increased by 44 percent. The overwhelming majority of deaths, 610 of them, are of non-indigenous people, including 27 females. Deaths of indigenous people numbered 109, some 15 percent of the total. While 15 percent of prison inmates are on remand, a disproportionate number of deaths in custody are on remand. This reached 37 percent of custodial deaths in 1997. Over the 18-year period, 42 percent of deaths were by hanging and 33 percent by natural causes. However, among Aboriginal people, death from illness and natural causes exceeded deaths by hanging.[11]

Since the Royal Commission into Aboriginal Deaths in Custody, the number of deaths of both indigenous and non-indigenous people in prison has more than doubled, from 33 deaths in 1990 to 75 deaths in 1997. At the same time the prison population has increased by 29 percent. Nationally, prison deaths rose 44 percent during 1997, from 52 to 75. This figure is the highest number recorded during the 18-year period, with New South Wales, Western Australia and the Northern Territory also recording 18-year highs.

Forty-eight people died in prison during this time from homicide. In the four years from 1994, 22 homicides have occurred representing 46 percent of the total

45

homicide deaths recorded during the 18-year survey. New South Wales has recorded 23 homicides, the greatest number of any state at 46 percent.[12]

What is clear from the evidence is that despite the high profile of death-in-custody enquiries, prison custody deaths are increasing, particularly among non-indigenous people. This provides grave cause for alarm.

The Wood Commission into Police Corruption

In 1995 the NSW government set up a Royal Commission to investigate the NSW Police Service. What emerged over the more than two years of hearings and submissions shocked Australians. Aided by a 'rollover door' tactic which enabled corrupt police to give evidence 'without prejudice', the commission heard of an epidemic of fabricated confessions, planted evidence, illegal phone taps, systematic perjury, denial of suspects' rights, framing of innocent people, assaults to induce confessions, bribery and general corruption that reached way beyond a 'few bad apples' within the force to the highest echelons of the criminal justice system. This included allegations of corruption against judges, politicians and police in the highest ranks. In a now infamous deposition on 9 October 1995, ex-Detective Sergeant Trevor Haken told the commission he had committed perjury on numerous occasions and explained his actions by saying, 'It is part of being a detective. Giving false evidence was purely a matter of course.'

The final report, while confirming the major allegations, lacked any real cutting edge that might have rooted out the causes of the corruption. It sought structural changes to policing but failed to promote community accountability to any marked degree. Hundreds of convictions were deemed to be 'unsafe' following the commission's findings. Some imprisoned on false evidence have been freed. But many others will not easily gain access to the false evidence that convicted them and remain the victims of corruption.

Private Prisons

The advent of private prisons in Australia during the 1990s has further entrenched a retributive philosophy of criminal justice. There are now seven private prisons in Australia, and more than 20 per cent of Australian prisoners are lodged in them.

The first was built at Borallon, outside Brisbane, and opened in 1990. Long hailed as the jewel in the crown among private prisons, Borallon receives only selected inmates. Excluded from eligibility are protection prisoners, reception prisoners, those requiring extended hospital or infirmary care, those currently subject to separate confinement or special treatment orders, those with psychiatric problems or illnesses and those who are actively suicidal or currently experiencing suicidal tendencies requiring a prevention programme.

The Arthur Gorrie Correctional Centre in Queensland opened in 1992, the

Junee Correctional Centre in NSW in 1993 and the Fulham Correctional Centre in Victoria in 1997. Victoria also hosts the Port Phillip Private Prison built by the British company Group 4 and the Metropolitan Women's Correctional facility at Deer Park, the first private women's prison outside the US. The largest private prison in Australia is the maximum-security high-tech Metropolitan Remand and Reception Centre in Victoria, built to house 900 inmates. By the end of 1997 Victoria's private prisons held 45 percent of the state's prisoners. The ironic twist is that this expansion of the prison system comes at a time when the crime rate in Victoria is falling by approximately 4 percent a year.

The Port Phillip Private Prison had the rockiest start. It was opened with great fanfare by Corrections Minister Bill McGrath in August 1997. He said it 'heralded a new era' and 'would set new standards for correctional facilities'. Regrettably, these standards have proved to be new low standards. By January 1998 five men had died in custody and enormous tensions had developed within the prison. So bad was the situation that Senior Magistrate Brian Barrow twice recommended that no Aboriginal person be sent there.

In early March 1998, after an official police/prison investigation, a Coroner's Court was told that the prison was 'inadequately staffed and has major design faults which have led to the deaths of at least two inmates'.[13] By this time nearly half the prison's staff had resigned. That same month the Community and Public Sector Union claimed there had been more than 100 suicide attempts and that drug overdoses were a daily occurrence. Within days a six-hour riot broke out which almost completely destroyed a 52-bed unit and caused nearly $300,000 worth of damage. Then two more inmates committed suicide. A few days later, in response to a breakdown between management and staff, the Prison Officers' Union imposed a 23-hour lockdown until conditions improved.[14]

Thus in six months, from mid-August 1997 to mid-March 1998, this brand new state-of-the-art private prison had become a nightmare for all concerned. Neither Correctional Services Chief John Van Groningen, State Premier Jeff Kennett nor Corrections Minister Bill McGrath would take responsibility for what Justice Frank Vincent, chairman of the Parole Board, called 'a predictable series of events'.[15]

To the superficial observer, private prisons may seem to offer much, including less government spending and better programmes. Their PR is excellent. But it is mainly illusory. While all contracts are shrouded in secrecy and financial figures are hard to get, it is clear that they generally cost more to the taxpayer in the long run, have fewer benefits for both staff and inmates, provide less public accountability and simply send unknown quantities of tax funds into private pockets. Programmes and staff wages are the first things to be cut when extra profits are needed. This means longer lock-up periods, fewer amenities. Private prisons also need high crime rates and lots of offending in order to survive.

Juvenile Justice

Following on the New Zealand example, Australian authorities have moved in some states to introduce a restorative philosophy to parts of the juvenile justice system. For example, in NSW a trial scheme pioneered at Wagga Wagga has been modified and is now used state-wide. Under the Young Offenders Act 1997, police have been given clear guidelines to use their discretion regarding interventions, which range from street warnings through cautions to youth conferences or even court. Sadly, certain crimes are excluded from the process. These include sex crimes, those involving a death, serious drug offences, serial offenders, breach of violence orders, many traffic offences and most minor drug offences. These exclusions will, judging by the New Zealand experience, severely limit the effectiveness of the new processes.

Convenors selected from lay applicants across the state have been appointed to 16 centres to convene the conference of offenders, their families, the victims and their support people and seek agreement on the appropriate way to deal with the offence. Unlike New Zealand, NSW did not close any of its juvenile detention centres when the act was introduced, nor did the government replace existing legislation. Given the vested interest inherent in any traditional structure and the difficulty of changing traditional mindsets, such actions may yet prove to be fatal flaws that prevent the act from succeeding fully.

However, there is a dark side to juvenile justice in parts of Australia. In NSW the Royal Commission exposed the huge number of state wards who enter the juvenile justice system. They are the responsibility of the Department of Community Services. About 170 per 100,000 children are in the care of the department. While in care, female state wards enter the Department of Juvenile Justice (DJJ) at a rate of 1 in 5. Female children from the general population enter at a rate of 1 in 2500: that is 20,000 per 100,000 compared with 40 per 100,000! There are no figures for male state wards. What is known at present is that DJJ consists of about 15 percent state wards and 30 percent Aboriginal children. Therefore fewer than 3 percent of the state's children make up almost 50 percent of the kids in jail.[16]

Youth laws have got tougher. In Queensland, for example, amendments have been made to juvenile justice legislation which allow for huge increases in sentences for juveniles, including life sentences. Queensland has also given the police powers to fingerprint and register formal cautions on a juvenile's criminal record even though they may not have been convicted of a crime.[17] In NSW many argue that the Children (Parental Protection and Responsibility) Act 1997 and the Crimes Legislation (Police and Public Safety) Amendment Act 1998, which significantly increase police powers, discriminate needlessly and unfairly against young people.

It seems that as soon as legislation allows for some restorative justice processes among juveniles, the same law-makers undo the good work with further punitive legislation.

Women in Prison

In the past 10 years the number of women in Australian prisons has more than doubled. This is partly as a result of sentencing policy but mainly as a result of the upsurge in drug-related offending. This type of offending is greater in percentage terms among women than men. In 1988 approximately 80 percent of female crime was drug-related.

Like the men, the majority of women in prison are young and poor. They are not well educated, most of them having had less than three years of secondary education. Over three-quarters are in low-paid jobs or unemployed, fewer than half are married or in de facto relationships. Most are convicted of drug-related crimes, welfare fraud and spouse homicide, in that order. As the churches' report found, there was some evidence that women also suffer from discriminatory sentencing in regard to prostitution (where prostitutes but few clients are jailed) and spouse homicide (where they receive harsher sentences than men – even where the women have been subject to years of violence). Women are more likely to be imprisoned for first offences and less likely to be included in programmes that are an alternative to prison.[18]

Aborigines in Prison

Far and away the most appalling dimension of the Australian prison system is the number of Aboriginal people there. In 1997, despite constituting only 2 percent of the national population, they constituted 18.7 percent of people in prison. Police custody statistics are even more appalling. A nationwide survey undertaken in August 1995 by the Aboriginal and Torres Strait Islander Commission (ATSIC) found that Aboriginal people and Torres Strait Islanders constituted 31.8 percent of all people held in police (as distinct from prison) custody. This ranged from highs of 80 percent in the Northern Territory and 52.8 percent in Western Australia to a low of 4.6 percent in Victoria. Their overall custodial rate was 27 times that of the rest of the population, varying from a low of six times the rate in Tasmania to 39 times the rate in Western Australia.[19]

As the churches' report observed, part of the reason for the high imprisonment rate has been the discriminatory laws aimed at Aborigines. They charged that since the beginning of European occupation, Aboriginal people have been denied the vote, disqualified from various forms of social security, denied the right to buy liquor, discriminated against in labour laws, had their children taken away without real cause, and been subjected to the whims of so-called protection laws.

Aboriginal people find themselves discriminated against at every step of the legal process: in the chances of being charged, in the difficulty of getting legal assistance and bail, and in the severity of the sentence passed.[20]

Conclusion

The obvious conclusion one must draw from this brief outline is that the retributive justice system in Australia does not serve its citizens well. Its prison empire is expanding. At \$A50,000 per head[21] the nation is being badly short-changed in its penal policy. Australia imprisons Aborigines at a scandalous level. Its philosophy of retribution has brought nothing but mayhem and widespread distress to families caught up in it, and death and disaster to Aborigines. It has guaranteed a growing level of crime and wasted billions of dollars of taxpayers' money. At this point, while there are glimmers of light in areas of juvenile justice, even this does not reflect a widespread or confident commitment to a fairer and more healing form of criminal justice.

Footnotes

1. *Prison, the Last Resort,* report of the Combined Australian Churches, 1989, p8
2. *Common Wealth for the Common Good*, Australian Catholic Bishops' Conference, Collins Dove, Victoria, 1992, p49
3. Australian Associated Press, 15 October 1998.
4. *Common Wealth*, op cit, p72
5. *The Age*, Melbourne, 29 May 1992
6. *Bulletin*, 18 January 1994
7. *Prison, the Last Resort*, op cit, p11
8. *Corrective Services, Australia for the June Quarter,* Australian Bureau of Statistics, 30 September 1998.
9. *Prison, the Last Resort*, op cit, p21
10. Ibid.
11. Vicki Dalton, Australian Institute of Criminology, research paper, *Prison Deaths 1980-1997 : National Overview and State Trends,* No. 81, March 1998
12. Ibid.
13. *Herald Sun*, 8 March 1998
14. People's Justice Alliance report, *Framed* 35, Winter 1998
15. *The Age*, Melbourne,11 March 1998
16. *Framed* 32, Summer 1996
17. *Framed* 31, Spring 1996
18. *Prison, the Last Resort*, op cit, p21
19. Aboriginal and Torres Strait Islander Commission, research paper, *Keeping Aboriginal and Torres Strait Islanders Out of Custody,* December 1996.
20. *Prison, the Last Resort*, op cit, p13
21. *The Bulletin*, 11 January 1994

CHAPTER FOUR

Retribution: the British Way

Prison is an expensive way of making bad people worse.

Government White Paper, House of Commons, 1990

Ripon is a small northern Yorkshire town of 12,000, sited on the Ure River. As long ago as the year 934, King Athelstan granted the church there the right to offer sanctuary. This meant that law-breakers could not be prosecuted within certain boundaries but instead, after seeking sanctuary, were handed over to the canons of the cathedral. From them they could usually hope to receive just and humane treatment.

Ripon also has one of the earliest prisons in England, euphemistically called 'the House of Correction'. It was built in 1686 alongside an already existing debtors' prison. In England the poor have always had to pay their dues. In 1815 it was decided to add a prison block and to lock up wrongdoers other than vagrants, with separate wings for men and women.

The treadmill was used extensively in Ripon from 1820 to 1866, and the stocks were last used in 1859 for a man found drunk in Allhallowgate. Treadmilling was gruelling and unproductive. Up to 10,000 treads a day were made by prisoners going nowhere. Ten prisoners at a time could be 'corrected' on this diabolical machine.

To visit the Ripon Prison and Police Museum is to recall the history of punishment in Britain in the past 1000 years. It is also to come up against a cold hard fact: the philosophy of Ripon's early days is still the driving force behind British criminal justice today. Ripon's philosophy of 1686, a mixed cocktail of 'correction' and punishment tempered by a dash of incentive and reform, is the same philosophy that produced the amendments to the Criminal Justice Act in 1993.

Yet it need not have been so. The Strangeways riot in Manchester in April 1990, following so soon on the riots in Hull, the Isle of Wight and Gloucester, and the burning of Northeye, should have produced a turning point for the British penal system. The riot could have been a catalyst, or even an excuse, for long-overdue reforms to the philosophy of retribution that has dominated the monstrous history of penal sanction in Britain.

Britain has practised them all - from a massive array of executions in the 19th century (over 200 offences attracted the death penalty), through transportation first to the United States and then to Australia, then the period of the 'hulk' ships off the coast, followed by the draconian days of Victorian prisons with their floggings, hard labour and spartan living conditions, to the modern, soul-destroying, electronically controlled maximum- and medium-security institutions. All follow the same retributive philosophy - punish and avenge. All use the same dehumanising techniques - isolation, boredom, dependency, coercion.

Strangeways came at a time when penal reform was already on the front pages. The riot brought nightly scenes of chaos and disorder into the lounges of the nation via television as the men on the roof clung to their defiance.

Just how far modern Britain has moved from any semblance of a just and fair society was reflected in those distant rooftop figures. For 25 days they waved from the rooftops, trying to communicate to the wider public their despair, their anger, their hopelessness, while police sirens wailed every time they tried to speak. Mostly unemployed, mostly addicts of one form or another, mostly homeless, many psychiatrically disturbed, they represented a class of people structured out of mainstream life in Britain. They had nothing to lose by their action.

As prison chaplain Willie Slavin says, prisons increasingly have acted as a backstop for the social services.

> Prisons have become a 'third world' in our midst. Here is the flotsam and jetsam of our society, the redundant and the rejected. They suffer massively from alcoholism, and increasingly from drug addiction. Often they have been involved in the black economy, or in petty crime such as stealing vehicles. Clearly missing are those who mainly benefit from crime: the financiers who launder ill-gotten gains, well-heeled gangsters, tax evaders, cowboy operators, police who are perjurers, abusers of women ... Almost all come from the marginalised sections of the community.[1]

A caring government should have been able to look beyond the immediate problems caused by the riot and listen to the governor of the prison, Brendan O'Friel, when he made his plea for a more humane system of justice. He spoke of 'an explosion of evil' that occurred when the pent-up emotions of the inmates were unleashed in an orgy of violence and revenge. He believes that official policy towards inmates is still clouded by the 'hulks' mentality of the 19th century, when hulks moored off the coast kept prisoners out of sight, out of mind.

The situation had been brought about by a whole range of interconnected social polices that needed to be addressed. Inside the prison, the situation of long remands, protection prisoners, overcrowding (up to three in a cell built for one), lack of education facilities and programmes, and the plight of mentally disturbed inmates all cried out for immediate attention. The outside needs of more jobs, better housing, drugs in the community, the spiritual malaise, poverty, poor parenting skills, racial issues, were all apparent to community workers and local leaders. What was clearly needed was a widespread policy of change.

It was not to be. Instead, Strangeways came and went and it was business as usual for the authorities. Until the next time. And the next. And the next, when the same explosive cocktail of causes will ignite into another riot, in another place, over the same issues.

How did the criminal justice system get so bad that thousands get locked away in little concrete rooms for years on end? What pressures lead them eventually to revolt as they did at Strangeways? How did this violent and degrading retributive system ever get a grip on Britain and later her colonies?

The criminal justice history of most cultures – Polynesian, African, Celtic to name but three – has been entirely different. According to the Jubilee Policy Group's report in December 1992, ancient cultures viewed crime essentially as a personal event. Although it breached the common welfare, the offence was still seen principally as a violation against the victim, and the offender was held responsible to settle that account with the victim.

To avoid an endless cycle of vengeance and violence, legal codes, issued between 2050BC and AD600 in places as far afield as Babylon, Rome and Kent concentrated on restitution as a means to wipe out the consequences of the offender's actions on the victim, to make up for the losses and to help restore community peace and order. The modern view of the state monopoly on justice arose to protect individuals from the uncontrollable violence of blood feuds. Private vengeance was taken over by the community to ensure it was limited to reasonable proportions. Restitution was not an end in itself. The commitment required by the criminal justice system was not only to address the wrong, but also to vindicate the victim, reconcile the parties, and re-establish community peace.[2]

The Jubilee Policy document goes on to explain how community-based justice gave way to a state-controlled process in Britain. It says that until the rise of the European nation states and the consolidation of the institution of the monarchy, the victim was always the central focus.

Some writers have pinpointed the paradigm shift away from this at the time of the Norman invasion. William the Conqueror and his descendants had to struggle with the barons and other authorities for political power. They found the legal process a highly effective instrument in asserting their dominance over secular matters and, through their control of the courts, in increasing their political authority.

To this end, William's son, Henry I, issued in 1116 the *Leges Henrici*, creating the idea of the 'King's Peace' and asserting royal jurisdiction over certain offences by which it was deemed to have been violated. These included arson, robbery, murder, false coinage and crimes of violence. A violation of the King's Peace was a violation against his person, and thus the King became the primary victim in such offences, taking the place of the victim before the law. The actual victim lost his position in the process and the state and the offender were left as the sole concerned parties.

As a result the system, rather than being concerned to make the victim whole, now focused on upholding the authority of the state. It centred on the offender, rather than the victim, since it was concerned with why the law had been broken, and how to stop it being broken again. Criminal justice became future-orientated, concerned rather to make the offender and potential offenders law-abiding, than to make them atone for their past offence. Restitution, being past-orientated and concerned with the victim, was gradually abandoned. Monies which would have been paid to the victim were now paid to the state, and thus took on a punitive rather than a compensatory role, becoming what we know as a fine. Many cruel and humiliating forms of corporal punishment were also used.[3]

Crime in Britain

Despite nearly 1000 years of punishment-orientated retributive justice, crime in Britain is endemic. Something is not working. However, about three-quarters of it is not recorded in the official figures.

The Home Office conducts annual surveys called the British Crime Survey. This does not consider offences already notified. It is based on interviews with one person over 16 years of age in each of 11,000 households. The results of this survey show that there are about 21 million crimes a year, four times the official figure. Many of these offences are of a very minor type that would be most unlikely to result in any form of sanction. Scotland has its own independent criminal justice system.

In 1988 the police in England and Wales recorded 3.7 million notifiable offences against property. In 80 percent of reported thefts, the value of the goods stolen was under £500, and in half of the cases less than £100. Violent crimes against the person, sexual offences and robbery amounted to 5.1 percent. Dealing with crime in England and Wales is expensive. The annual expenditure on the criminal justice system is £7 billion (about $NZ20 billion), an increase of 77 percent in the past 10 years.[4]

By 1991 the number of notified crimes had risen to 5.3 million. Ninety percent of those were crimes against property; one-third of these involved either stealing cars or having goods stolen from them. One-quarter involved burglary. Another 18 percent involved criminal damage and 6 percent were violent crime, including sexual offences.

Vivien Stern, director of NACRO, the National Association for the Care and Resettlement of Offenders, provides some interesting data. Of every 100 offences committed, 41 are reported to the police. The police analyse and sift the information they have been given, reducing the number to 26. They are successful in laying a charge in seven of these cases, and then the criminal justice process starts. There is an outcome in four of the seven offences: one offender will admit guilt and be cautioned, three will be convicted.[5]

In other words, far more people commit crime than ever come to the notice of the police. It confirms what criminologist Allan Nixon always said about the them-and-us attitude that most people have towards offenders. He used to say that most people were prone to law-breaking when it suited them, but that only a few ever got caught up in the criminal justice system.

This may be for a variety of reasons, among them the fact that serious crimes committed by 'blue-collar' offenders will be more severely policed than either 'white-collar' crimes or minor ones.

Education, race, class and location largely determine whether a person ends up in the criminal justice system. A recent survey showed 15 percent of prisoners had a reading age of 10 years or less, and 30 percent had played truant at school. Over 80 percent of prison inmates have no school qualification. Several recent reports have also accused various police forces in England and Wales of racism in their approach to their duties. Special programmes are now run in some forces to help police recognise their own basic racist tendencies.

Racism is not confined to policing. There are structural problems elsewhere. Sir Sonny Ramphal, former Secretary General of the Commonwealth, in a lecture to the British Bar Council in 1990, said:

> Speaking of Britain, the legal system has attracted considerable public criticism both as regards the profession and also the way the courts treat the black population ... The concept of 'equality before the law' can be an extraordinarily difficult one to realise in a multicultural society where law is, inevitably, and for reasons of history, in the hands of a single dominant culture.

Britain has always been a class-ridden society and this is reflected in the prison statistics, especially in relation to the unemployed. Even more striking is the relationship between unemployment and imprisonment. Researchers who had analysed trends in crime and unemployment rates since the war calculated that, after allowing for any increase in crime, for every 1000 people unemployed in England and Wales, there were 14 more receptions into prison. For every 1000 more young people unemployed, an extra 56 young people were jailed.[6]

The National Prison Survey found that 33 percent of prisoners had been unemployed, compared to 10 percent of the general population. Another survey found that 64 percent of young offenders were unemployed when arrested. The same survey found that 20 percent of prisoners were mentally disturbed, and three percent had 'mental disorders of the kind which would justify compulsory detention in hospital for treatment'.[7]

Homelessness is a major problem for prisoners. Adrian Speller of the British Council of Churches Penal Policy Group says in his book *Breaking Out* that it has been estimated that as many as 58 percent of those released from prison in London and the southeast may be without a home to which they can return. In other parts of the country it is between one-third and one-quarter. Without a base in the community, the chances of successful resettlement are slim. Without an address, it is difficult for ex-prisoners to claim social security benefits. Without reasonable accommodation, it is extremely difficult to obtain work. There is evidence from Home Office studies that accommodation obtained by homeless ex-prisoners is usually at a lower level than that which they had before imprisonment.[8]

Only half the prisoners released in 1991 said they would be going back to their previous accommodation. A quarter of young people remanded in custody expected to be homeless on release, joining the estimated 135,000 young people in Britain without a home. In a survey of homeless people, 35 percent said they had spent some time in custody.[9] Before they came to prison, 83 percent had somewhere relatively settled to live. Only seven percent lived in hostels or on the streets. By the time they had to leave prison, half of those who had somewhere to live had lost their homes.[10]

Home Office research shows that, as in other similar countries, re-offending rates for ex-prison inmates in Britain are extremely high. Among teenagers, a whopping 92 percent re-offend within a two-year period. In other words, only eight juveniles out of every 100 'go straight' upon release. For youths under 21, the reconviction rate is 71 percent within two years and 82 percent within four. For adult males, 57 percent re-offend within two years and 68 percent within four. And for adult women, the re-offending rate is 40 percent within two years and 48 percent within four.[11]

Fast Forward
Britain has always imprisoned in disproportionate numbers the downtrodden, rejected, homeless, dispossessed and victims of prejudice and economic injustice. As Vivien Stern of NACRO said in delivering the Allan Nixon Memorial Lecture:

> Our prison system is a monstrous leftover from an earlier age. When you walk into one of our old Victorian prisons you feel you are stepping back into another century – the bare grey walls, the little dungeon-like windows, the prison officers in uniforms signifying a bygone notion of authority, the gruesome humiliating rituals, such as slopping out.[12]

Sadly, things have taken a turn for the worse. What had seemed like the light at the end of a long tunnel has been extinguished. The late 1980s had brought a surge of hope to compassionate people involved in prison work: it seemed that at long last Britain would adopt a more modern humane attitude towards offenders and its prison system. This had followed on a reduction in criminal offending in 1988-89, and a realisation within government circles that the cries from the trenches were genuine and needed attention.

Douglas Hurd had replaced Leon Brittan as Home Secretary in late 1983 and had taken his duties seriously. A light was dawning on the wider echelons of Conservative Party policy-makers and the government that things had to change. Under Hurd at the Home Office a new strategy developed. Its first component was in the way crime was presented. It was to be always placed in context.

For example, to counter the tabloid mentality that everyone should be cowering in their homes because of the murderers, rapists and muggers on the loose, the British Crime Survey came up with a statistic that an adult in Britain could expect to experience a robbery once every five centuries, an injurious assault once every century, for the family car to be stolen once in every 60 years, and could expect to be burgled once in every 40 years.

The message went out, proven from the statistical information, that levels of crime were not related to levels of imprisonment. Nor were they related to the severity of punishment from the courts. They were related to whether people locked their homes and cars, kept a dog, whether local authorities put up good lighting and had adequate public transport from the city to the suburbs for the drinkers at the end of the night's revelry.

More deeply, it was suggested they were related to social factors – for example, how people brought up their children, the level of discipline or lack of it in the home or school, the working of the labour market, levels of affluence and housing conditions. Indeed, the Home Office actually commissioned research that set out 'to explore the range of factors, particularly economic factors, believed to be related to crime'.[13]

The study concluded that economic factors have a major influence on trends in both property and personal crime. It appeared that:

> … in the years when people are increasing their spending little, or even reducing it, property crime tends to grow relatively quickly. Whereas in years when people are rapidly increasing their expenditure, property crime tends to grow less rapidly or even fall.[14]

The government Green Paper 'Punishment, Custody and the Community', published in July 1988, was followed by a supplementary paper, 'Tackling Offending: An Action Plan'. This led to a White Paper, 'Crime, Justice and Protecting the Public' being presented to the House of Commons in February

1990, calling for wide-ranging reforms in how criminal justice was to be serviced.

In many ways the White Paper was conservative. It adopted the sour-sweet approach, maintaining a clear focus on punishment. It held to the retributive philosophy that 'punishment has a major part to play in reducing crime, but its role must not be overstated'. It also concluded that 'long prison sentences are the right punishment for certain types of serious offence'. Long-term prisoners were to be kept in longer. Crimes of violence were to be punished more harshly. The paper made it clear that the government's aim was to punish, and that criminals should get their 'just desserts'.[15]

> Punishment can effectively denounce criminal behaviour and exact retribution
> for it. The sentence of the court expresses public repugnance of criminal
> behaviour and determines the punishment for it.[16]

At the same time it was a reform paper, providing a shift in emphasis. It recognised that prisons no longer provided realistic rehabilitation. A shift in philosophy was needed. The paper said it was once believed that prison, properly used, could encourage a high proportion of offenders to start an honest life on their release. Nobody now regards imprisonment, in itself, as an effective means of reform for most prisoners. No matter how hard prison staff try to inject a positive purpose, prison remains a society that requires virtually no sense of personal responsibility from inmates. Normal social or working habits do not fit.

The opportunity to learn from other criminals is pervasive, the paper found. For most offenders, imprisonment has to be justified in terms of public protection, denunciation and retribution. Otherwise it can be an expensive way of making bad people worse.[17]

The White Paper encouraged compensation to victims, developed a system for unit fines, promoted community-based options to imprisonment 'as being better for the victim, the public and the offender than a custodial sentence'. It gave the courts new powers to combine penalties such as compensation, supervision and fines. It promoted community service orders and probation as alternatives to imprisonment. It demanded that before it gave a custodial sentence, a court had to be satisfied that the offence was so serious that a custodial sentence was justified, and necessary to protect the public from serious harm. The court should also give reasons for its decision.[18]

The paper also recognised the limitations of deterrence, describing it as a principle with immediate appeal. Most law-abiding citizens understand the reasons why some behaviour is made a criminal offence, and would be deterred by the shame of a conviction or the possibility of a severe penalty. There are doubtless some criminals who carefully calculate the possible gains and risks.

But much crime is committed on impulse, given the opportunity being presented by an open window or an unlocked door, and it is committed by offenders who live from moment to moment. Their crimes are as impulsive as the rest of their reckless, sad or pathetic lives. It is unrealistic to construct sentencing arrangements on the assumption that most offenders will weigh up the possibilities in advance and base their conduct on rational calculation. Often they do not.[19]

It also provided for a marvellous new unit payment system of fines. This was to overcome the obvious injustice under the prevailing system whereby the courts took little account of the income of the offender. People were fined according to the offence, regardless of their income. This was particularly obvious with automatic fines. The net result might be that two people, one a millionaire and the other a beneficiary, would be convicted of the same offence and fined equal amounts. For the millionaire it would be no punishment at all. For the beneficiary it might mean a period without food or an inability to pay a power account or the rent.

The principle of the unit fines system was that an offender paid a certain percentage of disposable income per week. An offence might be serious enough to be judged to be worth a fine of 10 units. An offender with a disposable income after meeting all basic needs of $20 a week would pay $200 as the fine. Another poorer person with only $5 disposable per week would pay $50. The philosophy underpinning this approach is based on fairness and economic position before the law, and the principle that rich and poor should be treated equally by the law, but not necessarily treated the same. Such a philosophy is of the essence of true justice.

In 1988, 16,800 people had been imprisoned for fines default: 3 percent of the prison population. Most simply could not afford to pay. This results in a grave injustice and stigma for the defaulters, their families, and the taxpayer, who had to pay up to £300 a week per capita for each one imprisoned.

After considerable community and parliamentary debate, legislation was enacted in 1991 in the Criminal Justice Act. The next four months saw 4000 fewer in prison, a marked rise in community service orders, and a lessening of probation and suspended sentences.

Return to Square One

This brief respite in a 1000-year history of retributive punitive action was not to last. The right wing of the governing Conservative Party cried foul when they saw their position of privilege before the law being eroded. Several highly publicised cases of recently released offenders committing crimes and some obviously absurd abnormalities in the unit fines system combined to form the base from which a backlash resulted.

A well-constructed and directed media campaign sought to have the old regime reimposed, with heavy prison sentences as its central platform. Alongside this came a series of strident speeches from successive new Home Secretaries, Kenneth Clarke and Michael Howard, advocating a greater use of imprisonment. This led to the 1991 act being considerably weakened in 1993 by amendments including the abolition of the unit fines system and a tougher sentencing policy all round.

Ironically, two of the three Home Secretaries (Justice Ministers) mentioned were themselves convicted of law-breaking in court decisions handed down in November 1994. The High Court ruled that Douglas Hurd, who had introduced the White Paper in 1990, acted unlawfully in authorising aid for a controversial Malaysian dam project. The court upheld an unprecedented appeal against a £234 million ($NZ607m) subsidised loan that the British government admitted became 'entangled' with a huge British arms deal with Malaysia. The government is required by the judgment to make good the £25 million a year deficiency in the aid budget caused by the loan.

In the Appeal Court, hard-line Minister Michael Howard, who scuttled the progressive elements that flowed from Hurd's White Paper, was judged 'to have acted unlawfully, abused his power, and flouted the will of Parliament' in cutting compensation for crime victims.

The Chief Inspector of Prisons in England and Wales inspected Wandsworth Prison in London in April 1989. The prison held about 1500 male prisoners; its usual capacity is 1254. The Chief Inspector found that prisoners were issued with one bucket or bowl and one towel. They used these for all their personal washing and also for washing their plates, knives and forks. Not all prisoners had a bath or shower each week. The shower room was described by the Chief Inspector as 'a ghastly place with the atmosphere of an earlier century'.

In the segregation unit, where prisoners were isolated either for punishment or for their own protection, there was no opportunity to empty their lavatory buckets from 2.30pm until the following morning. Some prisoners did not get clean clothes for two or three weeks and were not able to wash their clothes themselves. Racial harassment of black prison inmates was also reported. The Chief Inspector concluded in his report:

> For prisoners, life at Wandsworth was a deadening experience broken only by conversation about routines or a future life of crime.[20]

Pentonville, in North London, which dates from 1842 and has about 650 inmates, was in March 1994 also the subject of a scathing attack by the Chief Inspector of Prisons, Judge Stephen Tumim. He described health-care facilities as 'grossly inadequate, run-down, cramped, dirty and unfit for patients'. His report described the 55 asylum-seekers and refugees incarcerated as being 'distressed, despondent and in some cases desperate'.[21]

During the 1990s British prisons again became in many instances overcrowded, violent cesspools of humanity in which, as Brendan O'Friel observed at Strangeways, the weak have become 'contaminated' by the wicked. Prisoners have been degraded by the conditions meted out to them by a vindictive Conservative Government, spurred on by a media war for sales. Already British prisons have come under scrutiny by their European neighbours, who generally speaking treat their prisoners much more humanely and imprison far fewer per head of population.

In 1992 the British government published a study based on 4000 interviews from every prison in England and Wales. It showed the majority of prisoners were from unskilled or low-skilled backgrounds, that more than one in four came from disrupted family backgrounds, with four out of 10 under 21 years of age having been in care at some stage. It found prison breaks up marriages and that this had happened to more than half those serving five to 10 years in prison. They were less qualified, mostly unemployed, one-third had another family member in prison, and many had a history of violence against them.[22]

Another major development in the 1990s was the number of private prisons built. The first in Britain, called the Wolds, was built for £30 million and opened in 1992 in North Humbershire. It was built by Group Four. Since then there have been numerous prisons built by private contractors – in Rochdale, Hereford, Worcester and Doncaster to name four. Many have had major problems with staff morale, security and violence, both from staff and inmates. Partly this has been due to an inherent weakness in the private prison concept, which is that profits can only be increased when conditions and wages are cut. In 1996, the Director General of the Prison Service, Richard Tilt, said '…the great majority of the cost reduction comes from the payment of much lower wages and poorer conditions of service for staff working in the private sector'.[23]

Britain continues to imprison its poor at alarming rates. In 1994, 22,723 people were imprisoned for defaulting on fines – an increase of 36 percent for men and 68 percent for women since 1990. In 80 percent of the cases the cost of incarceration exceeded the amount of the fine. In 1994, 503 men and 260 women were imprisoned for their failure to pay fines for not having a TV licence.[24]

In 1996 the prison gates clanged shut behind 83,000 people. But for some their prison stay was short: 8500 of them were in prison for not paying a fine. Some 29,000 were imprisoned for burglary and other property offences. Violent and sexual offences accounted for 16,600 and drug offences for 6000. So just over one-quarter of those entering prison each year had been convicted of violence or drug offences.[25]

The number of women in prison in England and Wales rose by 57 percent between 1992 and 1995, and in June 1997 there were 2664 women prisoners. Two thirds of women locked up in prison before their trial in England and Wales do not get sent to prison when their case comes to court.[26]

So bad did things become that David Wilson, head of the Prison Service, resigned in April 1997 on conscience grounds, citing the shameful state of Britain's overcrowded jails and the 'tabloid, short-term, prison-works' criminal justice policy as the principle reasons. Quoted in the *Guardian Weekly* (27 April 1997), he warned that Britain was 'wasting billions of pounds on social failure'. He said that the increase of 20,000 prisoners in the previous four years, mostly for relatively minor offending including fines default, reflected the courts 'responding to politicians talking up law and order issues and creating a climate of fear'.

A New Broom?

In 1996, under the Conservative government and Home Secretary Michael Howard, a White Paper proclaimed that 'prison works'. It argued:

> First, by taking offenders out of circulation it prevents them from committing more crime. Second, prison protects the public from dangerous criminals. Third, prison and the threat of prison act as a deterrent to would-be criminals. Finally, time spent in prison can be used to rehabilitate offenders.[27]

Two years later, a new Labour government gave a totally different appraisal in its White Paper. It warned that 'the huge rise in population during the last five years is unsustainable. Unless halted, and in due course reversed, it will end badly.' It goes on:

> If our prisons are to be anything other than human warehouses, it is essential that constructive regimes exist to provide inmates with training, education and help in facing up to their offending behaviour. It is also essential, and in the interests of society, that prisoners are prepared for re-entry to the outside world when they are eventually released, as most will be.[28]

Late in 1998 the government passed the Crime and Disorder Act which sought to put a fresh face on fighting crime. It had three key themes. First, reforming youth justice to focus efforts on preventing offending by children and young people. This is the principle aim of the youth justice system. Second, building safer communities, through new local partnerships and by giving better protection against anti-social behaviour, sex offenders and offenders misusing drugs. Third, criminal justice reform seeks to improve performance, reduce delays and promote public confidence in the system.[29]

Regarding youth justice reform, the aim is to focus on better early intervention to prevent young people offending. A Youth Justice Board for England and Wales has been established to monitor performance across the youth justice spectrum. Locally, multi-agency youth offending teams have been established, bringing together the police, probation, social services, health and education.

The act provides for child safety orders, local child curfews, intervention with the parents of children, a fresh look at truancy, the practice of reprimand and final warning for offending children, two new community punishments, the reparation order and the action plan order, the abolition of *doli incapax,* the ancient belief that children of 10-13 aren't responsible for their offending, and for serious offenders the introduction of new detention and training orders.

The act also provides for new partnerships within local communities to reduce crime, and new penalties for crimes of a racial, sexual, violent nature and those involving harassment or intimidation and drug misuse.

Reaction to the new legislation has been varied. Many are appalled at the punitive focus on young people and the abolition of the *doli incapax* law, which has been grounded in British Common Law for centuries. Even Lord Bingham, the Lord Chief Justice, has expressed reservations about some dimensions of the act. In the Home Affairs Committee Report of the House of Commons he speaks of 'uncertainty' about some provisions. And there is no guarantee that provisions regarding drug-addicted inmates will work. The report considers 'prison is not, generally, effective in reducing inmates' drug habits and long-term effective protection of the public could be more effectively achieved by giving some offenders community sentences in which they would get help in breaking their habits'.[30]

Home Secretary Jack Straw's new broom will not come cheaply. In 1998/99 the prison system in England/Wales is expected to cost £1.545 billion. The cost per prisoner per week in England and Wales in 1995/96 was £466.[31]

Conclusion

Things have changed a bit in Ripon now. The old prison closed down in 1877. Did the Home Secretary who ordered its closure recognise that retribution was an ineffective and dehumanising way of treating human beings? Regrettably, the philosophy did not die with him. As we enter a new millennium, retributive justice is still alive and kicking.

Britain continues to apply a demonstrably failed retributive philosophy to its criminal justice system. The vitriolic ranting of the tabloids feeds the insatiable dark side of the British psyche. The public seeks simplistic solutions to complex social problems, including crime.

Yet despite hundreds of years of punishment and vengeance, crime is on the increase. Twice as many British people now commit crime as they did 40 years ago. Prison has solved nothing. It has simply proved beyond a shadow of a doubt that it plays a major role in ensuring a continued high level of crime and criminal behaviour.

The trumpet call for vengeance and punishment remains loud and clear throughout the land; the scapegoating of the poor is alive and kicking. The failed philosophy of Ripon has entered the very psyche of British national consciousness and the events of the past few years show it to be well entrenched.

Footnotes

1. *The Tablet*, London, 27 November 1993
2. Report, 'Relational Justice - A New Approach to Penal Reform', Jubilee Policy Group and Prison Fellowship, England and Wales, in association with the Prison Service Chaplaincy, Cambridge, December 1992, pp9-10
3. Ibid, pp10-11
4. Vivien Stern, *Crime, Policy and the Role of Punishment*, 19 April 1993
5. Ibid
6. Catholic Social Welfare Commission report, *A Time for Justice*, 1982
7. Vivien Stern, op cit
8. Adrian Speller, *Breaking Out*, Hodder and Stoughton, London, 1986,
9. NACRO annual report, 1992-93
10. Vivien Stern, op cit
11. *The Guardian*, 24 June 1994
12. Vivien Stern, Allan Nixon Memorial Lecture, Auckland, New Zealand, June 1990
13. Ibid
14. Trends in Crime and their Interpretation: A Study in Recorded Crime in England and Wales, Home Office, 1990
15. White Paper, Crime, Justice and Protecting the Public, February 1990, House of Commons, England.
16. Ibid 2.4
17. Ibid 2.7
18. Ibid 4.10
19. Ibid 2.8
20. *Report on HM Prison, Wandsworth, by HM Chief Inspector of Prisons*, Home Office, London, 1989
21. *The Independent*, 22 March 1994
22. Vivien Stern, *A Sin Against the Future*, Penguin Books, London 1998
23. Ibid
24. *New Internationalist*, No. 282, August 1996
25. Home Office, *Prison Statistics, England and Wales*, 1996
26. White Paper, Office of the Home Secretary, 1996
27. White Paper, Office of the Home Secretary, 1996
28. House of Commons Report, Home Affairs Committee, 1998
29. Jack Straw, Home Secretary, speech to Magistrates' Association, Blackburn, 25 June 1998
30. *The Tablet*, London, 3 October 1998
31. *HM Prison Service, Corporate Plan*, Home Office, 1996

CHAPTER FIVE

The Caging of America

Amnesty International, whose previous worldwide campaigns have targeted such well-known human rights violators as China, Rwanda and Guatemala, has now turned its attention on the United States. The London-based human rights organisation launched the campaign on 6 October 1998 detailing cases of police brutality and violence against prisoners, among other violations of international standards. Human rights violations in the US occur in rural communities and urban centres from coast to coast. They are committed by sheriffs and judges, by Immigration and Naturalisation Service officials, and by police and corrections officers in jails and prisons across the country.[1]

Three decades after the war on crime began, the United States is warehousing more and more poor people in its prisons in an ever-expanding prison-industrial complex is rivalled only by the military-industrial complex in size, cost and influence.

The prison-industrial complex is a set of bureaucratic, political and economic interests that encourage increased spending on imprisonment, regardless of the actual need. It is not only a set of interest groups and institutions. It is also a state of mind. The lure of big money is corrupting the nation's criminal justice system, replacing notions of public service with a drive for higher profits.[2]

The prison-industrial complex is not a conspiracy, guiding the nation's criminal justice policy behind closed doors. It is a confluence of special interests that has given prison construction in the United States a seemingly unstoppable momentum. It is composed of politicians, both liberal and conservative, who have used the fear of crime to gain votes; of impoverished rural areas where prisons have become a cornerstone of economic development; of private companies that regard the roughly $35 billion spent each year on corrections not as a burden on American taxpayers but as a lucrative market; and of government officials whose fiefdoms have expanded along with the inmate population.[3]

The raw material of the prison-industrial complex is its inmates: the poor, the homeless, the mentally ill, drug addicts, alcoholics and a wide assortment of violent sociopaths. About 70 percent of inmates in the United States are illiterate. Perhaps 200,000 of the country's inmates suffer from serious mental illness. A generation ago such people were handled primarily by the mental health, not the criminal justice, system. Sixty to 80 percent of the American inmate population has a history of substance abuse.[4]

Mentally ill offenders are often caught in the system because mental health treatment is unavailable to the poor. For example, in 1960 there were 40,000 patients in state mental hospitals in California. Today there are 4500, half of whom are civilly committed and half of whom are forensic patients. Within Californian prisons approximately 10 percent of the population is suffering from schizo-phrenia, bi-polar disease or clinical depression. In the county jail system, 15 percent are severely mentally ill.[5]

The prison-industrial complex now includes some of the nation's largest architecture and construction firms, Wall Street investment banks that handle prison bond issues and invest in private prisons, plumbing-supply companies, food-service companies, health-care companies, companies that sell everything from bullet-resistant security cameras to padded cells available in 'vast colour selection'. A directory called the *Corrections Yellow Pages* lists more than a thousand vendors.[6]

Prisons have replaced factories as the economic centrepiece of many small towns. In the US, the days are gone when people lined up to chant 'not in my back yard' when a new prison was proposed. In most areas they are welcomed with open arms. They do not use a lot of chemicals, do not create noise or atmospheric pollutants and do not lay off workers during recessions.

Private prisons are the fastest-growing segment of the prison-industrial complex. Both the Bush and Reagan administrations welcomed and encouraged their development. But it is the Clinton administration that has endorsed them most enthusiastically. It has encouraged the Justice Department to place illegal immigrants and minimum-security inmates in private prisons in an ever-increasing effort to reduce the federal workforce. Today nearly 30 states make use of private prisons and nearly 90, 000 inmates are being held in prisons run for profit.

In 1997 a Prudential Securities report on private prisons described some of the potential risks for the industry. These included a falling crime rate, shorter sentences, alternative sentences and changes to the nation's drug laws. Nevertheless, the report concluded, investment is still worthwhile as 'the industry appears to have excellent prospects'.[7]

As Norwegian criminologist Nils Christie, author of *Crime Control as Industry*, points out that just as steel companies need iron and timber companies need trees, so prison companies use people as their raw material. Much of the profit private companies make comes from paying lower wages to prisoners and prison staff and failing to provide the services most likely to turn prisoners into productive members of society upon release. Profit-making companies prefer to avoid the costs of drug treatment, group counselling and literacy training. So lucrative is the investment in private prisons, the Corrections Corporation of America, the biggest private prison company in the world, announced that it would build three prisons in California entirely on spec – that is, without any contract to fill them. 'If you can build it in the right place,' a CCA executive said, 'the prisoners will come.'[8]

The Cold, Hard Facts

There are three principal prison systems in the US. At the county and city level is a system of jails. At the state level is a system of state prisons. And interspersed within every state is a comprehensive system of federal prisons.

The growth in the US imprisonment population has been extraordinary. In 1968 the prison population of the US was 188,000. By 1998, just 30 years later, US prisons and jails held a total of 1.9 million people. In addition, in 1995 more than 3.1 million people were on parole and 700,000 on probation, a total of nearly 4 million, representing a more or less fourfold increase over 16 years. Consequently, in 1995, there were 5.4 million Americans in prison or within the judicial system, accounting for 5 percent of men aged 18 and over, and one in five black males.[9] The percentage increase has been 7.8 percent annually since 1985.[10] At the end of 1985, one in every 329 US residents was incarcerated. By mid-1996 it was one in every 163. Since 1990 the average growth in the total population in custody has been 1686 each week.[11]

This leaves the United States with the highest imprisonment rate in the world, with 645 detainees per 100,000 of the population in 1997. This is five times the 1973 figure, and between six and 10 times that of countries of Europe such as France, Germany, Ireland, Greece, Sweden and Holland.

Yet serious crime has been dropping. The number of crimes reported in 1997 was 18 percent below the 1992 figures. This decrease is true even for murder, which is considered to be the most reliable crime figure as nearly all murders are reported. From 1992 to 1996, the figure dropped nationwide by 20 percent. Most of the newly imprisoned are there for non-violent offences relating to either drugs or parole violations.[12]

The cost to the American taxpayer has been horrendous. About $30 billion is now spent annually on the US prison system. From 1980 to 1996, the cost of building and operating state and federal prisons and local jails soared 443 percent, from $7 billion to $38 billion. Since 1992, four states have allocated more than $1 billion to prison spending – California ($3.2 billion), New York State ($2.1 billion), Texas ($1.3 billion) and Florida ($1.1 billion).

Of course the money has had to come from somewhere. It has come from cutting resources to social welfare, education and public health programmes. For example, since 1994 the annual budget of the California Department of

Corrections has been higher than that allocated to the University of California. The budget that Governor Pete Wilson proposed that year was designed to get rid of 1000 jobs in higher education in order to fund jobs for 3000 prison wardens.[13] Florida spends more on 56,000 prisoners than on 203,000 university students. New York's prison budget increased in 1996 by $761 million while its state and city university systems declined by $615 million.[14]

The advent of the New Right idelogy in the 1990s has led to a dramatic change in how public monies are being spent on the poor. Loic Wacquant, a lecturer at the University of California at Berkeley, writing in *Le Monde Diplomatique* in September 1998 in an article headed 'Imprisoning the American Poor – From Welfare State to Prison State', said:

> What matters more than all the statistics is the rationale underlying the shift from social welfare to a toughening in penal policy. Far from being inconsistent with the neo-liberal programme of deregulation and decline of the public sector, the rise in prominence of the US penal system reveals the true picture, reflecting a policy of criminalising poverty. This inevitably goes hand-in-hand with the imposition of insecure and underpaid jobs, as well as the restructuring of social welfare programmes to make them more restrictive and punitive.
>
> Nowadays the US prison system performs a role in regard to those groups who have been rendered superfluous or who no longer fit as a result of the restructuring of both employment relations and public welfare: the shrinking working class and the blacks. As a result it has become a vital instrument of government by poverty, used to underpin the principle of flexible working at the point where the market in unskilled labour, the urban ghetto and the 'reformed' social services meet.[15]

Despite the fact that the nation did not experience an increase in crime during the era of the massive escalation of prison-building, the prison population trebled as the threshold for admission to prison was lowered. Non-violent offenders have accounted for 84 percent of the increase of prison admission since 1980. California's $5.5 billion three-strikes law captured twice as many people for simple possession of marijuana as for murder, manslaughter and rape combined. The National Council on Crime and Delinquency projects that if current 'get tough' proposals like truth-in-sentencing and three-strikes-you're-out were fully implemented, the prison population would leap from 1.9 million to 7 million![16]

California has the nation's largest prison system and its most overcrowded. In 1998 it had a population of 159,000 inmates, despite spending $5.2 billion on new prison construction over the previous 15 years. A further $6.1 billion will be needed over the following decade just to maintain the current level of overcrowding. About half of those released each year are illiterate and 85 percent are substance abusers. In 1997, two-thirds of those sent to prison in California were parole violators. Of the 80,000 returned to prison, 60,000 had committed a technical violation such as failing a drug test, 15,000 had committed a property or drug crime and only 3000 had committed a violent crime.[17]

This enormous and expensive system has essentially become a revolving door for the poor, the marginalised, the drug-addicted, the dysfunctional, the illiterate, the unemployed. They go in, they do time, they come out. Their paroles are breached, they return. At $30,000 per inmate per year, it's an expensive way to house someone.

Nearly all 50 states have established mandatory sentencing laws that require prison terms for certain offences and mandate a minimum number of years the offender must serve behind bars. Thirty-four states have 'habitual offender' laws requiring enhanced prison terms for repeat felony offenders, sometimes without regard for the seriousness of the crime. In a study conducted by the Justice Department in 1994, one-third of all federal prisoners incarcerated under mandatory laws for drug offences were considered low-level offenders. In Michigan, which has probably the harshest mandatory sentencing involving drug convictions, it is not unusual to find prisoners serving 10 years for a murder sentence, while others serve life in prison without the possibility of parole for a non-violent drug conviction.[18]

US Prisons are Brutal

The inhumanity of the American penal system is hard to believe. Cold prison statistics hide the harsh reality of life behind bars in the United States. This quote from Supreme Court Justice Harry A. Blackmun in February 1992 says it all:

> Various kinds of state-sponsored torture and abuse – of the kind ingeniously designed to cause pain but without a telltale 'significant injury' – lashing prisoners with leather straps, whipping them with rubber hoses, beating them with naked fists, shocking them with electric currents, asphyxiating them short of death, intentionally exposing them to undue heat or cold, or forcibly injecting them with psychosis-inducing drugs – techniques commonly thought to be practised outside this nation's borders, are hardly unknown within this nation's prisons.

(Hudson v. McMillian, 25 February 1992)

Perhaps the most troubling aspect of the human rights situation in US prisons is a trend that could be labelled 'Marionisation'. In 1983 the federal prison at Marion, Illinois, implemented a series of extraordinary security measures. By 1995, 36 states had followed in creating their own super-maximum-security institutions. One such prison is in Colorado.

> The Federal Bureau of Prisons has opened a new top-security prison in Florence, Colorado, on the site of an old radioactive dump. There the prisoners have an average sentence of more than 40 years. In the cells the furniture is immovable and there is no soap dish, toilet seat or toilet handle, as all these could be made into weapons. The cells have cement floors painted grey. The building is designed

so that the prisoners will not be able to see other cells or the Rocky Mountains through the small windows. The visiting room has a glass window that can stand two hours of being beaten with a hammer. Visitors can communicate with the prisoners they are visiting by a phone. When the 'worst' prisoners leave their cells their hands will be handcuffed behind their backs. They will be shackled in leg-irons and accompanied by three guards. These prisoners have no television in their cells and they will be allowed one 15-minute phone call every three months.[19]

If for some reason an inmate has to leave the cell, he or she is strip-searched, which often includes a humiliating anal probe. Each will be shackled around the waist and handcuffed. The food may be tampered with, while medical care may be non-existent. The inmate is totally under the control of mainly white-supremacist prison guards, whose hatred of them and their beliefs soon becomes abundantly clear. One must remain constantly on the alert against mental and physical deterioration. In effect such prisons are used as social-control mechanisms. They serve political functions.

At the Public Safety Building in Syracuse in upstate New York, the prison that housed New Zealand Ploughshares peace activist Moana Cole for a period in 1991, inmates are tortured. A report in the *National Catholic Reporter* in October 1992 claimed that prisoners were handcuffed to the bars of their cells for days at a time.

In 1990 there were 56 murders in penal institutions and thousands of serious assaults.[20] In 40 states and the District of Columbia, courts have ruled that prison conditions violate federal or state constitutions.[21] This means their conditions do not meet minimum standards fit for human beings.

According to the *New Internationalist* (March 1992), beatings of prisoners are routine during cell transfers. Rectal probes are said to be used to intimidate and rape prisoners moved out of certain high-security prisons. The loss of privileges and withdrawal of visiting rights by families are routinely used to intimidate prisoners.

Brutality reeks from every encounter one has with the penal system in the United States, be it in a local county jail, a state prison or a federal one. Handcuffs and leg-irons are routine. Moana Cole, who weighs just 45kg and was in prison for peaceful non-violent actions, was handcuffed and put in chains to visit a dentist in the local town. Leg-irons were clapped around her ankles. The chains from these led to her waist where there was a leather belt, with further chains to her cuffed hands. Two guards had to support her getting into and out of the dental chair. Prior to this she had to wait in a crowded waiting room for her turn. Ciaron O'Reilly, her co-defendant, was flown several thousand kilometres to a prison in Texas in handcuffs and chains. This reflects a system built on violence and humiliation, not respect for human dignity.

Prison rape is as American as apple pie. In September 1982 *Time* ran a special report on US prisons, describing them as a mess, with punishments ranging from the purgatorial to the hellish. Professor Sean McCouville, a professor of criminal justice in Illinois, says that among the biggest problems facing American prison administrators are prison gangs, assaults, rape and the extortion practised on weaker inmates by the tougher ones.[22] The number of men raped in US prisons each day may exceed 25,000. Women, who make up 4 percent of the prison population, also suffer rape and abuse daily.

According to *Prison Law Monitor*, one in five prisoners is raped.[23] Tom Cahill, a specialist in the field of prison rape, says prison rapists typically victimise young heterosexual first offenders. He claims the boredom, frustration, sexism, racism and outright terror combine to create an atmosphere of barbarism behind bars.[24]

Rape is simply a fruit of the violent ethic that pervades American prisons. Deaths, stabbings, beatings, riots and suicides make up the everyday diet of many institutions. In a two-year period in the early 1980s, 225 inmates and 11 guards were killed by other inmates, and inmate suicides totalled 263. The pattern has been maintained into the 1990s, with 54 inmates and two guards killed in 1990.[25]

The War on Drugs and Addicts

Legislators in the US are obsessed with the 'drug crisis'. By this is meant the use of illegal drugs such as crack, marijuana and heroin, as distinct from legal drugs such as alcohol, tobacco and coffee. The launching of the 'War on Drugs' by President Bush has escalated the numbers in prison and resulted in an erosion of basic civil rights. To advance this campaign, law enforcement powers have been expanded. For example, the US Supreme Court ruled in June 1996 that police officers could stop motorists for minor traffic violations even if the real motive was to look for drugs. As a result, in 1995, six out of 10 of those newly convicted were put in prison for possessing or dealing in drugs.[26]

Yet health experts, law enforcement personnel, judges and others agree that the 'War on Drugs' has been a failure in curbing drug use and trafficking. They agree that most of the people convicted as part of the anti-drug frenzy would be better served by anti-drug prevention programmes. Unfortunately that reality has not prevented the introduction of additional legislation such as bills to increase marijuana penalties tenfold, attempts to do away with drug treatment programmes for prisoners and attempts to increase the number of mandatory minimum sentences.[27]

The fact that so many freely available drugs are illegal makes for a most unstable social situation and a major cause of the criminalisation of so many. The arrival and widespread use of crack made it an easy currency in the ghettoes and among the poor and led to an upsurge in other crimes including gang war and murder. The rate of imprisonment of drug offenders has reached a proportion where, for example, in California in 1998 there were more than twice the number imprisoned for drug offences than were imprisoned for all offences in the state in 1978.

New York drug laws mandate prison terms of 15 years to life for selling two ounces or possessing four ounces of a narcotic substance – harsher sentences than for rape or murder. According to the *CURE-NY* newsletter (Fall, 1998), more than 20,000 people, most of them minor players, are now locked up in New York's prisons for such offences. About 3000 are there for possession alone. New York taxpayers spent $850 million to build cells to hold these people, and continue to spend $300 million a year to warehouse them. Convictions are based on the weight of drugs. As a result, drug kingpins almost never get caught, while low-level 'mules', many of them women, serve very long sentences. About 95 percent of the women charged as drug couriers have had no previous criminal involvement. The children of these women get shuffled to foster parents or reluctant relatives. The destruction of families is rampant.

Of the 130,000 substance abusers in California's prisons, only 3000 are receiving help behind bars and only 8000 are enrolled in any kind of pre-release programme to help them cope with life on the outside.

Although the prevalence of illegal drug use among white men is approximately the same as that among black men, black men are five times as likely to be arrested for a drug offence. As a result about half of the inmates in the United States are African-American. One out of every 14 black men in the country is now imprisoned. One out of every four black men is likely to be imprisoned at some point during his life.[28]

Yet there is little help in prison for drug addicts. The number of drug treatment slots in American prisons has declined by more than half since 1993. Drug treatment is available to just one in 10 of the inmates who need it.[29]

Caging Teenagers

In the past century no country has set about systematically imprisoning its teenagers with greater relish than the United States. Draconian juvenile justice legislation has been introduced to try juveniles as adults. This process is reminiscent of the processes used in 18th-century Europe, where juveniles were tried and penalised as adults. This resulted in children as young as seven years of age being hanged for theft. Since 1992 every state except Hawaii has decided to allow some juveniles to be tried in adult jurisdictions.[30]

The tone for these changes was signalled in May 1997 when the House of Representatives passed a bill that would give $1.6 billion to states that agreed to toughen the handling of juvenile offenders who commit serious felonies. The fact that serious juvenile crime rates had been falling for several years proved no hindrance to a vengeful Congress. For example, juvenile murder arrests declined by 3 percent from 1993 to 1994, 14 percent from 1994 to 1995 and another 14 percent from 1995 to 1996.[31] Nor were they impressed with the fact that juveniles commit suicide eight times as often in adult prisons and jails as they do in juvenile detention.[32]

The 1997 Juvenile Control Act has, among a raft of other punitive measures, mandated adult prosecution for juveniles who commit serious federal violent crimes and major drug trafficking offences, and established enhanced mandatory prison sentences for the same juveniles who use firearms in the course of their offending. Most states have similar legislation.

More and more juveniles are being sentenced to death. In January 1998 there were 63 juveniles on death row. Two-thirds of this group are minorities, and two-thirds of their alleged victims are white. The US is one of the few countries in the world that executes juvenile offenders. They join five other known for this practice – Pakistan, Saudi Arabia, Iran, Nigeria and Yemen. The US has executed six juvenile offenders this decade: more than any other country. Yet juveniles on death row are often the victims of recent, horrific abuse themselves. A 1988 study by Georgetown University neurologist Dr Jonathan Pincus and New York University psychiatrist Dorothy Lewis found that of 14 condemned juvenile offenders studied, all 14 had suffered serious head injuries as children, all had serious psychiatric problems, all but two had been severely beaten or abused as children, and five had been sexually abused by relatives. Only two had IQ scores above 90.[33]

It seems that these moves have had little impact on crime reduction. According to a study by the National Center for Initiative and Alternatives, Connecticut has the highest juvenile-to-adult transfer rate and Colorado the lowest, yet their youth crime rates are the same. Since the 1970s, New York has been automatically trying as adults juveniles 16 and over charged with serious crimes. In that time its juvenile crime rates have doubled.[34]

Women in Prison

The number of women sentenced to a year or more in prison has grown twelvefold since 1970 and conditions have deteriorated markedly for women in prison as inmate numbers have risen. There are now 128,000 women in US jails and prisons. Two-thirds of these are mothers of dependent children: more than 1.5 million children have a parent behind bars.

Half of these women are black and two thirds have had children before they were 18 years old. They are nearly all in jail for drug possession or sale, immigration violations, prostitution or money crimes. About 10 percent of the women admitted to prison are pregnant, and virtually all were the sole support for their children. While in 1979 the proportion of women imprisoned for non-violent offences was 51 percent, that proportion 20 years later had risen to 75 percent.

Racist as Well

Civil rights were won for Afro-Americans more than two decades ago. But what was won in the legislature is lost daily in the courtrooms. Across the country, blacks have their basic right to a fair trial and good representation trampled on by the demons of a racist criminal justice system. Mandatory prison terms for many offences mean that hundreds of thousands more are now penalised unjustly in the prison system than were ever penalised in the worst days of discrimination.

In 1995, of 22 million black adults, 767,000 were in prison, 990,000 were on probation and 325,000 others on parole – a total of 9.4 percent caught up somewhere in the grip of the prison system. As far as whites are concerned, an estimate that is on the high side puts the figure at 1.9 percent for a population of 163 million adults. Over his lifetime, a black male has a one-in-four chance of spending at least a year in prison, and an Hispanic a one-in-six chance, whereas a white has just one chance in 23. This phenomenon is even more marked among young people, prime targets of the criminalisation of poverty. More than one-third of blacks aged between 20 and 29 years are either in prison, under the authority of a judge responsible for the execution of sentences, or awaiting trial. In the big cities the figure is substantially higher than 50 percent, and in some places in the heart of the ghetto, in excess of 80 percent. Blacks account for 13 percent of drug users but one-third of those arrested and three-quarters of those imprisoned for drug offences.[35]

In 1986 some 609,690 black men were under the control of the criminal justice system, while only 436,000 were enrolled in college.[36]

These figures are merely the tip of the iceberg. Each one represents a person with a life story. Every prisoners' rights groups in the country tells the same story. The defendants are all poor. Most have had court-appointed attorneys for their cases, many of whom are white middle-class graduates of law school anxious to gain a little experience, but not necessarily committed to their client's wellbeing. The net result is a mountain of horror stories of poorly defended young blacks going to prison and even to death row after minimum defence in what amounts to a sham of a hearing.

As Bonnie Kerness writes, if you are poor, young, male and of African descent in the US and you get arrested, your bail is likely to be set so high that you become an economic hostage. The phrase 'innocent until proven guilty' will have little meaning. You will sit in a cell for up to two years without even having been found guilty of anything. You will certainly not get a trial by a jury of your peers, and you are quite likely to be pressured into forgoing your right to a trial altogether. You will be defended by a poorly paid public defender who has a caseload so vast that you cannot possibly be treated as a priority. Finally, you will receive a sentence 30 percent longer than a white person would receive for the same crime. You have seen the same thing happen to your father, your uncles, or your cousins.[37]

While nationwide about 25 percent of all black males will be in the criminal justice system at some time, in Washington DC, home of the US president, the Congress and the Supreme Court, close to half of all black men will see the inside of a prison before they reach the age of 24.[38]

Canadian Quaker and international prison abolitionist Ruth Morris says that taking the racism out of criminal justice systems would be like taking the religion out of churches or the sex out of marriage – it cannot be done because the major thing justice systems exist for is to maintain racial and class systems and barriers. Retributive justice, classism and racism are like Siamese triplets. You cannot change any of them without affecting the others because retributive justice systems exist mainly to reinforce the racial and class strata in our society.[39]

Three Strikes and You're Out

Early in 1994 California passed the Jones-Costa Three Strikes Law. It is generally referred to as the 'three strikes and you're out' law, a phrase taken from baseball terminology. Its goal is to put repeat offenders into prison for sentences of 25 years to life without possibility of parole. The law will imprison for life any defendant who is convicted for a third offence if that person has two previous violence convictions – even if the third conviction is for a non-violent felony such as passing a bad cheque.[40] Since its inception, three-quarters of the people sentenced under the 'three strikes' laws are being sentenced for non-violent offences. In December 1996, 150 people were serving life sentences for petty theft.[41]

A network of underwriters, builders and correction officers has a powerful financial interest in perpetuating and expanding the boom in the prison industry. One group of the beneficiaries, the prison guards of California, contributed $1 million to help Republican Pete Wilson become governor. In return, the governor initiated the most expansive prison construction programme any state has ever undertaken. He has also approved the guards' request for more benefits.[42] The guards have been well rewarded for their investment. In California a prison guard now earns 30 percent more than a university lecturer!

The Californian legislation has become the model for the rest of the country: more than half the states have debated or introduced 'three strikes' legislation. While it varies from state to state, basically it has three provisions. For first-time felony offenders, the statute leaves intact the prior-sentencing guideline. For second-time offenders, the new law doubles the minimum required sentence. The centrepiece of the legislation is its 'three strikes' provision, which mandates that state courts sentence to an 'indeterminate term of life imprisonment' those individuals previously convicted for two or more serious and/or violent felonies. While the rhetoric implies a life sentence without possibility of parole, in effect a convicted three-time felon will now have to serve triple the first-time sentence, with a minimum of 25 years' imprisonment.[43]

Legalising Murder – the Death Penalty

Perhaps nowhere is the violence of the US culture more marked than by the acceptance by up to 80 percent of the population of the death penalty. More than 500 prisoners have been executed since 1976, when deliberate death by the state was again declared to be constitutional. Recent federal legislative changes add more than 50 fresh offences to those already carrying the death penalty and more than 3000 prisoners await execution. Most are black, poor, young, male and have been poorly represented by state-assigned lawyers at their trials.

One popular misconception is that imprisonment is a more expensive option than a 'simple' execution. Not so. In recent times studies have shown that execution is a more expensive way to dealing to offenders than even imprisonment for life. In Texas, a death penalty case costs taxpayers an average of $2.3 million, about three times the cost of imprisoning someone in a single maximum-security cell for 40 years. In Florida each execution is costing the state $3.2 million. In financially strapped California, one report estimated the state could save $90 million each year by abolishing capital punishment. The New York Department of Correctional Services estimated that implementing the death penalty would cost the state about $118 million annually.[44]

An American Association for the Mentally Retarded fact sheet states that six people known to be mentally retarded were executed in 1995. By 1998, 11 of the 40 death penalty states had passed legislation to prohibit this. Since 1970, according to a House judiciary sub-committee report, 75 people have been released from death row with evidence of their innocence. At least 23 others have been executed.[45]

Interestingly, in April 1994, Supreme Court Justice Harry Blackmun, who had upheld death sentences throughout a lengthy term on the court that had seen 228 people executed, declared his opposition to all death penalty laws.

> Rather than continue to coddle the court's delusion that the desired level of fairness has been achieved and the need for regulations eviscerated, I feel morally and intellectually obliged simply to point out that the death penalty experiment has failed. It seems that the decision whether a human being should live or die is so inherently subjective, rife with all of life's understandings, experiences, prejudices and passions, that it inevitably defies the rationality and consistency required by the Constitution.[46]

Pope John Paul II again called for the total elimination of the death penalty in his 1998 Christmas message to the world. He was only confirming what the Catholic Church has officially taught for several years.[47]

Conclusion

The American criminal justice system is now so adversarial that actually getting some sort of justice is incidental to the process. At the start of the new millennium, nearly 2 million American citizens are in prison and the numbers are skyrocketing. Retribution and vengeance are at the heart of the nation's approach to crime and punishment. They form an expensive, harsh, despairing and wasteful option in a hungry nation with huge social problems and structural injustice.

Whichever way we look at it, the well-meaning experiment by American Quakers to develop the penitentiary as a way of reforming criminals has backfired horribly. The United States is quickly becoming an imprisoned land, with fear of crime imprisoning more and more of those who are not already incarcerated. The 'land of the free' is becoming a society of the caged.

Footnotes

1. *National Catholic Reporter*, 16 October 1998, launching *Rights for All*, Amnesty International's report on US human rights abuse.
2. *Atlantic Monthly,* December 1998
3. Ibid
4. Ibid
5. Ibid
6. 'The Prisons Industrial Complex', *Multinational Monitor*, November 1996
7. *Atlantic Monthly*, op cit
8. Ibid
9. *Le Monde Diplomatique*, 8 September 1998
10. Vivien Stern, *A Sin Against the Future*, Penguin Books, London, 1998
11. Ibid
12. *US News and World Report*, 25 May 1998
13. *Le Monde Diplomatique*, op cit
14. *The Campaign for Equity-Restorative Justice*, introductory booklet, January 1999
15. *Le Monde Diplomatique*, op cit
16. *Multinational Monitor*, op cit
17. *Atlantic Monthly*, op cit
18. *US Prison Build-up*, Pat Clark and Laura Magnani, American Friends Service Committee, March 1998
19. Vivien Stern, op cit
20. *New Internationalist*, March 1992
21. *National Catholic Reporter*, 13 August 1985
22. *Christchurch Star,* 8 March 1985
23. *The Progressive*, November 1985
24. Ibid
25. *Christchurch Mail*, 23 August 1993
26. *Le Monde Diplomatique,* op cit
27. *US Prison Build-up*, op cit
28. *Atlantic Monthly,* op cit
29. Ibid

30. *Time*, 21 July 1997
31. Ibid
32. Ibid
33. *Time,* 19 January 1997
34. *Time*, 21 July 1997
35. *Le Monde Diplomatique*, op cit
36. *Young Black Men and the Criminal Justice System – A Growing National Problem*, Sentencing Project, Washington DC, 1990
37. *Catholic Worker*, March-April 1993
38. *New Internationalist,* March 1992
39. Ruth Morris, Allan Nixon Lecture, Auckland, June 1994
40. *Harvard Law Journal,* Vol. 107, 1994, pp2123-28
41. *US Prison Build-up*, op cit
42. Robert F. Drinan, *National Catholic Reporter,* 9 September 1994
43. *Harvard Law Journal,* op cit
44. Richard C. Dieter, 'What Politicians Don't Say about the High Costs of the Death Penalty', article in *Studies in Prolife Feminism,* Winter 1995.
45. Radelet and Bedau, *In Spite of Innocence*, North Eastern Press, 1992.
46. *National Catholic Reporter,* 22 April 1994
47. Paragraph 2267 of the *Catechism of the Catholic Church* (Second edition, 1997) bans the death penalty, stating the conditions for its acceptance 'are now very rare, if not in practice non-existent'.

SECTION TWO

Restorative Justice

Instead of defining justice as retribution, let us define justice as restoration.
If crime is injury, then justice will repair injuries and promote healing.

Howard Zehr

CHAPTER SIX

The Maori Restorative Tradition

An elderly Far North Maori has been banned from his home marae for a sex offence. A spokesman said the offender was a very active member on the marae, and was very embarrassed and humiliated by his actions. The six-month ban was a suitable penalty.

The case follows recent publicity about marae hearings in the Waikato that have resulted in seven Maori elders being stripped of their kaumatua status. The process, developed by the Hamilton child and protection agency Kokana Ngakau, has resulted in 18 cases of physical and sexual abuse being taken back to various marae.

Maori lore has a way of addressing Maori grievances, with court sessions being held on marae in accordance with tikana Maori, and whanau determining the sentence. Some court sessions had taken up to three days of non-stop discussion to resolve.

NZPA, September 1993

It will have come as a considerable surprise to most New Zealanders to learn that Maori have a traditional integrated system of criminal justice and that in some areas of Aotearoa to a degree it is still being used. The general perception among Pakeha is that such 'quaint customs' died out over a century ago.

Clearly this is not the case. Despite the strongest efforts of the 'one law for all' brigade, there obviously has been a parallel system of justice operating alongside the dominant English-derived system.

Modern Case Histories
Aroha Terry of Tainui, an expert in sexual abuse cases, claims marae justice is more effective than the traditional Pakeha justice system. In the latter, a person can be locked away for a few years in jail and no-one hears about it. They never have to face their accusers or take responsibility for their actions, and they never have to change. There is no healing for the victim, no healing for the whanau. In the Pakeha system there is no appropriate procedure for the whanau, and no empowerment for them to make decisions.

Under marae justice it is just the opposite. The purpose of marae justice is a healing for all: it is not a battleground. The process is primarily about hearing and helping the victim, healing the whanau, and helping and healing the perpetrator. It works for all three.

> Marae justice is set up to meet victims' needs. It is not about squashing the offender into the dirt. It is about recognising who got hurt – to hell with people saying society is the victim: it was *me*, not society, that got hurt.
>
> Marae justice takes the responsibility away from the victim and places it where it belongs – with the offender. It is particularly appropriate for dealing with sexual offences. The offender is the one who puts all the crap on the victim. We're so scared, we're so tidy in our little whares, in our lives, picking on the victim. It's all so wrong. I say go back to the offender and say, 'Hey, this is your problem.'[1]

Waha Stirling of Ngai Tahu and Ngati Porou na Whanau Apanui, in speaking of his youthful days in the 1930s and 1940s on the East Coast, remembers that most cases of wrongdoing involving criminal behaviour were dealt with on the local marae by elders. Cases included all petty offending such as stealing and assault as well as more serious ones of sexual and child abuse. The police were only called in for more serious offending.

The process used was one of bringing the families together and talking it all through in a way that is very similar to the process now used in Aotearoa under the Children, Young Persons and Their Families Act.

The whanau of both sides in a complaint were invited to a hui. The accused needed to plead guilty and not hide what had been done. It was up to the accused's whanau to get to the root of the matter before the hearing began, and elicit a guilty plea if this was the case. In a sense the whole whanau was on trial so this usually wasn't hard to do. At the hui the elders would take the offender to task, with the kuia being particularly prominent in shaming the offender and the whole family. Often they were all reduced to tears.

Then, consultation between the parties would take place as to a suitable way of dealing with the matter, so as to heal any hurts and restore things to 'normal' again. Things stolen would have to be recovered or compensation paid. Damage would have to be repaired. The penalty usually also involved some compulsory work – sometimes offenders would be sent off to work on adjacent cattle stations if there was not enough work for them around the marae or village.

Hohua Tutengaehe of Ngai Te Rangi and Ngati Ranginui recalls a case when, as a 14-year-old boy in the late 1940s, he was asked to act as recorder in an attempted rape hearing. The attempt had got to a point where the assailant had allegedly removed the young woman's underwear before the assault ceased. The chief called a hui of the rangatira of each of the local marae. After whaikorero, the process began.

First the victim came in accompanied by her parents, her aunts and uncles, sisters and brothers and the whanau of the grandparents. Then the whanau of the assailant arrived. They sat on opposite sides of the meeting house.

The boy, who admitted to the offence, was about 17 years old, the girl a year younger. As soon as the boy pleaded guilty, a session of lectures started from the kuia, the old women present. They berated him for his behaviour, for the sacred tapu he had broken by attacking a young woman, for the shame he had brought on himself, his whanau, his people. In next to no time he and his family were reduced to tears.

Following that, the penalty was pronounced. It was decided that for the first 12 months, whenever there was a wedding or a tangi, the family of the boy had to supply all the meat and vegetables. In addition, he had to paint the meeting house. When they examined the meeting house they found that the weatherboards and roofing iron were decayed, so the family had to replace these.

After some time, because the meeting house belonged to them all, the girl and her whanau went along to help prepare the meals for the boy's family while they were working. The two sides came together in a gesture of reconciliation. Eventually they all settled down and together repaired the dining-room and the surrounding fences. The whole process took about two years.

This was modern Maori justice in action – restorative, healing, reconciling. There were no names on the criminal pages of the media, no police record to haunt the boy in his future life, and the victim received due recognition in the process and was healed of her trauma.

But marae justice is not just something from the past. In an *Inside New Zealand* television documentary, *Marae Justice*, shown in Aotearoa in August 1994, actual marae hearings were filmed and shown nationwide. These were examples employing a traditional Maori justice setting where the whanau acted as prosecutor and sentencing court.

We were taken to the Korapatu Marae where a 24-year-old local woman alleged she had been raped and sexually abused repeatedly between the ages of eight and 16 years. Three brothers were among her abusers. She described how she had been treated as a slave and raped repeatedly.

> It would happen once a day. Sometimes once a week. We thought it was normal.
> I can remember being dragged under the house. If I didn't go I got a hiding. I
> just let them do what they wanted. I was so terrified – I was really scared. I don't
> know why they hated me so much. I was just a little kid, trying to live, trying to
> survive.[2]

The three offending brothers had been summoned by the whanau to the hearing. Such is the power of the whanau that there is no escaping from them if they wish to remain a part of it. The family sit in judgment on the allegations; there were no lawyers, no judge, no police.

Aroha Terry, as advocate, read out the charges of multiple rape, sexual violation and abuse. All listened in silence. Each of the three men pleaded guilty. One added he was glad it had come out into the open. Another said he took full responsibility for what he had done. They all then listened to the woman speak of her pain, her abject suffering over many years, her feelings of rejection, distrust, hatred, anger. She finished by saying that after many months of counselling prior to the hearing, she now felt ready to forgive them. What had moved her finally to that point was hearing them acknowledge what they had done was wrong, that they took full personal responsibility for their actions, and that they deeply regretted the hurt and pain she had suffered.

The aroha present enabled healing and reconciliation to occur. The openness of the accused and their acceptance of responsibility coupled with a desire to change their behaviour and make some amends meant progress could be made towards healing for all.

The sentence for the three men as decided by the whanau was severe but positive. The whakama that each had experienced by appearing before other family members and their acceptance of responsibility and pleas of guilty were taken into consideration and given considerable weight.

Each was to undergo extensive counselling and commissioned to go to work on behalf of the whanau and tell others of the need to end sexual abuse. They had to speak to groups and families of their own experiences and offences, and encourage others to treat their children and their whanau with respect. This process was to be carefully monitored to make sure that there was full compliance.

The victim expressed delight at the progress made. She said she 'felt good' that the balance had been partially redressed and the men had acknowledged their offending. She was glad there were no more skeletons in the cupboard. Maori women generally found it hard to speak out, but she was glad that she had.[3]

Another woman featured in the same programme alleged abuse by her stepfather.

> I figured that if he abused me as the eldest, he might leave my sisters alone. I felt like I wanted to kill him. He used to hold me down over the wash-house sink with the broom handle. He told me he would kill me if I told Mum. I used to get into the shower and bath-tub and try and scrub myself clean.[4]

The stepfather pleaded guilty at a marae hearing. The whanau stripped him of his mana and matuatanga and kaumatua status and banned him from the marae. But eight months later when filming took place he was in denial. He claimed he was drunk all the time, and had never abused anyone.

There was a time when belonging to a gang almost certainly meant having to be involved with rape in order to be seen to be 'staunch'. Such was the case with Black Power, probably New Zealand's best-known gang. For years women were treated as objects to be enjoyed at gang members' behest, and no amount of imprisonment for rape and other charges of violence made any difference. Prison was seen as a place to recruit new members. The traditional retributive justice process could not stem the violence towards women. In effect it increased it.

Then came a dramatic shift in attitude. At their 1978 national convention, Black Power, led by their president, Rei Harris, banned rape. Rediscovery of traditional Maori justice and values had a significant part to play in this conversion. So too did the strength and integrity of the president and some of his chief supporters.

But for some old habits die hard. There were subsequent cases that Black Power dealt with themselves. Bill Maung, former judge and legal adviser to Black Power, has talked about how the gang dealt with such violations of their moral code.

He tells of one incident when a young woman came to the Wellington chapter and reported that she had been raped by three of their members. She preferred not to go to the police, so it was agreed they would be dealt with on a marae. Amster Reedy of Ngati Porou, at that time a lecturer at teachers' college and a kaumatua, was one of about 50 who gathered to hear the case: Maori wardens, social workers, whanau, Black Power members.

After hearing the young woman's story, the hui reflected on what should happen to the three young men. One of them came from Taranaki and his kuia berated him tearfully, saying that their tribe had always walked with pride, and now he had made them all crawl seeking forgiveness. One suggestion was that they should all be exiled from Aotearoa forever, banished and forced to leave the country and the people they had so betrayed.

The offenders then took the floor and admitted the rapes. Their remorse was overwhelming, their desire to change and do reparation genuine. Pills and alcohol had obviously been contributing factors, though they claimed no mitigation from that source. They experienced tremendous shame in front of their whanau, their peers, their tribes. They vowed never to re-offend.

Then the young woman spoke, saying that she forgave them. Later, in explaining why, she said that for once in her life she had felt in control of a major situation, so she felt she could afford to be generous to them given the sorrow they had expressed.

Finally the penalty was spelt out. Quoting an old Maori proverb, Reedy noted that shame would be their principal punishment. There was, he said, no more powerful punishment in Maori society than whakama. People had been known to will themselves to death because the finger of shame had been pointed at them. The young men were also placed under close supervision and ordered to pay $20 a week each from their meagre incomes to the woman for six months. This constituted about a quarter of their incomes.

None of the men involved re-offended. One later committed suicide, though no definite connection was made with his rape offence. Another became a strong family man and a leader in the development of his whanau and people. Under Pakeha law, says Maung, they would still be sitting on all their anger in prison, while the woman, after a degrading court experience, would have become a marked woman and would have had to leave town.[5]

In the Whanau Awhina programme at the Hoani Waititi Marae in West Auckland, marae justice using traditional and modern insights seems to be working well. John Perkis, the justice programme chairman, says that 'the purpose of the process is the restoration of a person's mana. To restore him or her to society with mana intact, on the marae we don't discriminate. Raggy-arsed guys are treated the same as the prime minister.'[6]

An evaluation of the marae process by the Crime Prevention Unit concluded that Whanau Awhina is working. The rate of recidivism for clients who completed the pilot period was 22 percent, compared with 10 percent at nearby Waitakere's police diversion scheme. If the comparison seems unflattering, the report also shows 80 percent of Whanau Awhina's clients had considerable criminal histories, whereas the police diversion scheme usually deals with first offenders.

Marae chairman Pita Sharples says that 'Maori being dealt with by Maori is a key factor in achieving results. It's a process of healing. We deal with the circumstances of the case rather than just with the offence. For two to three hours we look at the charge and circumstances and make an action plan. Families are welcomed with a karakia (prayer), with kuia and kaumatua present. Then the real dynamics, the impact of the marae, takes over. That's been our methodology. We're quite proud of the results achieved.'[7]

Whanau Awhina's achievements depend on the passion and commitment of a volunteer panel well skilled at responding to mute shrugs, one-word answers and long silences. Questioning can be torrid, panel members stern. Family group conferences become emotional as more information is elicited. Inevitably, panel members know the offender's extended family. The panel formulates a plan to break the offending cycle. Idleness, lack of motivation, poor education, low self-esteem, unemployment and financial hardship emerge as the main contributing factors. An offender's community service is often based around marae projects.[8]

Judge Coral Shaw of Henderson is a great admirer of the programme and insists that programmes like Whanau Awhina should be properly funded and included within the legal framework of New Zealand.[9]

The Traditional Approach
Prior to European contact, Maori had a well-developed system of custom and practice that ensured the protection of individuals, the stability of social life and the integrity of the group.

The system of governance within the Maori system was based on tikana (justice or fairness as evidenced in customary practice). The relationships between people were at the heart of tikana. Protocol was the method by which these relationships were established and maintained.

This is demonstrated in the karanga (the call onto the marae), the mihi (the greeting), the hongi (the touching), kaitahi (eating together) and moetahi (sleeping together), which were important features of any gathering and remain important today.

Fundamental to the definition of relationships was whakapapa (genealogy), which established the historical basis for current relationships. The reality of social life was played out in the whanau and hapu structures: the immediate family and wider clan that stand behind each individual member of the community. The interests of whanau and hapu were the yardstick by which justice was measured – not the interests of the individual. It was through whanau and hapu that the health and stability of society were maintained – not through the actions of individuals.

Essentially the system was akin to what is now referred to as restorative justice. There were a number of important elements in this. When there was a breach, community process enabled a consideration of the interests of the whanaungatanga (social group) and ensured the integrity of the social fabric. Through whanau or hapu meetings, and on occasion iwi meetings, the voices of all parties could be heard and decisions arrived at by consensus (kotahitanga). The aim was to restore the mana of the victim, the victim's family and the family of the offender, and to ensure that measures were taken to restore the future social order of the wider community. Because these concepts were given meaning in the context of the wider group, retribution against an individual offender was not seen as the primary mechanism for achieving justice. Rather, the group was accountable for the actions of the individual (manaakitanga) and that exacted compensation on behalf of the aggrieved.

So is the marae justice outlined in the cases above a modern version of traditional Maori justice, or one culturally influenced by Pakeha traditions?

Moana Jackson of Ngati Porou and Ngati Kahungunu says that research shows that this type of marae justice is a product of the Crown which, early this century, set up marae or Maori Committees under Maori Council legislation. They were set up not to respect the articles of the Treaty of Waitangi, but to destroy Maori social and judicial structures. A specific purpose of the legislation was to break down surviving iwi and hapu authority by replacing them with Crown-funded bodies.

He says that these committees practising 'marae justice' had very limited authority and very limited subordinate jurisdiction to 'hear' cases on a marae. The structures formed part of the subordination of Maori decision-making to one Pakeha law. He believes its use today confirms that subordination.[10]

Edward Shortland, Protector of Aborigines, writing in 1856, described his understanding of Maori law. He said Maori sought compensation rather than punishment for the injury or crime. He complained that their methods of redress were often unjust in his opinion, 'with innocent persons being made to suffer for the faults of others'. For instance, in cases of adultery, the relations of the guilty parties were liable to suffer, and sometimes even the relations of the injured husband.[11]

He saw the question of honour and satisfaction as a major component of Maori understanding of justice. He wrote that the friendly involvement of a stranger in their quarrels was never taken amiss by Maori and it often enabled a peaceful settlement by helping the weaker party save face and withdraw. He noted that Maori always sought to take their stand and make a point, even if eventually they conceded the argument.[12]

Criminologist John Pratt confirms the restorative nature of the process. He writes that the purpose of the justice system, which usually took the form of a hearing on the marae (area in front of the meeting house or wharenui) or inside a special meeting house called a wharerunanga, was to investigate the matter and try to restore the balance that had been disturbed. This usually meant redressing the harm done to the victim.

The quantity of redress would depend on the degree of the offence: a form of compensation (utu) for some, with mediation to remove causes of tension. Other offences – say some breaches of tapu – would be seen to be so serious that death would be demanded. Whatever, the interests of the victim and his or her family or tribe were central to the administration of justice. Indeed, the victim's 'right' to justice could be handed down from one generation to another and could be pursued against the wrongdoer and his next of kin or tribe. Hence the importance attached to dispute proceedings, which might last for days while a resolution was being negotiated.

Pratt says that here, as well, the justice system did not exist in isolation from the rest of society (as with the elitism and professional dominance to be found in the European model) but was completely integrated within it, rooted in the everyday experiences of Maori people. The most prevalent sanction seems to have been utu – and the usual method of securing satisfaction in this way would be for the offended party and his kinsmen to act as a raiding party (taua muru) and plunder the offender and his kin. The scope and extent of the raid would have been agreed in advance.[12]

Shortland presented a 19th-century Pakeha version of how Pakeha generally viewed Maori behaviour. He wrote that thieving was not regarded as disgraceful, and was therefore a common vice of the youth of the country . However, when a thief was detected, he was not allowed to escape without punishment. Once, when Shortland was absent, his house at Maketu was broken into by two young men, who stole some small items. They were soon discovered, and most of the property was restored. Afterwards a public meeting was called to deal with the matter. It so happened that one of them was the son of a chief, who owned a piece of land near his house. Shortland had wished to include the land within his boundary. The owner refused to part with it, as the soil was rich and the situation convenient for a garden. Now he offered it voluntarily as compensation for the theft.[13]

Another major component of Maori law was muru, which in essence amounted to compensation. It was enforced by a raiding or stripping party. A person may have been guilty of some offence or may have suffered an accident. In either event muru was appropriate. While Europeans dreaded the arrival of the stripping party – the taua muru – the Maori would welcome it. For them it would be a point of honour to have food ready for the stripping party on their arrival. Their social position would be enhanced, not diminished, by the rigour of the stripping.[14]

Not every tribe followed the same pattern or employed the same sanctions. Teone Taare Tikao, a leading chief of Ngai Tahu at the turn of the century, explained his tribe's approach to muru.

> Muru was not common in some parts of the South Island, but we had it in Banks Peninsula. Tapui, a son of Whiua, was taken prisoner by Te Rauparaha to the North Island, where he married a Ngati-Awa woman. They came to Akaroa at the time of the rongopai (when peace was made and Christianity came in). He died and a North Island man of Akaroa took her to wife. She was a putao (widow), and this was not according to custom, so the relatives felt they must muru him and kill someone else. So the people went to plunder him but there was not much to take. The woman died soon after. In the old days the muru party would have taken the goods and burnt the house, but they did not go so far [this time].[15]

Differing Features

The fundamental differences between Maori and Pakeha law were many and varied. The whole English system of courts with prosecutors, judges and lawyers skilfully weaving their way through legal precedents and volumes of law and acts of Parliament was totally alien to Maori. So too was the notion that the English law dealt only with the individuals involved. Maori law always presumed a collective or corporate responsibility for offending and restoration while Pakeha law looked only at the individual and his or her guilt.

The Maori concept was built on the most fundamental of all Maori values – that we are all part of one another. The Pakeha concept was built on the notion that each person is individually responsible for his or her own plight. Maori found imprisonment abhorrent, whereas Pakeha took it to be the norm.

In two areas in particular was there a fundamental difference in terms of redress. Utu, or compensation and satisfaction, was an important concept at the very heart of Maori justice. It found no comparable expression in English law. And muru, a formalised concept of retributive compensation, was a feature central to Maori but alien to English law.

In ancient times not all cases ended up in complete reconciliation. Maori justice provided the death penalty or banishment from the tribe as appropriate sanctions on occasions. But the aim was always restorative: restore the mana of the tribe and of the offended parties. If the victims were of high birth, then sometimes only drastic measures such as death could achieve this. While execution may appear to be harsh to modern eyes, it should be noted that at this point in history, England had more than 200 offences that warranted execution, and a further quota that resulted in transportation to the colonies as convicts.

Hohua Tutengaehe recalls hearing from his mother that the brother of the Ariki, a very high chief, had raped a woman of high birth. The hearing was held at a hui on the marae and it was the unanimous decision of the rangatira present that he would have to pay with his life for assaulting the tapu of the tangata. He was executed publicly on the marae by his older brother, the ariki, so that 'the stain and blemish was removed from the aristocracy of ancient bloodlines'. He was clubbed in the temple. Before the execution, the brothers clasped each other in tears, with the doomed man's last words to his brother being, 'Kei te pai (it's all right).'

Not all murderers were executed. Shortland recorded the case in 1844 of Hinekina, of the Hapu Katahuriri. She lived at Moeraki with a Pakeha by whom she had two children, plus a child of about 12 years old by a former husband. The child went missing unexpectedly and the mother was unable to explain its absence, so Te Ruakaio, a near relative of Tuhawaiki, and two other women went searching. They eventually found the child's body in a waterhole and some whalers from the settlement helped them retrieve it. When confronted with the dead child, Hinekina confessed to the killing.

> The natives generally, as well as the Europeans, were very indignant. Hinekino subsequently fled to Waitaki, but has been brought back by the European who lived with her, with whom she still remains.[17]

After the Treaty

The settler government was in no mood to allow such a widely divergent system of justice to exist parallel to its own imported British system. Yet the Treaty of Waitangi clearly stated that Maori laws and customs were to be maintained. Maori law and the process of Maori justice have an inherent validity as taonga (treasures) and as an expression of rangatiratanga (authority) guaranteed in article 2 of the treaty document.

As Moana Jackson said in a recent submission to Parliament:

> Under article 1 of the Maori version, the Maori gave kawanatanga to the Queen. To the Maori this term meant simply that the Queen should provide for the good

order and security of the country by exercising control over the Pakeha settlers, while recognising the special rights which accompanied the tangata whenua status of Maori. Recognition of these rights carried with it an acknowledgment of the laws and institutions existing within Maori society. To ensure their maintenance within a rapidly changing world, the Maori saw those laws as operating in a parallel system to that of the Crown.[18]

Pakeha clearly saw it differently, and to them kawanatanga corresponded to a more absolute concession of sovereignty, resulting ultimately in the supremacy of the Pakeha way. Jackson again:

> The undertaking to preserve 'other properties' in article 2 was translated to include 'all things highly prized such as their own customs and culture'. However, although Maori law was frequently described as a 'quaint custom', it has never been regarded as sufficiently quaint to be protected under article 2. Neither has there been an acceptance of the Maori belief that the 'tino rangatiratanga' guaranteed over those customs was an assertion of authority and control. Any recognition of Maori law, Maori authority and Maori participation in general law-making processes was excluded. In effect, this has been used to deny Maori involvement in, and thus excluded Maori values from, the law-making process.

Article 2 of the Maori version of the treaty guarantees the right of rangatiratanga over taonga or prized things. In article 4 the treaty ensures protection of 'te ritenga Maori', that is, the basic threads of law, religion, language and other taonga that wove Maori society together. Those articles in conjunction recognise the general authority of Maori people to monitor the conduct of their own.[19]

In other words, Maori were guaranteed that their system of law would be protected and allowed to develop under the terms of the treaty. That they have not been thus allowed is clearly evident. The law of Aotearoa has been consistently in breach of the Treaty of Waitangi virtually since its signing.

What were the particular ideals and institutions of Maori law at the time? Did they contain a clearcut code of behaviour and how widely was it accepted?

Jackson, in his parliamentary submission, argued that such a code clearly existed. The system was clear and defined, and Maori people knew which acts were unacceptable – hara or crimes. The definition of hara rose from a framework of social relationships based on group rather than individual concerns. The rights of individuals, or the hurts they may suffer when their rights were abused, were indivisible from the welfare of the whanau, the hapu, the iwi. Each had reciprocal obligations found in a shared genealogy, and a set of behavioural precedents established by common tipuna.

> Those precedents became te tikanga o nga hara (the criminal code) and were accepted as binding because they 'were the law that came from the wisdom of our past... which binds us to our tipuna'. They became part of the process by which certain acts were made subject to sanction. These definitions of

unacceptability were based not so much on the fact that people had individual rights, but rather that they had collective responsibilities. They were based too on the specific belief that all people had an inherent tapu that must not be abused, and on the general perception that society could only function if all things, physical and spiritual, were held in balance.

Jackson goes on to explain that the commission of nga hara would damage that tapu and upset that balance. Constraints on behaviour, a criminal law, had to be developed to preserve harmony within and among individuals and their community. That law was not an isolated set of rules to be invoked only upon an infringement of accepted behavioural limits. Neither was it part of a distinct discipline to be 'learned' separately from the spiritual and religious beliefs of society.

Instead, it grew out of and was inextricably woven into the religious and hence the everyday framework of Maori life. It reflected a special significance that was manifest in the spiritual ties of the people to their Gods, and the whakapapa shared between individuals and the ancestors who bore them. The Maori lived not under the law but with it. This inter-relationship affected the definition of the criminal act itself, the ideas of responsibility for it, and the process by which the hara would be redressed.

Jackson says that because individuals were inextricably linked by whakapapa to their whanau and iwi, so were their actions the unavoidable responsibility of the wider group. An offender could not be isolated as solely responsible for wrongdoing; a victim could never be isolated as bearing alone the pain of an offence. There was a collective rather than an individual criminal responsibility, a sense of indirect as well as direct liability.[20]

As in indigenous cultures the world over, the inter-relationship between the deities, the ancestors and the living thus provided the base of definition of both crimes and responsibility. Certain acts were criminal not so much because of the immediate imbalance they caused or the social dysfunction they created, but because of the behavioural prescriptions laid down through the interdependence of the living and the ancestors. The act itself was less important in explaining offending than the reasons why it was defined as unacceptable.

John Pratt says the act of rape was thus a hara punishable by death, not just because it physically hurt the victim, or because, as in early English law, it damaged a chattel owned by a man. Rather it was forbidden because it violated the inherent tapu of women. It thus in turn upset the spiritual, emotional and physical balance within the victim herself, and within the relationships she had within her community and tipuna. The act of rape was therefore proscribed to protect that balance and to preserve her tapu. The crime of incest was similarly predicated in a specific weave of ancestral and spiritual prohibition.[21]

Jackson says that in this sense, Maori law was no different from the laws of other indigenous peoples. The purpose of the legal process was to ensure order and the survival of the collective and the individual. The nature of what was to survive, what was to be ordered, was an intricately interwoven taniko centring on group relationships, and the respect and reverence for tipuna and land from which the sense of order came. The law thus embodied ideals, hopes and potential, as well as a longing for harmony. It strengthened and directed individuals and iwi. The nexus between the spiritual and the temporal was so close as to refuse separation. The links between culture and matauranga were so close as to be indivisible in the process of defining wrongdoing.[22]

It is clear, Jackson says, that in pre-colonial times there were specially trained tohunga or experts in the law who chaired or supervised hearings. It was not just the kaumatua who sat in judgment – the hearings included experts in law and Maori legal processes.

There were educated and trained tohunga who dealt with legal matters in concert with representatives of the disputant whanau. These representatives were often pakeke, but the process could not function without those trained to administer it.[23]

He says that if Maori are to reclaim their own judicial authority then it will not be as some 'informal' process that anybody can call or set up. Its principal aim will be that of mea tuhonohono, a process designed to ensure ongoing 'bringing together' or harmony. It will be a process involving all parties, mediated by appropriate tohunga, backed by the authority to impose sanction, and implemented to seek the restoration of balance.[24]

One System, Not Two
The prevailing belief among 19th-century government officials and settlers was that the British system was the best in the world. They never really sought to understand the different goals and processes of Maori justice. The Treaty of Waitangi was soon forgotten.

The British government was not keen to allow two parallel systems – one retributive, one primarily restorative – to develop in its new colony. Pratt explains that in the last century, the British Colonial Office and New Zealand governments pursued a policy of assimilation toward Maori people in regard to their modes of punishment and dispute resolution.

Although Maori were formally made citizens of New Zealand under the terms of the Treaty of Waitangi in 1840, the concept of citizenship was seen as having much wider meaning than this. It referred to the various modes of behaviour, practices, social codes and institutions that together represented 'the British way of life' in the 19th century. The assimilation process referred to the methods by which Maori people gradually achieved this status and in return for which had to give up their land, culture and institutions, including the power to punish in their own way. They were expected to stop being Maori and, instead, to act and behave as Europeans.

This is not to say that Maoridom itself was dismantled, to disappear forever. What it did mean was that Maori were ultimately forced outside of and excluded from official power and administration. Any subsequent assertion of it would take the form of resistance to European citizenship and the British way of life, on which official power had come to be based.[25]

The New Zealand government was hell-bent on a process of assimilation, meaning that traditional Maori customs that in any way affected European settlers had to be removed. Within months of the signing of the treaty, Governor Hobson reflected the views of the settlers when he sought to impose the British legal system upon Maori and Pakeha alike. Hobson believed Maori habits to be so different to those of civilised life, and their practices so repugnant to the customs of Englishmen, that he scarcely hoped to preserve peace when the settlers became more numerous. He also looked to the simple assertion of his authority, rather than some system of practical co-operation with the chiefs, as the solution to New Zealand's difficulties.[26]

Maori culture, traditions and values were not to be allowed to develop alongside those of the Pakeha society if there was any way they would undermine the ideology, identity and power of the new government. Pratt confirms that the form of colonisation and legal protection envisaged by Glenelg (Secretary of State to the Colonies based in London) assumed that assimilation of the Maori into 'the British way of life' would be the result and that they would become British citizens in the widest meaning of the term.[27]

Thus the decimation of the traditional restorative philosophy of Maori justice was set in place by British officials in London, many of whom never set foot on New Zealand soil.

There were some in New Zealand who tried to modify English law to accommodate some aspects of traditional law. In 1844, under Governor Fitzroy, the Native Protectorate Department proposed the establishment of Native Courts, which would be administered by the Protector and local chiefs. Mixed juries would be used for serious cases. As Pratt notes, judgments would be recorded in the manner of British practice, and thereby establish judicial precedent and certainty. Meanwhile the presence of the chiefs would give the proceedings added authority. It was hoped the practice of muru would fall into disuse.

In cases other than rape and murder, a Maori would be allowed to go free on payment of a £20 deposit. In cases of theft, Maori offenders could escape imprisonment by paying four times the value of the goods stolen – recognition of the utu principle – and utu could also be enacted by Maori complainants against Pakeha defendants. In addition, 'people of the native race were not liable for imprisonment for debt'. The principle was extended in the Fines for Assaults Ordinance 1845: the court was given the power to award compensation from the fine imposed provided that the sum so awarded did not amount to more than half the fine levied.[28]

Fitzroy's policies were very much out of step with the wishes and views of the European settlers. For them, the misguided philanthropy of the Colonial Office was actually preventing the advancement of civilisation. In their eyes, formally recognising the indigenous punishment process would only help prolong Maori culture. It could only be harmful for the 'natives' as well as hindering their own plans for settlement.

Alan Ward gives credit to Fitzroy's effort to include restorative dimensions in the law, saying it was a genuine attempt to make English law more acceptable to the Maori by incorporating a useful point of custom (utu).[29]

The rejection by London of Fitzroy's Native Exemption Ordinance was to have far-reaching consequences for race relations and the administration of justice in New Zealand. The effects are still with us. Fitzroy's successor, Governor Grey, was instructed by London to amend the ordinance to allow British law to assume undoubted supremacy.

In 1846 Grey moved to systematically undermine the traditional authority of chiefs by appointing magistrates who would have summary jurisdiction over everyone, Maori and Pakeha. This was a major first step to total dominance of the legal processes by English law.

Some elements of Maori law did prevail for some years afterwards. The Native District Regulations Act 1858 specified that Maori, through local runanga rather than chiefs, could dispense justice in minor matters. These matters included drunkenness and the control of dogs.

A ministerial memorandum of 1861 outlined the government's intentions. Here the government was speaking with a forked tongue, for while it did empower local runanga in minor matters, it further disempowered Maori by refusing to allow dimensions with no place in English law to be used. These included such things as breeches of tapu, and making taua muru on the innocent relatives of offenders. This latter process was part of the notion of collective responsibility. Even so, restoration rather than retribution remained at the heart of runanga justice.

Governor Grey in 1862 clarified the position of runanga further. Grey explained that there would be village runanga (composed of elected villagers) under the auspices of new officers called civil commissioners. Grey explained that his policy through the runanga would propose local laws concerning cattle pounds, fences, branding cattle, thistles and weeds, dogs, spirits and drunkenness, putting down bad customs of the old Maori law such as the taua muru, and the various things that especially concerned the people living in the district. They would also make regulations about schools, roads (if they wished for them) and other matters which promoted the public good of that district.[30]

In effect, the runanga seem to have functioned in ways not too dissimilar to the subsequent development of borough and county councils. Regular use of runanga for the purposes the colonial government intended failed to materialise as bigger issues such as the struggle over land assumed prominence.

In modern times there have been various attempts by Maori to regain control of their judicial processes. In 1998 the New Zealand Maori Council recommended that essential elements of any future legal system in Aotearoa based on restorative justice should:

- Give Maori a stake in the justice system by giving them control of the decision-making processes;
- Properly identify the communities to which Maori belong and where their offending must be dealt with;
- Allow Maori to identify those who should take responsibility for the process;
- Formally recognise the validity of community process as a legitimate alternative to adjudicatory process;
- Resource communities to set up restorative justice processes and to provide for the outcomes agreed to through these processes;
- Develop the resources within the communities to provide for the needs of families and children before offending occurs;
- Provide for safety nets within the community that will lessen the chances of offending, monitor those at risk, and develop community supports;
- Develop rules about when back-up systems can be used to provide for partial, temporary or permanent withdrawal of offenders from the community through adjudicatory process when this is the only method likely to protect the safety of citizens.[31]

Conclusion

There have been many other modern examples of local Maori communities dealing with offenders accused of various types of criminal activity, ranging from stealing to rape. The cases of the kaumatua in the Far North in September 1993, of other Waikato kaumatua stripped of their status by marae justice and the ambit of cases dealt to in the Whanau Awhina programme give but three of many indications that the parallel Maori process continues in various ways, in various places and is expanding.

Footnotes

1. *Inside New Zealand* documentary 'Marae Justice', TV3, August 1994
2. Ibid
3. Ibid
4. Ibid
5. Pamela Stirling, *NZ Listener*, 14 May 1990
6. Liz Mahoney, *NZ Listener*, 18 April 1998
7. Ibid
8. Ibid
9. Ibid
10. Letter, Moana Jackson to the author, 17 October 1994
11. Edward Shortland, *Traditions and Superstitions of the New Zealanders*, Longman, Brown, Green, Longman and Roberts, London, 1856. Reprinted by Capper Press, Christchurch, 1980, p236
12. Ibid, p238
13. John Pratt, *Punishment in a Perfect Society, The New Zealand Penal System 1840-1939*, Victoria University Press, 1992, p35
14. Shortland, op cit, p240
15. O. Wilson, *From Hongi Hika to Hone Heke*, John McIndoe Ltd, Dunedin, 1985, p127
16. *Tikao Talks*, told by Teone Taare Tikau to Herries Beattie, Penguin, 1990, pp153-54
17. Shortland, letter to Fitzroy, 1844, Papers Relative to New Zealand, No. 71. Also found in *The Southern Districts of New Zealand* by Edward Shortland, 1851, reprinted by Capper Press, Christchurch, 1974, pp132-33
18. Moana Jackson, 'Criminality and the Exclusion of Maori', from *Essays on Criminal Law in New Zealand – Towards Reform*, edited by Neil Cameron and Simon France, Victoria University Press, Wellington, 1990, p32
19. Ibid, p33
20. Ibid, p30
21. Pratt, op cit, p13
22. Jackson, op cit, pp27-28
23. Moana Jackson, paper 'A Maori Justice System', Maori Law Society Annual Hui, Te Herenga Marae, 26 August 1994
24. Letter, Moana Jackson to the author, 17 October 1994
25. Pratt, op cit, p13
26. Alan Ward, *A Show of Justice*, Auckland University Press, Oxford University Press, 1973, p58
27. Pratt, op cit, p32
28. Ibid, p42
29. Ward, op cit, p67
30. Pratt, op cit, p53
31. *Restorative Justice – A Maori Perspective*, submission to the Ministry of Justice on behalf of the New Zealand Maori Council, August 1996. Compiled by Donna Durie Hall.

CHAPTER SEVEN

A Gift to the World:
Youth Justice in Aotearoa

Children's Court, July 1964:

Three youths, each aged 16, appeared today for sentence on six charges of car conversion. Stephen Menzies, Jason Pirihio, and Robert Pound had pleaded guilty to the charges. They said that they were bored and just having fun. They had not damaged the cars. All the offending had taken place on the night preceding Otago's challenge for the Ranfurly Shield.

The magistrate, Mr Raymond Brown SM, said that the community was fed up to the back teeth with young hooligans stealing as they wished, and joy-riding around town. He said that he planned to put a stop to such anti-social behaviour before it got out of hand. He added that he hoped the effect of his sentence would deter other young people from following in the defendants' footsteps. He sentenced each defendant to borstal training. This is a variable sentence ranging from four months to two years to be served at Invercargill Borstal.

Social Welfare report, July 1994:

A youth aged 16 who admitted stealing a total of six cars over a 12-hour period on a recent Friday night met with representatives of his family, the police, the Department of Social Welfare and four of the car owners in a family group conference convened by Ms Cecily Hamara. After opening with karakia, the kaumatua of the family spoken of his embarrassment that one of his nephews had got himself into so much trouble.

Constable Bernice McGara, from the Youth Aid section of the police, read out the summary of facts. This included the information that one of the cars had a front fender damaged and another had interior damage. The young man then admitted the offences, saying he had been 'out of it' on drugs at the time. One car owner angrily said that didn't help him get to an important meeting on time and he had ended up paying $56 for a taxi. Another said he had appreciated the youth's guilty pleas but wondered whether or not the whole episode not might be repeated once this case was over. A third said that he had lost his $200 no-claim bonus claim from the insurance company and wondered how the youth felt about that.

The co-ordinator said it was up to the group to arrive at a suitable penalty. After further discussion among family members, who spoke of their experience of the youth, his inability to make friends and his waywardness at school, the family retired to discuss what they thought an appropriate penalty might be. After a cup of tea the conference reconvened and the family put forward their proposal. They suggested that the youth repay both the money for the no-claim bonus and the taxi fee. Further to that, he agreed to see a counsellor with a view to entering the Odyssey House drug programme.

He accepted the offer of one of the car owners to be taught to drive properly and eventually get a licence. In exchange he agreed to cut that owner's lawns each Saturday during the following summer. All present agreed on this procedure.

Right now a revolution is occurring in the field of youth justice in Aotearoa. A new paradigm of justice is operating, which is very traditional in its philosophy, yet revolutionary in its effects. A restorative philosophy of justice has replaced a retributive one. Ironically, 150 years after the traditional Maori restorative praxis was abolished in Aotearoa, youth justice policy is once again operating from the same philosophy.

With the introduction of the Children, Young Persons and Their Families Act in 1989, the Labour government initiated the most sweeping reform of juvenile justice our country has seen this century. In fact it appears as a new concept, and in many parts of the world its implementation in New Zealand is being watched with increasing envy.

No longer are young offenders immediately arrested, charged and taken before the Children's or Young Offenders' Court and dealt with like adult offenders. In the vast majority of cases, after they have been apprehended by the police they are restored to their families and with considerable speed a new less formal process gets under way.

Its aim is to restore the wellbeing of the community by having the offenders face up to their responsibility for their crime. Victims, who are normally shut out of the process, are offered an opportunity of being involved in the follow-up. As Australian criminologist John Braithwaite points out, this reforming has the effect of bringing shame and personal and family accountability for wrongdoing back into the justice process.[1]

Judge F. W. M. McElrea, Youth Court liaison judge for Auckland, suggests that there are three radical changes involved in this new process. They involve the transfer of power from the state to the community, the use of the family group conference as the mechanism for producing a negotiated community response, and the involvement of victims as key participants, making possible a healing process for victim, offender and the community.

In the old model of justice the judge is in control, representing the state and exercising authority given by the state either to impose punishment or to direct intervention in peoples' lives for 'welfare' reasons. By contrast, in the new model the principle task of the judge is to facilitate and encourage the implementation of solutions devised through the group family conference procedure, and to act as a backup if these solutions are not implemented.[2]

Judge Michael Brown, principal Youth Court judge for New Zealand, asks judges to aid this process by asking who is the community? What are its strengths? How are those strengths best made use of? He notes that the concept of a judge trying to facilitate the strengths of others and bring them to the fore is radically different to the controlling position of the traditional judge.

At the heart of the revolution in youth justice in Aotearoa is the transfer of power from the state to the family group conference. In the traditional court, the key players are the judge, the prosecutor, the defence lawyer and the offenders. With the family group conference the key players are the offender, his or her family, the victim and their support group, with the facilitator, the police and other professionals all present in 'helping roles'. They assist the process so that the offender, within his 'family group' – which may or may not include only his immediate birth family – is helped to recognise the damage done and can be confronted by the victim as to the negative effects being experienced. Often victims have become more nervous, less trusting and retain considerable anger about the offence.

A key player in the family group conference is the victim. This represents a radical departure from the retributive system still prevalent in our adult system. The victim is encouraged to join the conference, express feelings about the offences, and then be part of the discussion of what might be a suitable sanction for the offender. This is acknowledged as usually being a very healing process for most victims, provided they are given adequate time and opportunity to be properly involved.

The Process
It is the role of the Youth Justice Co-ordinator to convene the family group conference, with the help of social workers. Generally the offender's family nominate the venue, which can vary. Sometimes their own homes are best suited, sometimes a church hall, a friend's home, a marae. Sometimes even a police cell has been used, though this is not usually considered to be appropriate.

Often the proceedings are opened by the offender's family. Many start with karakia or prayer. What happens next is worked out by the participants: there is no set formal procedure. Often the co-ordinator, after introducing people, will have the police summary of facts read. This can be challenged by the offender and may be amended on the spot. The offender then is usually invited to respond. If the offender denies the allegations, the conference is adjourned to enable a Youth

Court hearing to be held. In the vast majority of cases the offender admits guilt, sometimes offering an explanation as to why he offended.

Then the victim is invited to respond. This can take a variety of forms. A fleshing-out of how the incident has affected the wellbeing of the victim will usually follow. For example, if a burglary has been admitted, it may emerge that the property stolen had belonged to a grandmother and had sentimental value, that the ring taken was perhaps a dead mother's wedding ring, that the clothing stolen was to have been worn at a wedding, that the tools taken were work tools and irreplaceable.

Sometimes women express their feelings that in invading their home, a burglar has invaded their very privacy. Some describe this feeling as being akin to sexual violation. The offender may find out that the victim now cannot sleep at night, is scared of the dark, or has withdrawn from community groups because of mistrust of strangers.

This will usually all come as a complete shock to offenders, who thought they were only pinching a few things to trade for drugs. Deborah Hollings, a lawyer with wide experience in youth justice, says it never appears in the summary of facts, and very rarely in the victim impact reports, that this was not just a car being stolen. This offence wrecked a very important part of the victim's life.

That sense of meeting eyeball to eyeball is a very important aspect of the family group conference (FGC). It means the young person cannot remain aloof; he has to be confronted by his victim. It is also a chance from the victim's viewpoint to get his anger out, a chance to state the repercussions, and a chance to reach across communities. Often there is a racial aspect there as well.

Hollings says there is also the process of the victim actually being reaffirmed, because the last time he saw his offender may have been in a dark alleyway. This time he is seeing his offender surrounded by his family, who are frequently crying with shame. In some 50 percent of cases (Hollings' guess) the offender is also crying with shame. The victim is re-empowered by that process.[3]

Usually there follows an apology. The highly charged atmosphere, the tearful response of many, often means the offender is overcome with remorse at realising the damage caused. At this point the real healing begins because, to use a term coined by Judge McElrea, 'responsible reconciliation' begins.

Then the penalty is discussed. All have a voice as to what is appropriate. The victim's views are again obtained at that point. Usually they are interested mostly in putting the wrong right, in reparation, in an apology, in having the young person come and work for them or a member of their family. Sometimes that conflicts, interestingly enough, with the police view.

So the victim is very powerful, they have a power of veto, as does everyone else in the FGC. The police then give their views as to what they would see as appropriate. The co-ordinators state the type of penalties they would see as appropriate for the type of offence and what funding is available from the department.

At that stage the family group retires on its own. Then the FGC comes back together, reunited, and the family spokesperson stands up and announces what the family has resolved in terms of penalty. There are sometimes further negotiations if the police or the victim are not happy, but usually there is agreement.

The meeting will then generally wind up with everyone having the chance to say how they feel about the process and sharing any other thoughts. Usually that ends with everyone saying that they wish the best of luck to the young person. Most cases end on that very positive note. Then the family close the meeting in a way appropriate to them.[4]

Research conducted by Dr Gabrielle Maxwell, senior research officer for the Commission for Children, and Dr Allison Morris of the Institute of Criminology, Cambridge, shows that the FGC does not always follow this rather idyllic process. In research covering the first three years of the process, in an average of 42 percent of cases the professionals did not leave the families alone to discuss a proposed penalty. In one area of the country this was 63 percent – nearly two-thirds of the cases.[5]

Sadly too in most cases the background to the offending was not discussed at any length. An exploration of the factors leading to the offending was either rare or made in random or haphazard fashion. Alcohol or drug use, for example, was raised and discussed for only some of the young people whose pattern of offending seemed to involve substance abuse.[6]

Despite some of these initial hiccups, this is clearly an exciting development in the field of criminal justice in Aotearoa. In effect the state has been removed from the centre of the justice equation and replaced by those most affected: the offender, the victim, and their families, who make up the community. For the victims there is a special place. While all their scars may not be healed initially and while full satisfaction may not be achieved, at the very least they are invited into the heart of the process.

As criminologist John Braithwaite says, sometimes moving gestures of healing come from the victim side. They waive their right to compensation from an unemployed young offender who cannot afford it. They invite them to their home for dinner a week after the conference. They help to find an unemployed young offender a job, a homeless young person a home. In one amazing case, a female victim who had been robbed by a young offender at the point of a gun had the offender live in her home as part of the agreed plan of action.

People can be amazing when they are enmeshed in institutions that invite them to care about each other instead of hate each other. The surprising thing is that victims, who so often call for more blood in traditional Western justice systems, in New Zealand frequently plead with the police to waive punishment and 'give the kid another chance'. Partly this happens because victims get an insight through the process of dialogue into the shocking life circumstances the young offender has had to confront.[7]

Given the weaknesses inherent in human nature and the scarred backgrounds of many offenders and victims, it is remarkable what can be achieved. Often it takes a group consciousness to shake the bravado and macho attitude and allow something of the pain of the victim to penetrate the tough exterior.

Braithwaite points out that young offenders use a variety of techniques to protect themselves from the shame of what they have done. This collective encounter with the harm done is the best chance for piercing the barriers young offenders have erected. Quite often the anger or grief of the victim will miss its mark, going straight over the head of a young offender, on whom it has no emotional impact. But the grief of the victim might pierce the heart of the offender's mother as she sits behind him. Then it can be her sobbing that rips away the armour that protects the offender's emotions.

In short, the strength of the New Zealand process is that it is neither individualistic nor dyadic (as in traditional US victim-offender mediation) but that it engages multiplex communities of concern. Emotions of shame and feelings of responsibility are often brought out because shafts of emotion bounce from person to person within the room in unpredictable ways. When collectivities as well as individuals are targets of shaming, it is harder for responsible individuals to shrug off the shame.[8]

The ideal would be full reconciliation and healing, and it will happen in some instances. In most, particularly where there is personal injury involved, it probably won't. But at least in putting a human face on the crime it opens up the healing process. And that has to be good for everyone.

Background to Change

The Children, Young Persons and Their Families Act only came into existence in 1989. It was born out of the frustration of many in the juvenile justice field who found that the philosophy underpinning the former system left two major negative effects. The first was an orientation towards more offending, the second was the encouragement towards dependency on welfare as a way of life.

Previously youth offenders had often ended up in child welfare residential homes or, after serious offences, in detention centres (youth prisons), corrective training institutions or borstal. Here they were placed in state custody with other youthful offenders from similarly deprived backgrounds. For many such institutions provided their first real bonding with peers. For others, a real identity developed with a 'bad boy/bad girl' image that could only lead to lives as adult criminals. For all, new anti-social behaviour patterns were developed, along with new criminal skills.

The end result for too many was that such residential institutions became the first step along the road of habitual criminal behaviour and a lifetime in and out of jails. Prison chaplains and others well remember observing numerous reunions as new inmates arrived in prison and were reunited with old friends from one or other of the state's many residential homes.

Michael Doolan, Southern Regional Manager of the then New Zealand Children and Young Persons Service, nominated several other factors that led to the radical change towards a restorative philosophy.

- There was a growing dissatisfaction among practitioners (reflected in the wider community) about the effectiveness of work with young offenders. Practitioners laboured under the unreal expectation that they could control offending behaviour through treatment programmes. Gradually a loss of confidence in the goal of rehabilitation built up. The loss of confidence, when not explicit or recognised, was often expressed as failure to resource the work adequately, a marked lack of enthusiasm for doing the work at all, and advocacy for ill-defined preventative work directed towards at-risk young people with all its net-widening effects.
- There were new and more determined efforts by Maoridom to secure self-determination in a monocultural legal system that demonstrably discriminates against Maori and places little value on Maori customs, values and beliefs. The Maori renaissance contributed, in turn, to a renewed awareness of the plight of Pacific Island cultures in New Zealand society.
- Related to Maori concerns, but also an issue for the wider community, was the growing rejection of the paternalism of the state and its professionals, and a need to redress the imbalance of power between the state and its agents and individuals and families engaged by the criminal justice system.
- Sixty years of paternalistic welfare legislation had little impact on levels of offending behaviour. Costly therapeutic programmes that congregated young offenders, particularly in residential settings, emerged as part of the problem rather than as part of the solution. Decarceration and de-institutionalisation became the buzz words for both those seeking to free up locked-in resources for other uses and those seeking more positive outcomes for individuals.
- Concerns emerged for more decided justice, in both process and disposals. Courts were beginning to dismiss cases where prosecuting authorities had failed to exercise strict procedural safeguards in the questioning and/or arrest of juveniles; the indeterminate guardianship order as a response to the serious young offender was being used less and less. Increasing numbers of young offenders were being sent to the adult court for sentence (over 2000 in 1988), an indication of the inability of the juvenile system to deal with them effectively.[9]

Doolan also pointed out that previous diversion schemes for young offenders often had the opposite effect of what was intended: they ended up in more trouble rather than less. They had been largely constructed around panels of officials and professionals – the Children's Boards and Youth Aid Conferences – and functioned as quasi-judicial bodies. They have always been by-passed whenever police exercised their powers of arrest. With more than 60 percent of young offenders appearing on arrest, less than 40 percent of those who appeared had been considered for a diversion option. Worse still, there was evidence that the diversion mechanisms were having a net-widening effect, by drawing into their ambit very petty offenders who should and could have been handled in much less formal ways.[10]

The new Labour government of 1984 determined to overhaul what was clearly a leaking and creaking system. They appointed a working party that year to investigate how best to change the policy and process of dealing with young offenders. The party issued a working document in December 1984, which resulted in new legislation being introduced in December 1986. This proposed legislation met with widespread criticism, especially from Maori and Pacific Island leadership. It was also criticised by professionals for being top-heavy and bureaucratic.

The government listened and, when re-elected in 1987, set up another working party to advise a parliamentary select committee on how the bill needed to be changed. This committee travelled all over Aotearoa, listening to submissions on marae and from Pacific Island groups as well as from the general public.

The result was that at the second reading in Parliament in 1989 the bill reflected a whole new approach to juvenile offending, which later that year was passed into the Children, Young Persons and Their Families Act. This act is a tribute to the possibilities Parliament has to offer this country when time is taken for consultation and proper due process.

Success Rate

The beauty of the restorative justice policy and process introduced by the act is that it works in the vast majority of cases. Not only does it place responsibility clearly with offenders to deal with their own behaviour and its effects, but it encourages and empowers families to work together to overcome difficulties. In as much as at-risk families need some legislative framework within which to operate, this act provides it. A 90 percent agreement rate at family group conferences is testimony to the ability of parties to resolve most cases of youth offending. The mechanism used is a negotiated settlement rather than an imposed solution from the top.

It should be noted that not all juvenile offending ends up immediately with a family group conference. Some serious offenders are arrested by police in much the same way that adults are. They are then brought to the Youth Court. Then, if the charge is admitted, an FGC is held within 14 days. If it is admitted and the youth is remanded in custody, it is held within seven days. If the youth has initially pleaded not guilty but the charge has been proven in a Youth Court, an FCG is then held.

Maxwell and Morris researched the effects of the act in its first three years of operation and their findings were very positive. They found that 95 percent of young people are being made accountable for their anti-social and criminal actions. This is a remarkable figure. Sanctions evolving from the FGCs include apologies and active penalties such as fines, reparation, donations to charity, community work, work for the victim, driving disqualification and curfews.

Court appearances have plummeted. From a rate of something like 64 per 1000 young people appearing in court each year, it has dropped to 16. A third of young offenders used to appear in the court. Now it is only 10 percent, and the proportion who receive court orders has also decreased. Of the 10 percent who appear in court, only 5 percent actually end up with court orders because the court accepts the recommendation of the FGC. Residential custody is also far less common – less than half the previous figures – and the length of residential sentences has been decreased enormously. Now only about 2 percent of young offenders end up with a residential sentence, which is an astonishing transformation.[11]

There are many other positive qualities associated with this restorative process. In most cases, the family group conference is convened in half the amount of time that it used to take to get an case heard in the court. It is also much more culturally sensitive, with whatever is culturally appropriate being the norm. That is a massive change inside a short space in time. The involvement of families is a crucial concept. Often families are at their wits end as to how to deal with a particularly anti-social member. The group conference can often strengthen their resolve and determination to persevere.

The family involvement will obviously have appeal to those conservative political and church groupings in the community who are strong in promoting traditional values. Often for such groups punishment has been seen to be the primary way of coping. Now there is a new mechanism that strengthens the whole bonding network of the family.

Official post-election papers from the Justice Department in December 1993 indicated that the number of prosecuted cases for defendants aged 17, 18 and 19 years had dropped by 27 percent in the five years from 1987-92. Clearly the youth justice process, while not solely responsible for such a marked decline in offending, played a significant if not a dominant part.[12]

It has to be noted that not all family group conferences succeed. In a small number of cases the whole process becomes a complete fiasco. Victims remain in a 'hanging' mood and veto all attempts at reasonable sanction. Offenders sometimes remain arrogant and unmoved. Families sometimes fight and squabble among themselves and are unable to reach consensus. Bearing in mind that many families are almost dysfunctional, that some have a history of neglect, drugs and violence going back years, and that some have very few social skills in terms of relationships, it should come as no surprise that such is the case. But the failure of the few should not detract from the success of the many.

Conclusion

Many claim that the restorative process adopted with juvenile offenders in Aotearoa is the most important positive piece of social legislation adopted in a generation. This claim is not misplaced. That the dominant Pakeha culture chose to learn from Maori and other Polynesian traditions and apply the lessons to the whole community, regardless of race, is cause for pride.

It is early days yet for the Children, Young Persons and Their Families Act. It will need protection from hard-line elements in the community who lust for blood and have done in every century. It will need fine-tuning as experience throws up new insights that will improve it.

It will be hard – if not impossible – to prove its strengths to the doubters because its strengths will be in its promotion of personal responsibility among young offenders, their maturation into young adults, the strengthening of family ties and community bonds, and its positive flow-on effect to a rising generation of children. In time it will be easier to see its impact on crime rates and imprisonment numbers. But such bald statistics will never tell the full story of its impact.

It has been a radical step and obviously a positive one. Now other countries are looking at our model of restorative justice among juveniles with an eye to reviewing their own systems. It leaves open the possibility that if such a philosophy works so well for adolescents, could it not also work for adult offenders?

Footnotes

1. John Braithwaite, 'What is to Be Done About Criminal Justice?', *The Youth Court in New Zealand: A New Model of Justice*, Legal Research Foundation, Publication No. 34, 1993, p37
2. F. W. M. McElrea, panel discussion, *The Children, Young Persons and Their Families Act – A Blueprint to Be Applied to Adults?*, New Zealand Law Conference, Wellington, 1993, p2
3. Deborah Hollings, ibid, p9
4. Deborah Hollings, ibid, p10
5. Gabrielle M. Maxwell and Allison Morris, *Family, Victims and Culture: Youth Justice in New Zealand*, Social Policy Agency and Institute of Criminology, Victoria University, Wellington, 1993, p92
6. Ibid, p88
7. Braithwaite, op cit, p39
8. Ibid, pp37-38
9. M P. Doolan, 'Youth Justice – Legislation and Practice' in *The Youth Court in New Zealand : A New Model of Justice*, Legal Research Foundation, Publication No. 34, 1993, pp19-20

10. Ibid, pp21-22
11. Gabrielle M. Maxwell, panel discussion, *The Children, Young Persons and Their Families Act – A Blueprint to be Applied to Adults?,* New Zealand Law Conference, Wellington, 1993, pp5-6
12. Justice Department papers to the Minister of Justice, December 1993

CHAPTER EIGHT

Aboriginal Australia: Betwixt and Between

An Aboriginal man charged with murdering his de facto wife wanted legal history made in his bid to get the Supreme Court of Western Australia to recognise the bona fides of tribal law. Neville Gable, 36, has asked the court to release him from custody so that other members of the Wongi people can fulfil tribal law and punish him by spearing him in the upper legs. Gable, a camp-dweller at Nannygoat Hill in Kalgoorlie, is charged with murdering his de facto wife by stabbing her in the throat with a knife at Ningomia Village, an Aboriginal settlement near Kalgoorlie, on 12 June 1993.

Last Monday, Gable asked Judge Yeates to release him on bail so he could be subject to the traditional spearing. Once completed under police supervision, he would return to custody to await the preliminary hearing of the murder charge against him. A Wongi elder, Mr William Wesley, told the court on Monday that if Gable was subject to the punishment, a senior male member of Gable's family would supervise the spearing to ensure that it did not get out of hand. Otherwise, brothers of Gable would be punished but without supervision. The court rejected his application for temporary bail.

The Australian, 3 September 1993

It ill behoves a non-Aboriginal to try to give an overview of Aboriginal customary laws. For a non-Australian, an occasionally visiting New Zealander at that, to attempt this complex task appears cheeky at best and somewhat arrogant at worst. Given the fact that there are more than 700 languages and tribal groupings spread over almost the entire continent of Australia, such a challenge would seem to be too much for even a taskforce of the most eminent scholars.

This is therefore merely a modest attempt to indicate some of the outline of traditional, restorative Aboriginal law and justice. I am not trying to teach anything at all to the more than 265,000 Aborigines who belong to these tribes. Studied properly, their 40,000-year history can teach Westerners much that our own cultures have lost.

It is interesting to note that the Constitution of Australia does not mention Aborigines, nor does it protect their rights as the indigenous people of the continent. Neither does the legal system within Australia guarantee Aborigines the right of self-determination within the nation.[1]

It should also be noted that there are two indigenous peoples in Australia, the Aborigines and the Torres Strait Islanders. It is principally upon traditional Aboriginal customary law and practice that this chapter will focus.

Offending Within the Tribe or Clan

Despite some apparent illustrations to the contrary, formal gatherings in the nature of law courts did not happen in early Aboriginal Australia. They have no system parallel to that which white Australia adopted upon colonialisation, and as generally understood in modern city states. But their councils did have authority to discipline erring members and they appear to have functioned with some similar philosophy aimed at restoring the wellbeing of the community.

Such councils of elders seem to have been fairly common, but generally they are exceedingly informal and while they meet to settle disputes, among other things, they do not try to handle all types of these, nor do they always act in a judicial capacity.[2]

In researching this chapter I found that it is primarily to anthropologists that one must go for information pertaining to traditional customs and law. Probably the most accomplished team of anthropologists Australia has produced in the area of Aboriginal traditions are Ronald and Catherine Berndt and it is from their writing, spread over nearly five decades, that much of the material is drawn.

The Berndts' research indicates there are generally two categories of offending within the tribe or clan. Breaches of sacred law, that is, regulations, taboos, codes of behaviour that are thought to have a clearly supernatural basis form one clear grouping. The second comprises offences against people or property.

Given the variation in tradition that exists among the 700 tribal groups, it is difficult to pinpoint consistently applied processes whereby disputes are resolved. Ronald Berndt speaks of the seemingly casual meetings that frequently occur on the men's sacred ground, a little distant from the main camp. He has been present at many of these gatherings, at which discussion ranges from the trivial to sacred secret matters, including resolution of dispute.

The most serious disputes are said to be instigated by 'women and corpses'. The first points to a wide range of 'causes', including jealousy, adultery, elopement and so forth. The second relates to the search for a scapegoat upon whom blame may be laid for a death, with subsequent retaliation or punishment. Some of the procedures whereby a decision is made (such as inquest or divination) or retaliation takes place (for instance a revenge expedition or sorcery) are institutionalised means of resolving difficulties at the social rather than at the purely personal level.[3]

Minor disputes can be settled by other forms. The Berndts explain that a first way is typified by the north-eastern and western Arnhem Land *magarada* or *manejag*. There is a judicial quality in this, insofar as the major aim is the settlement of a dispute, and all interested parties are represented. But before the meeting the accused has already been judged guilty and may have even admitted culpability. Acceptance of responsibility or a guilty plea is an important feature of all restorative systems.

Although the *magarada* is spoken of as a peacemaking ceremony it is better styled 'trial by ordeal' or 'settlement by combat'. It is clear that this procedure of conventionalised retaliation is a legal one, and closely related to a system of law. As Warner mentions, a *magarada* is not held straight after an offence, but after people have had time to cool down.

The two opposing groups, painted in white clay, stand just out of spear-throwing reach. Members of the aggrieved party advance towards the opposite side in a totemic dance, then walk back again. The others do the same. Now they are ready for the 'duel'. Men of the accused group run irregularly across the ground, and with them run two men who are closely related to both sides. Spears are flung at them – but usually with the stone or iron blades removed. They can dodge, but they must not throw back the spears, or the abuse that accompanies them. This takes the edge off the injured clan's anger.

After a brief lull, the accused man or men run across the ground. This time the blades are left in the spears and flung at him one after another. Elders from both sides try to restrain the participants, warning them to keep their tempers in check. Finally the accused man's party dance across to their opponents. If they spear him in the thigh the matter is at an end and both groups join in dancing. Ideally the thigh wound is enough, but sometimes the accused is killed.[4]

The Berndts' research shows that this process has its counterparts in other regions, with a slightly different emphasis in each case. These practices include the conventional thigh wounding of the Western Desert, and among the Maryborough (Queensland) people. This type of settlement lacks the formality of legal proceedings. It lacks the embodiment of official justice with the power to regulate in the traditional Western legal sense. But the key to the proceedings is that both parties are interested in bringing about a reconciliation between the parties. It is essentially a restorative process, not a retributive one.

In all cases we have outlined, while there is so much verbal emphasis on revenge, it is plausible to infer that underlying this is a general aim of achieving order and balance. An injury is done, the status quo is upset, retaliation provides a means by which this may be restored. Peace should follow the application of law.

Offences against property are rare among Aborigines. Ownership of land is communal, and Aborigines' non-materialistic culture means that few offend.

Offences against the person are more common and are dealt with in a variety of ways. These can range from ridicule and criticism to a spearing in the thigh with a wooden spear. This is a very traditional Aboriginal mode of punishment for serious offending. Death can be the penalty for some murders.

Customary Law

What are Aboriginal customary laws, and, given the complex tribal structure, can they be systematically codified? Law professor James Crawford of Sydney and formerly Commissioner in Charge of the Law Reform Commission's Reference on the Recognition of Aboriginal Customary Laws, writes that Aboriginal customs and laws are part of an oral culture. In terms of that culture it is usual to speak of 'The Law' rather than of laws. The emphasis is on unity and immutability rather than on plurality and change. There are no written codes or statements of customary laws such as are found in some other countries.

There is a considerable amount of general anthropological discussion on Aboriginal traditions and practices, including especially marriage, kinship, hunting and fishing practices, relations to land and dispute resolution. There is no agreement by anthropologists on important issues such as, for example, whether in Aboriginal traditional communities there were institutional authority structures for dispute resolution. However, there is agreement among anthropologists that Aborigines had and continue to have a definable body of rules, practices and traditions accepted by the community.[5]

Elsie Roughsey of the Lardil tribe relates her memories of the inter-connectedness of her traditions.

> Out bush there was no-one to worry you, only the laws and customs you proudly hear, see and learn to do the right thing. If you do the wrong thing, you punish yourself by mulgree. You forget what you are told when eating anything strange that the salt water disagrees with, you forget to wash before moving into some places you should not go with the certain smell of food... well, you get sick or die. These laws were proved, and were passed down to the tribes.
>
> The tribal culture has been looked carefully through... where danger lies and the wrong is done, and where protection must be guided to all who move around these areas. If you are careless and disobey the laws, there is always a trouble in the end... the law of creation, *mulgree*, I have seen things happen, I know they were true. I have seen many sacred dangerous spots. I have seen proved of how it was done, and how a witchdoctor cures a person from being ill, and death... also healing touch, the chanting, the brushing of special leaves by warming on the fire and carefully pressed on the sick person, and very strangely to see, the person is well all of a sudden. Many people may not believe the fact, but it is very real and it is true.[6]

The Berndts speak of Aboriginal law and customs flowing, like that of all indigenous peoples, from their understanding of the world and the interconnectedness of all of creation. The law is there to keep things in the proper balance. The Aboriginal Australian view of the world, of people and nature, was, broadly speaking, a religious one where the traditional past lived in the present, perpetuated in and through ritual and myth.

> Life was organised fundamentally in religious terms; and the deeds and pronouncements of the creative and spirit beings of the mythical past served as a 'charter' for contemporary behaviour – not merely on the ritual ground, but in everyday life.[7]

This flows on into dispute management. The Berndts explain that quarrels and fights do occur, but within set rules of killing or making peace. In traditional Aboriginal Australia behaviour is always framed in terms of the past. To put it a little differently, the mythical characters instituted a way of life that they introduced to human beings, and because they themselves are viewed as eternal, so are the patterns they set.

They point out that the dramatising of sacred mythology affirms the social identity and solidarity of those taking part. As well, the combination of positive pressures predisposes participants to accept traditional dictates of right and wrong. The sanction of religion supplies a moral basis to society's actions.[8]

The Berndts go on to explain how this translates into everyday behaviour patterns. They point out that whether they represent good or evil, mythical figures are said to have laid down precepts that people are expected to follow today. They defined the broad roles to be played by both men and women in such matters as sacred ritual, economic affairs, marriage, childbearing, death. They warned that if people behaved in such and such a way, certain consequences would surely follow: that various taboos and avoidances had to be observed and that various relatives should not be intimate with one another. They set patterns of behaviour for members of the particular social and cultural group in which their power is acknowledged.

References to this particular dimension, not limited by time, and often translated by the words 'Eternal Dreaming', underlie the Aborigines' traditional reliance on a body of knowledge and belief that is relevant not only to the past, but also to the present and the future. Within this scheme is provision for change and individual interpretation. The mythical beings are believed to have been responsible not only for creating the natural species (including humans), but also establishing an Aboriginal way of life, its social institutions, its pattern of activity, and a moral order.[9]

Ronald Berndt points out that the two most distinctive elements of Aboriginal life are the maintenance of the status quo and the fact that Aboriginal society is kin-based, and so, consequently, is its law. He says that in any given conflict a person can ideally depend on a number of others to defend or assist him. The kinship system, with its set of conventional behavioural patterns, provides a frame of reference for this. It constitutes a blueprint for social action, a guide to which people are expected to conform.[10]

Kopara

An understanding of Aboriginal law requires some knowledge of how settlement was obtained for outstanding debts and duties unfulfilled. The process is called kopara, which means a debt must be settled in a definite standardised way. As Ronald Berndt explains:

> Because social relationships are reciprocal and not one-sided, and because of the inter-meshing of obligations, there are pressures against leaving grievances, especially major grievances, outstanding for a definite period – unless the persons concerned are out of touch with one another. Moreover, settlement need not take the form of physical violence or the handing over of material goods. Nor is it framed simply in terms of person-to-person satisfaction, affecting only those immediately involved. The group as such displays an interest in maintaining the peace; and although this is not always achieved, mechanisms of institutionalised or, in effect, legal procedure are available – such as kopara, and penis-holding.[11]

Kopara applied to debt owed after gifts had been given for a marriage, when the man's family must respond to the 'gift' of a bride; after a birth, after circumcision, and especially after a death. On these occasions, ritualised responses need to be made to maintain the accepted spiritual balance of the family and tribe. Often the debt-settling process involved sexual activity among the various parties. Anthropologist A. P. Elkin describes one such settlement.

> [When the kopara party arrives to seek redress for the debt, the two groups] sit around separate fires a few yards apart and discuss the old and the new kopara.... A temporary exchange of wives between picked men and women takes place... the obligations will be finally settled by each side giving a wife to a man of the other moiety.[12]

Another compensatory process of restoration involves the rite of penis-holding. This symbolic action involving visiting males has an acceptance and healing dimension to it; a recognition of goodwill on the part of the participants and the forgiveness of previous grievances. Refusal to touch the penis can be construed as provocative. An appropriate relative can often stand in as a replacement for any of this sexual behaviour. For example, among the Wailbri tribe of Central Australia:

> A man publicly accused ... may try to place his penis in the hand of an actual or classificatory brother. If the latter permits this, he undertakes to plead for the accused and, should the plea fail, to fight beside him. The brother, however, cannot be forced to accept such a responsibility.[13]

Should the evidence not be accepted the matter is finished. In some ritual sequences involving grievances, a seated man may refuse to hold the penis of a visitor, thus provoking an urgent inquiry. In such instances a kinsman can offer his penis, the visitor reciprocates, and the grievance is settled. Should the accused be a woman, a different type of sexual ritual can be involved. If she is found to be *kopara*, she will offer herself to coitus to each of those who hold a grievance. Should the woman wish to evade this kind of 'payment' she too may arrange for another woman to stand in for her. The whole emphasis in this type of penalty payment is not to punish the debtor but to recognise that law has been broken and ritual is needed to restore the proper balance within the tribe.

Law Reform Commission Report

In 1986 the Australian Law Reform Commission issued its report on Aboriginal customary law. The commission rejected codification and the general incorporation of Aboriginal customary law into the general legal system of Australia, partly in response to the plea from Aborigines that their people would lose control over their laws and there would be unwarranted intrusion into or disclosure of secret matters. However, both parties did agree that in specific instances customary laws could be incorporated into general law. These would cover such areas as recognition of traditional marriage, hunting and fishing rights, distribution of property, and some parts of traditional justice and areas pertaining to criminal behaviour.

Many Aboriginal communities have moved to adapt to modern conditions in the dispute resolution processes. In some localities reliance is placed on the accepted authority of older men and women and there are some long-established procedures for resolving disputes. The intrusion of the general legal system has modified the application of traditional practices.

Some Aboriginal communities have developed new authority structures, including community councils and Aboriginal courts. Other communities, in order to distinguish various functions, also have chosen tribal councils to deal with more traditional matters. This has been done, for example, at Yuendumu (NT), Yirrkala (NT), Roper River (NT) and the Yungngora community (Noonkanbah, WA).

Three examples quoted in the report are of special interest. They reflect the varied approaches taken today by Aboriginal communities in more remote areas.

Edward River is a remote community with a population of 350-380, situated on the western side of the Cape York Peninsula. It is 550 kilometres north-west of Cairns. In essence 'old custom' is the Aboriginal way of resolving disputes at Edward River. It has a well-understood code of behaviour or 'right conduct', and there are clear procedures to be followed by those seeking redress for breaches of the code. Certain breaches bring automatic retribution by way of supernatural agencies. On the other hand, public disputes most commonly eventuated through the omission of kinship duties, breaches of bestowal expectations and arrangements, in instances of insult or real or threatened injury, and occasionally in cases of infidelity, trespass and homicide.[14]

Generally a dispute resolution would go through six stages, though all were not necessarily applied each time. It started with a *declaration* by the aggrieved person, followed by a *rejoinder,* a denial or countercharge. Then would follow public *argument* by both sides, aided sometimes by family or support people. Then followed *insult* and *physical combat.* This generally involved fighting with weapons between the parties, often escalating as others aligned joined in. 'Blockers' acting as umpires made sure things didn't get out of hand. *Separation* came eventually when parties decided they had had enough. The dispute resolution concluded with *reconciliation*, whereupon normal relationships resumed.[15]

The Yirrkala Community with a population of 700-800 is situated in north-east Arnhem Land in the Northern Territory, near the mining town of Nhulunbuy. The Yirrkala people also have a sophisticated and ritualised process of dispute resolution. It differs to a degree from the Edward River process but the end result is still reconciliation and peace. The grievance can be declared in one of several ways – a verbal declaration, a verbal declaration and a threat, or an assault or by destruction of property.

Disputes at Yirrkala covered a wide range of matters including failure to fulfil obligations to kin, domestic disputes, failure to recognise a person's specific rights over certain women, land, natural resources or ritual objects, breaches of religious restrictions, the failure to carry out sanctions imposed earlier and allegations of sorcery.

According to Dr Nancy Williams, who did extensive field work in the area, there are five basic characteristics of dispute settlement:

1. Intervention and subsequent management by a clansman with political authority.
2. Gathering and checking of evidence by the intervening clansman.
3. Obtaining an admission of all culpable acts (the 'true story').
4. Confirmation of findings and of action taken by those with authority over and responsibility for the principals in the dispute.
5. The application of sanctions.

An integral feature of this process is the moot, in which the disputants and interested parties are brought together so the matter may be discussed. This process can also happen within smaller family groups. The moot consists of four parts:

• Statements of the offence and breaches of law;
• Statements by people addressing themselves to the specific allegations;
• Response to those statements with the convenor urging the defendant to admit the extent of his or her culpable acts;

- Statements about the outcome and the composition of the dispute may be made by a number of people but should include the convenor, the offender and the aggrieved person.

The process is overseen by clan and sub-clan leaders so that a satisfactory result is achieved. Sanctions imposed have changed over the times. There is now greater emphasis on non-physical sanctions, although physical sanctions have not disappeared completely. The sanctions more readily applied are temporary exile from the community, restitution and temporary removal from employment.

At Yirrkala, traditional Aboriginal modes of dispute resolution continue to be affected by mainstream Australian law. A distinction is made between 'little trouble' and 'big trouble', which includes major serious assault and homicide.[16]

The Strelley Community, comprising 500-600 people, is situated about 40 kilometres inland from Port Hedland in Western Australia. It runs several pastoral properties which employ approximately half the people living there. It is the struggle for survival that has proved to have been the most dominant facet of modification of their dispute resolution. Decisions are made on a communal basis in regular meetings involving the whole community, with everyone being given the opportunity to participate. The accused person will sit inside a large circle strategically placed according to the position of the accusers and of their own families, who may have to speak on their behalf. Certain persons are assigned the role of negotiators. The meeting is highly organised and all attending understand their role. The protocol and structure is every bit as clearly defined as in a courtroom.

In order to deal with 'law and order' problems, the community selects what they call 'the 10-man committee'. The committee's function is to apprehend and bring wrongdoers before a community meeting. The meetings appear to follow traditional Aboriginal options regarding sanctions. They range from a admonition ('growling'), ridicule and shaming and a fine through to banishment (usually to a neighbouring community) and community work. In rare cases physical sanctions are applied ('a little bit of a hiding') but the community apparently does not approve of spearing. The reality of the broader legal system is accepted in a way similar to Yirrkala, with certain matters seen as being within local jurisdiction and others not.[17]

Professor James Crawford says the courts have on occasion taken customary laws of the defendant's community into account in determining whether a defence of provocation or duress was established sufficient to reduce charges of murder to manslaughter. To ensure that the law as represented by these decisions is applied fairly and consistently, the report recommended legislation expressly allowing that evidence of Aboriginal customary laws be admissible. The commission concluded that evidence of Aboriginal customary laws could be taken into account sufficiently in the general criminal law through the exercise of sentencing and other procedural discretions, and that a customary law defence was neither necessary nor desirable.[18]

However, the commission did recommend the creation of a partial defence, similar to a defence of diminished responsibility, which would operate to reduce the level of liability in particular cases from murder to manslaughter. This defence was thought to have several advantages: it would not involve condoning or endorsing payback killings or woundings, nor would it deprive victims of legal protection or the right of redress. But it would nonetheless represent a direct acknowledgment of conflicts that can occur between the general legal system and Aboriginal customary laws. It would allow the jury a role in mitigating degree of culpability, and would operate as an adjunct to the sentencing discretion.

This can best be seen in a test case decision in February 1994 in the Northern Territory. Wilson Jagamara Walker of the Walpiri tribe at Yuendumu in the central Australian desert was convicted of manslaughter for stabbing to death a fellow tribesman. The Chief Justice of the Northern Territory, Brian Martin, gave the victim's family six months to suffer a traditional punishment instead of going to prison. In this case the man was to be speared in both thighs. At the completion of six months, if the traditional 'payback' punishment had occurred, the court would have considered justice to have been achieved.

The Law Reform Commission also reviewed the desirability of developing mechanisms within Aboriginal communities to deal with criminal justice matters. It concluded that this time no such recommendation should be made, but did set out some broad guidelines should it be deemed appropriate to develop such a parallel system of justice in the future. These included:

- The Aboriginal group concerned should have the power to draw up local bylaws, including bylaws incorporating or taking into account Aboriginal customs, rules and traditions.
- Appropriate safeguards need to be established to ensure that individual rights are protected, for example, by way of appeal.
- Bylaws should apply to all people within the bounds of the community.
- If the court is to be run by local people they should have power within broad limits to determine their own procedure, in accordance with what is seen to be procedurally fair by the community at large. In any event, the community should have some voice in selecting the people who will constitute the court, and appropriate training should be available to those selected.
- In minor matters there need be no automatic right to legal counsel, though the defendant should in such cases have the right to have someone (a friend) speak on his or her behalf.
- The court's powers should include powers of mediation and conciliation, as well as powers to order compensation to be made. A court that is receptive to the traditions, needs and views of the local people may be able to resolve some disputes before they escalate, perhaps avoiding more serious charges.

- There should be regular reviews of any such court, undertaken in conjunction with the local community.

Black Deaths in Custody

A chapter on Aboriginal Australians would not be complete without reference to the appalling number of deaths of Aborigines in custody. The final report of the Royal Commission into Aboriginal Deaths in Custody was published in 1991. The commission had investigated the deaths of 99 Aborigines in custody during the period 1980-89. Custody here includes police lock-ups, prisons and juvenile detention centres.

The report concluded that there is something dreadfully wrong with modern criminal justice in Australia when so many die in state custody. The commission noted that Aboriginal people are incarcerated in police custody at 29 times the rate of the general population, and in prison custody at 17 times the rate of non-Aborigines.[19]

The commission found that the underlying issues of Aboriginal disadvantage generally – racism, poverty, alienation, powerlessness, hopelessness, alcoholism – contributed more significantly to the imprisonment of Aboriginal people than any degree of criminality on their part. In other words, Aborigines were in prison largely because of social and health factors.

In 1992 Amnesty International sent an investigative team to Australia to examine Aboriginal incarceration. It reported, among other important things, that:

> The criminal justice system makes Aboriginal people in Australia a group that is particularly vulnerable to the violation of their right 'to be treated with humanity and with respect for the inherent dignity of the human person', as set out in Article 10 of the International Covenant on Civil and Political Rights.[20]

They found that Aborigines were discriminated against according to some UN conventions. This is structured racism, and was consistent with the 1991 Report into Racist Violence conducted in Australia by the Human Rights and Equal Opportunity Commission. Amnesty International remains concerned that Aborigines continue to be subject to extremely disproportionate levels of incarceration and criminalisation. The title of its report, 'A Criminal Justice System Weighted Against Aboriginal People', aptly summarised its conclusions.

Reflecting on these stark findings, New South Wales judge Pat O'Shane comments that the picture today is as bleak for Aborigines within the dominant justice system of Australia as it was 15 years ago, and is not improving. She points out that Aboriginal Australians are over-represented in the criminal justice system, not only in comparison with non-Aborigines, but also in comparison with the world's other indigenous populations. She quotes Paul Wilson's research that shows where alienation from land occurs, extreme poverty, despair and violence develop. These have become endemic in Aboriginal communities.

Referring to racism in Australia, she points out that the objective evidence is that Aborigines suffer harsher penalties in courts than non-Aborigines from judicial officers, judges and magistrates.[21]

Conclusion

Reviewing the evidence on Aboriginal justice in Australia, one is left with the feeling that within their own communities a balanced approach to the preservation of family and tribal mores is maintained to a high degree. Traditional Aboriginal law has evolved over the more than 40,000 years that their people have lived in Australia.

As with all indigenous peoples, the protection of the tribe and the strengthening of family ties are paramount in their social rules and regulations. Their general approach to justice issues seeks to heal and restore breaches of community laws and values, even if at times their methods of doing so appear to the outsider to be somewhat harsh.

However, none of it is as harsh as what they undergo when they come into contact with the mainstream dominant culture and its justice system. The advent of the colonial system of government and its accompanying retributive system of criminal justice has brought devastation to Aboriginal communities. Aborigines are severely oppressed, as is confirmed by the findings of the Amnesty International report.

Footnotes

1. *Reconciling Our Differences*, ed Frank Brennan S.J. , Aurora Books/David Lovell Publishing, Melbourne, 1992, p2
2. W. L. Warner, *1937-58, A Black Civilisation*, Harper, New York
3. Ronald and Catherine Berndt, *Aboriginal Man in Australia*, Angus and Robertson, Sydney, 1975, p176
4. Berndt, *The World of the First Australians*, Aboriginal Studies Press, Canberra, 1992, pp350-51
5. James Crawford, 'The Recognition of Aboriginal Customary Laws: an Overview', published in *Aboriginal Perspectives on Criminal Justice*, Institute of Criminology, Sydney, 1992, p84
6. Elsie Roughsey Labumore, *An Aboriginal Mother Tells of the Old and the New*, McPhee Gribble Penguin Books, Victoria, 1984, p179
7. Berndt, *Aboriginal Man*, op cit, p174
8. Berndt, *The World of the First Australians*, op cit, p336
9. Ronald Berndt, *Australian Aboriginal Anthropology*, University of Western Australia, Perth, 1970, pp216-17
10. Berndt, *Aboriginal Man*, op cit, p169
11. Ibid, p190
12. A. P. Elkin, 'The Kopara, the Settlement of Grievances', *Oceania*, Vol. II, No 2
13. M. J. Meggett, *Desert People*, Angus and Robertson, Sydney, 1962
14. Australian Law Reform Commission, *The Recognition of Aboriginal Customary Laws*, 1986
15. Ibid
16. Ibid
17. Ibid
18. James Crawford, op cit, pp65-66
19. *Final Report of the Royal Commission into Aboriginal Deaths in Custody*, 1991
20. Amnesty International, Australia, *A Criminal Justice System Weighted Against Aboriginal People*, January 1993
21. Pat O'Shane, *Aboriginal Perspectives and Criminal Justice*, Institute of Criminology, University of Sydney, 1992, pp3-6

CHAPTER NINE

Western Samoa: Both Systems

A village chieftain was shot dead in front of his wife and five children on the orders of fellow chiefs in a small village here, Police Commissioner Galuvao Tanielu said on Wednesday. After killing Nu'utai Fatiala Mafulu, residents of the village of Lona in Fagaloa District east of here burned his home, shop, bus and pickup truck.

State-run Samoa Broadcasting Service said that Nu'utai was ordered killed because he opposed a night curfew and had not paid village council dues. Formerly, Nu'utai, who came from a family headed by a *matai* known as Matautia, had taken several legal actions against the village and the district, and was banned from both for life. Eight months ago he indicated he wanted to return and sent members of his family to make peace overtures.

AFP, 27 September 1993

The death in September 1993 of former Auckland taxi driver Nu'utai Fatiala Mafulu stunned Western Samoa and the Samoan community in New Zealand. The shooting took place at Lona in the northeast of Upolu Island. Cries of outrage greeted this deliberate killing. Questions immediately were raised as to how a village council of chiefs – a *fono* – could allow things to get so out of hand as to condone the killing of one of their own. It brought the Village Fono Act, under whose powers the chiefs claim to have been acting, into centre-stage spotlight.

An MP and former Samoan Minister of Justice, Ulualofaiga Talamaivao Niko, called for the arrest of the Prime Minister on the grounds that his party had been in power when the Village Fono Act had been passed in 1990. Under the act, *fono* were given the complete authority to deal with village justice, using the centuries-old system based on custom. The act does not define crimes or punishments or limit village chiefs' authority. Clearly, everyone agreed, the *fono* had over-reacted.

Nu'utai had lived in Auckland for 20 years but he longed for a return to his native village. Eventually, after peace overtures to the village elders, he was allowed to return with his wife and five children.

He built a shop and a bus shelter in the village. Tensions arose before the killing because of his apparent lack of respect for the traditions of the village and the position of the *matai*. A senior chief of Nu'utai's *'aiga* was disciplined by the *fono* over a land dispute and thereafter treated as an outsider. This, added to the apparent flouting of customs in the village, led things to boiling point, and the death of Nu'utai Fatiala Mafulu.

Subsequently, 41 people from the village were initially charged over the murder. Eleven charges were later dropped, and 24 people pleaded guilty to arson. The 37-year-old who fired the fatal shot was convicted of murder in March 1994. His death sentence was commuted to life imprisonment, effectively 10 years with parole. In April 1994, six *matai*, aged between 52 and 77, were charged with murder. They were alleged to have been at a Lona Village *fono* that passed a resolution that Nu'utai Fatiala Mafulu be killed and his home and property burnt. However, in October 1994 the murder charges were dropped and lesser charges of inciting others to damage a dwelling were substituted.

History

Western Samoa is a country with three sets of traditions, which often leads to clashes of values and customs. Traditional Samoan culture now blends in with major influences from European and Christian traditions. The origins of the people stretch back about 3000 years and are similar in many respects to other Polynesian communities living in the Pacific. Social structures have evolved over the centuries and, until the arrival of European immigrants in the early 1800s, centred on each independent village.

A people of the land and of the sea, Samoans' subsistence diet was culled from their crops and from the water. Land has always been a cause of great dissension among Samoans, with individual families rather than tribes having title. They also had a complex set of relationships with members of other villages. There was a complex set of titles to signify the importance of their elders, male and female. Lineage has always been important in Samoan life.

Far from being an isolated community, the Samoan village was the scene of frequent comings and goings. People engaged in such activities as the exchange of mats, the selection of titleholders, the celebration of births and the performance of funeral rites. It was in the course of this village visiting that Samoans expended much of their energy and resources and found much pleasure and pastime.[1]

Often there were matters of 'law and order' to be dealt with and the *fono*, consisting of the chiefs from all the families, was the decision-making body. In the 19th century, when there was usually no effective central government of any kind, the village itself was largely responsible for keeping order.

Some of the steps taken to achieve this end could be severe. For example, when a village was irreconcilably divided on any important issue, local or otherwise, the weaker party might be driven out in order to restore village unity. Individuals who committed serious offences were treated no less harshly. When travellers or visitors stirred up trouble or acted disrespectfully towards the village, even unintentionally, they were liable to immediate attack and expulsion by the *aumaga* (a group of untitled men).

The Samoans were so sensitive about village honour and the enforcement of local customs and regulations that their reaction against transgressors was liable to be hasty and violent. From the local point of view, these measures were about the only ones that could have been taken, and in so far as they freed the village of divisive elements, they were effective.[2]

Samoans are not a war-mongering people and often went to great efforts to avoid war between villages. However, when a village's honour was at stake because of some serious affront, war became a possibility. Two principally positive non-violent methods were used to prevent this happening if at all possible.

The first was to offer compensation, together with a formal gesture of self-degradation (*ifoga*). To perform the *ifoga*, the highest chiefs of the offending village had to go to the offended village that threatened aggression and there, on the *malae*, bow down and offer fine mats and the humbling of their dignity in satisfaction for the offence. Since this gesture was the greatest loss of face that a Samoan could suffer voluntarily – out of all proportion to the seriousness of most transgressions – it was never viewed lightly by either party to a dispute. A village would often choose to flee, leaving its houses and plantations to be destroyed, rather than apologise so abjectly.

When an *ifoga* was undertaken it was customary that the other party would accept the gesture and agree to a peaceful settlement. The whole idea of the *ifoga* is for the offending party to say to the offended, 'here we are, you can do anything you want with us'. The firewood and stones the offending party took with them symbolised this.

The other means of preventing war required the presence of a neutral party to stand between the disputants and propose terms of peace.[3]

Ifoga is still very much at the heart of judicial process today. The word literally means 'to bow'. An offender's entire extended family will sit with mats over their heads outside the home of a victim in a display of submission. This act of humiliation will almost always lead to reconciliation, which is at the heart of the concept. The offender is forgiven by the one wronged and reconciliation occurs.

When war had been fought between the men of the villages on neutral ground, at the point where honour was deemed to have been satisfied by mutual agreement, a formal meeting of reconciliation might then be held, officially ending the conflict. Sometimes, however, a much stronger party would simply overwhelm the adversary and loot and burn the village of the defeated. Much of the fighting was aimed to preserve village autonomy and self-respect. Independence and self-management are very important traditions for Samoans.

Local Government

There are two categories of chiefs in Samoa – the *ali'i* and the *tulafale*. Leaders of families within both are called *matai*, but their ranking is quite different. Malama Meleisea writes that the *ali'i* titles form links in the historical genealogies of the Samoans that go back to Tagaloa-a lagi.

In this respect *ali'i* titles were sacred titles that carried with them the mana of the gods. The rank of *ali'i* titles was also determined by descent from the gods – the older the title and the closer its origin to the sacred ancestors, the greater its mana and the higher its rank.

Tulafale titles did not depend on mana or sacred ancestry, although they originated from the same ancestral origins as *ali'i* titles. They were executive titles and carried with them special duties, which varied from family to family and village to village. Some were associated with service to an *ali'i*, some with war, or house-building, or carrying messages, or leading fishermen, or hunting, or reciting historical knowledge and many, many other roles.

Ali'i and *tulafale* had different roles in the government of villages. The role of the *ali'i* was to make the final decisions after listening to the advice of the *tulafale*, who spoke for and issued orders for the *ali'i*.[4]

All *matai* had authority over their extended families, which, in groups of up to 30, constituted a traditional Samoan village. Through marriage, all Samoans belonged to several extended families. At the centre of authority in the village sat the *fono* – council of *matai* – which made all the major political, food production and judicial decisions. Here decisions were made through negotiation, debate and compromise.

The *fono* made the laws of the village and if these were broken, the *fono* would decide how law-breakers were to be punished. They could exile a wrongdoer from a village or order the *aumaga* to beat him or inflict some other punishment such as forcing him to sit in the sun for long periods or to chew the burning teve root.[5]

Today, *fono* in the villages operate under the 1990 Village Fono Act and remain responsible for maintaining order and customs. They traditionally fine villagers for breaches of protocol and customs with penalties of money, food and fine mats.

Settler Influence

The arrival of European settlers had a massive effect on the social structure of Samoa. While there was no organised large-scale immigration, as there was to Aotearoa, missionaries and others brought news of the teachings of Jesus. Missionary societies were established to send pastors, priests and ministers to the islands to evangelise. Christianity was rapidly accepted by the people to the point where they were able upon Independence in 1962 to write into their Constitution the famous dictum *Faavae' i le Atua Samoa* – Samoa, founded on God.

Earlier Samoa came under the influence of the three great Pacific powers of the day, Britain, Germany and the United States. They snapped and snarled at each other over who would take over the islands and rule, and in the 1880s nearly went to war over the issue. Prior to this, the Samoans had asked the British to establish a protectorate over Samoa. Britain said it was only really interested in annexing Samoa, not offering it protectorate status. So the United States was asked, but it declined, being interested only in establishing a naval base at Pagopago Harbour. In 1889 the Berlin Act was passed, by which agreement the three major powers would jointly rule the Apia area through a joint council.

Germany had long held business interests in Samoa and had control of large areas of land. It brought in a considerable number of indentured labourers from Melanesia and China. By 1900 Germany took full control and officially colonised Samoa. Germany then maintained a colonial hold over central government until 1914 and the outbreak of World War I when New Zealand, at the behest of the British government, assumed control. The change in government was to make little difference to the quest by some for more centralised government and control.

The Rule of Law

Partly because land-grabbing had led to so many disputes among the people and partly because of inter-family disputes over titles, the German Administrator in 1903 instituted the Land and Titles Commission. This was the first major effort this century to centralise law. The intention was that this body would solve all remaining land and title disputes among Samoans. It consisted of four colonial officials and 14 Samoan advisers. In setting up the commission, the administrator sought to undermine the traditional Samoan decision-making process by rearranging the power positions of the *matai*. This move struck at the very heart of the order and degree of chiefly power.

The administrator reinforced his power at an important gathering of all the Samoan chiefs. He denied them permission to hold the gathering in a senior chief's village and instead demanded that it be held in Apia. This was a significant insult offered to the chiefs. He compounded this insult by then insisting that the same fine mats be given to each chief as if they were equals. This was a clear attempt at structural change to favour the colonial power.

This point has always been particularly difficult for foreign observers to appreciate, since they tended to see 'fine mats' as economic objects in themselves, as a form of money or capital. The apparent obsession of Samoan chiefs with 'fine mats' has thus often been interpreted as irrational greed. But *'ie toga* were not a form of money in the modern sense. Although *'ie toga* could be given in 'payment' for services such as house building or canoe making, there was no set 'price' for such services. The *'ie toga* was presented with the same ceremony as on any other occasion to honour the skill of the craftsman. In Samoan eyes, the number of *'ie toga* offered represented not objects but qualities – respect, prestige, gratitude, deference, recognition, obligation and so on.

A Samoan chief of paramount rank could not therefore give equal recognition to all the district chiefs. This would insult those whose historical and genealogical connections to the *Mata'afa* title had caused them to render the greatest service, or whose rank entitled them to the greatest rewards. It is precisely for this reason that gifts, in Samoan etiquette, are always publicly announced. Gifts make statements about relationships and about the nature of obligations, commitments and ties between givers and receivers.[6]

Eventually, after further liberalising changes this century, the commission was to remain as a permanent tribunal to arbitrate on matters of custom. Samoans have been encouraged to go to the commission for such judgments as are needed, but the tension remains as often those judgments are in conflict with local opinion.

Traditional Justice

This attempt to centralise village power and break down local decision-making, particularly in matters relating to justice, continued right up until Independence. Village *fono* began in the early part of this century to reassess their role in the maintenance of community relations and justice within the village. They set out rules and procedural guidelines to protect village interests. For example, when a trader ignored village rules and customs, they would punish him through sanctions and boycotts.

This produced the wrath of the central administration. One instance early this century (that has echoes in the death of Nu'utai Fatiala Mafulu) concerned a trader named Stopfkuchen, who ran a store in Salelologa in Savai'i. The *fono* ordered a boycott of his store because of his flouting of village customs. As a result of his complaint to the central administration, two *matai* were imprisoned and the *fono* warned against any repetition of such rulings.[7]

It should be noted that this occurred long before Samoans regained control of their own country and even longer before the Village Fono Act was passed.

In 1917 Logan, the New Zealand military ruler, issued a proclamation reiterating the primacy of centralised law and urging the *fono* to be temperate in their dealings with local people. Samoans responded by quoting their principle that all village rules were made by the *fono* with the intention of maintaining peace and the *mamalu* (dignity) of the community.[8]

What is of significance here is the notion that what is important to and constitutes 'fairness' in European eyes, may not have the same importance for Samoans, and vice versa. Meleisea explains:

> ...the system under which Germans and New Zealanders lived (in Samoa) was supported by an ideology of the priority of individual rights. The Samoan system was equally supported by an ideology of the priority of the collective interests of the *aiga* (extended family) and the *nu'u* (gathering of the people). The system therefore did not admit the notion of one individual wronging another. When an individual transgressed the system, the blame, punishment and shame were shared collectively by the *aiga*. Where the transgressor was untitled, his or her *matai* took formal responsibility.
>
> Relative evaluation as to the fairness or severity of a punishment can be determined meaningful only in the context of the values and ethics of the society whose law has been broken. For Samoans, the deliberations of the *fono* were the means of achieving decisions acceptable to all the *aiga* that comprised the *nu'u*, even for those *aiga* being punished. Very severe punishments, such as banishment, were decided by consensus in the *fono* where no reconciliation between parties was possible.

Banishment could never have been imposed by a minority because it had to be supported by the threat of violence from the *aumaga* if the decision was not obeyed. Force involved the pulling down of the house of the family who were under banishment orders, and destruction of their crops. In many cases the family facing social and political isolation would voluntarily accept such orders without the need for force. Banishments were seldom permanent and could be revoked after formal ceremonies of reconciliation.[9]

Local versus Centralised Government

There has never been a consistent code of traditional rules governing the whole of Samoa. Consequently, when Independence came in 1962 and a constitution was written, it was somewhat difficult to incorporate within the new structures a codified law that met the demands of the more than 80 percent who still lived in the villages, and the other grouping whose interest was in a more modern centralised form of government.

Several previous attempts to codify Samoan law had failed. Port laws were introduced by a British sea captain, Charles Bethune, in 1837. These sought to protect British interests and those of the London Missionary Society. They included no work on Sunday and curfew restrictions for visiting sailors. This was further developed the next year but restricted to the Pagopago and Apia harbours.

The next attempt came in 1839 from the British Consul George Pritchard, and later an attempt was made by American Charles Wilkes. Their efforts were partly to protect 'the poor Samoans', and partly to bring some recognised codes of behaviour for visiting crews. European settlers sought a renewed code in 1860 from Samoan chiefs. From that effort flowed what became known as Vaimaunga's Code. This contained 17 simple laws relating to property and trading rights, land sales, shipping, adultery, marriage, keeping the Sabbath, assault and murder, the carrying of lethal weapons, disorderly conduct and the regulation of liquor sales.[10]

Opposition grew to the code, and it was alleged that the chiefs of Vaimaunga had overstepped the mark in authorising it. The code was accepted in some places but not in others. In any event, it proved to be far from a universal centralised code; Meleisea points out that there was little evidence that its principles were enforced or taken seriously by Samoans.[11]

Consuls from Britain and later the United States and Germany sought to bring dimensions of their law to Samoa over the next 50 years, during which time municipal administrations were established. But with Europe at war little attention was paid to codifying the law of Samoa. The three governing nations were principally concerned with promoting their own interests rather than those of the indigenous people.

The Berlin Act of 1889 had failed to appreciate life in Samoa as it was lived, and had failed to come to grips with any centralised formulation of law. It did one important thing, though, and that was to establish the Supreme Court with a single Chief Justice of Samoa, to be nominated by the agreement of the three major powers. Yet despite its name, the court had limited power and most aspects of life relating to Samoans did not come under its jurisdiction. Samoan authorities retained jurisdiction over criminal matters, except where a European was involved.

In this century its powers would be greatly expanded as a United Nations Protectorate under New Zealand's administration. But clearly, in the lead-up to Independence, there were no clear lines of demarcation between traditional law and the jurisdiction of the *fono* on the one hand, and a centralised law and court system on the other.

Since Independence in 1962, Samoa has had to constantly face the dilemma of the traditional versus the modern ways of doing things. Many very articulate and educated young people wish the old traditions of decentralised government and the empowerment of chiefs and *fono* to continue on the grounds that such a system is local, practical, immediate. Moreover, centralised power leads too often to a morass of bureaucracy, inefficiency and disempowerment. For the majority of Samoans, small and local is beautiful.

The Constitution of Western Samoa embodies traditionalist principles and practices alongside those pertaining to a modern parliamentary democracy. This dual approach is a tension shared by other Pacific countries, most notably Papua New Guinea and to a lesser extent Fiji. The Constitution had been drafted after extensive negotiations between New Zealand and Samoan leaders. The surveys done had indicated a very high level of contentment with existing village structures. At the time of Independence, 86.7 percent of the population lived according to *fa'a Samoa*, the traditional Samoan lifestyle.

The Constitution takes precedence over *fono* law. As Sir Gaven Donne, Chief Justice and president of the Lands and Titles Court, said in a direction to the Samoan judges in 1980:

> Undoubtedly the customs and usages of Samoa in the past acknowledged the right of village councils and indeed the court to make banishment orders, but that custom ceased on 28 October 1960 when the people of Western Samoa through their representatives in a constitutional convention adopted, enacted and gave to themselves the Constitution.
>
> For several months before adopting the Constitution, over 170 of the most important chiefs and orators of Western Samoa, including the Tama-Aiga, deliberated on a Constitution and it was as a result of their deliberations and decisions that the Constitution was adopted and enacted. These leaders, who possessed wide knowledge of all the customs and usages of Western Samoa, decided that the written Constitution would be the supreme law and that any law in the Constitution that was contrary to the accepted customs and usages of Western Samoa that existed at that time completely superseded those customs and usages and that from thenceforth only the written Constitution would be followed and honoured.
>
> It is very important indeed that all Samoans understand that this Constitution is not *Papalagi* law that was imposed on Western Samoa. The Constitution was made by the highest chiefs and orators in the land and declared by them to be the supreme law of Western Samoa.[12]

One difficulty with the two legal systems is that they are based on two totally different philosophies. The centralised concept is based on English common law, which recognises the needs of the individual as paramount. From a criminal justice perspective, it is primarily retributive in nature. The traditional law is based primarily on a restorative philosophy, being principally concerned with the wellbeing of the community and the need to protect the interests of the majority. As Meleisea notes repeatedly in his study on this topic, the most important difference is in the notion of the right of the individual: an injury inflicted by one individual upon another is not seen in *fa'a Samoa*, as it is in Western law, as a case between two individuals, but as a case between two groups.[13]

Inevitably there are clashes between the rights of individuals guaranteed under the Constitution and the traditional norms of the villages as enforced by the *fono*. The Constitution, for example, is clear about the right of any individual to belong to any religion of choice, or none. But within the context of the *nu'u* and *fono*, this holds little sway. Village rules are village rules, in place to protect the good of the community. And no individual can challenge the rules (as in Western democracies) with impunity. Those who do can face severe sanctions, as Nu'utai Fatiala Mafulu found out to his cost.

The Role of Fono Today

Much of the reaction to the death of Nu'utai Fatiala Mafulu centred on the feeling that the *fono* had gone too far in its administration of penalties rather than that the whole *fono* concept needed to be scrapped.

The *fono* system has its strengths. There are only 382 (unarmed) police in Western Samoa for a population of 170,000 people. These include 18,000 *matai* in more than 300 autonomous villages. The fono retain immense influence in village life. Much of the customary land, covering 80 percent of land area of the islands, is tied up with *matai* and various rankings of chief.

An article in the *Island Business Review* explains that council rulings guide almost every aspect of village life and even today are only slowly being eroded by social changes, mobility and education. Villages often broadcast public notices over national radio. They publicise the times when a curfew for evening prayers will be enforced. There are also notices advising on bans for long hair, being drunk and disorderly, playing music too loud, using dynamite for fishing or women wearing shorts.

Fono are a crucial factor in grassroots economic development. They organise community projects such as the building of schools and churches, sanitation, and security. Other groups such as women's committees and untitled youth work with councils of chiefs to promote the general welfare of the village. This co-operation helps build a strong sense of identity based on a community with collective responsibility, not an individual. The few areas where councils hold little sway are with new settlements around the capital Apia, freehold properties, and leased or government lands.[14]

Fines are paid the same day by the family acting together rather than by the offender on his or her own. Collective responsibility is the order of the day. Apologies (*ifoga*) are also an important part of many proceedings. This involves family members covering themselves with fine mats and kneeling outside the family home of the victim until the apology is formally accepted.

The village *fono* acts as law-maker and judiciary, with no right of appeal. At the same time the system allows for apology and reconciliation so that even exiles may be welcomed back with full rights.

Some argue that the Village Fono Act of 1990 should be abolished. But it would seem that the legislation only officially acknowledged the process of that ancient jurisdiction, which has operated for hundreds and hundreds of years, and that even the presence of three empires in the 19th century could not change. The police chief supports the *fono* system of justice:

> Without the *matai* system we would run into difficulties. We rely on them as an enforcement agency as long as they do not encroach on criminal legislation that police should handle. There are advantages and disadvantages with the *matai* system, but I don't think our job would function properly without them. Where

there are differences the matter is often handled within the village before it reaches police. The traditional punishment is then used as mitigation in court. *Fono* are a state of control. Their authority is to keep order within their boundaries and organise community projects to benefit the villagers.[15]

The Secretary for Justice, Tuala Donald Kerslake, agrees. He says village law is more variable than the national system where the penalties are written down. For example, the maximum for rape is seven years and murder is commuted to life in prison. Its strength is that it is a system in a small area so it is easy to police. Village penalties are speedier: the chiefs meet, penalty is made, and the matter is settled that day. In the national system there are more procedures: you are questioned, arrested, charged, appear in court and plead. If you plead not guilty there are a series of adjournments and legal fees, before your case is decided. That may take months or a year. He sees the two systems continuing to co-exist.

Kerslake says it is common in the modern system for the family of the victim to ask for charges to be withdrawn because the matter has been settled traditionally. These settlements based on *fa'a Samoa* are also used in mitigation pleas during sentencing. Sometimes the victim will plead for the offender. Part of their survival has been by holding on to what has been their customs and traditions, because that is what makes them Samoan.[16]

Conclusion

Western Samoan law epitomises the clash between two philosophical bases underpinning separate law systems. When it acts with prudence and wisdom, the restorative nature of the *fono* system has enabled Western Samoa to remain relatively free of the major crime that now blights most nations. Clearly there can be excesses in its exercise of power. Clearly, too, individuals can feel aggrieved at the lack of individual rights compared with many other Western nations. But people in Western Samoa do not go hungry or homeless and are not regarded as worthless. There is a place in the society for everyone. Could this not be because the wellbeing and health of the community are the primary focus of its law?

Footnotes

1. R. P. Gilson, *Samoa 1830-1900: the Politics of a Multi-Cultural Community*, Oxford University Press, Melbourne, 1970, p47
2. Ibid, p48
3. Ibid, p49
4. Malama Meleisea, *Lagaga: A Short History of Western Samoa*, University of the South Pacific, Suva, 1987, p27
5. Ibid, p28
6. Malama Meleisea, *Change and Adaptations in Western Samoa*, University of Canterbury, Christchurch, 1992, pp33-34
7. Malama Meleisea, *The Making of Modern Samoa*, University of the South Pacific, Apia, 1987, p244
8. Ibid, p113
9. Ibid, p115

10. Ibid, p246
11. Meleisea, *Lagaga*, op cit, p33
12. *Samoan Times*, Vol. 14, No. 3, 23 January 1981
13. Meleisea, op cit, *The Making of Modern Samoa*, p214
14. *Islands Business Review*, November 1993, p23
15. Ibid, p24
16. Ibid, p15

CHAPTER TEN

The Celtic Tradition: Repairing the Damage

Fivefold are Crimes:
the crime of the hand, by wounding or stealing;
the crime of the foot, by kicking or moving to do evil deeds;
the crime of the tongue, by satire, slander or false witness;
the crime of the mouth, by eating stolen things;
the crime of the eye, by watching while an evil deed is taking place.[1]

For 1500 years, up until the time of the final Tudor conquest, the Irish had their own criminal justice system. The *Brehon* Laws were based on a philosophy of restorative justice. In the preceding centuries, when the country was still in effect ruled on a federal basis by Irish chieftains and kings, Ireland had enjoyed a developed social structure well in advance of many other countries of its size. Eventually the *Brehon* Laws were destroyed and replaced with the harsh retributive system of the coloniser.

The *Brehon* Laws take their name from the Irish word *Breitheamh*, which means a judge. A *brehon* was a local jurist who arbitrated disputes and imposed sanctions on behalf of the community. He was one of the important people in the tribe or village who, along with the chroniclers and storytellers, the bards, the musicians and the clergy, was entrusted by the people to maintain their culture and traditions for their own wellbeing, so they might be handed on to future generations.

Brehon Laws covered all criminal acts, from murder and cattle theft to dog fights and trespass. Many were strictly speaking not laws at all but codes of conduct and traditions guiding people's behaviour. They were formed from generations of wise decisions and sayings of the elders and they helped knit into cohesive units the varying elements within each clan, and between the different clans.

There were simple rules of hospitality such as, 'Whoever comes to your door, you must feed him or care for him, with no questions asked.'[2] And rules of neighbourliness such as 'Notice of a hound in heat and the mad dog must be sent to the four nearest neighbourhoods'[3] helped achieve community justice and peace in profound yet very practical ways.

No man was allowed to act as judge until he had studied the full law course and passed a rigorous public examination. The course of study for judge and law-agent, respectively, was carefully laid down. The *brehon* was an arbitrator, umpire and expounder of the law, rather than a judge in the modern sense. It appears that the facts of a case were investigated and ascertained by laymen before submission to a *brehon* for legal decision. The complainant could select any *brehon* he pleased if there was more than one in his district. Every king or chief of sufficient territory retained an official *brehon*, who was provided with free land for his maintenance and acted as registrar or assessor in the king's court.[4]

There were, it seems, at least in some places and during some later periods, two types of *brehon*, the *brithem* and the *aigre*. The former was a 'maker of judgments' or an 'arbitrator'. The latter can be equated with the modern barrister or advocate. As Fergus Kelly explains in his book *A Guide to Early Irish Law*, Uraicecht Becc distinguishes three grades of judges.

The lowest grade was competent to decide on matters related to craftsmen and had an honour-price of seven *sets* (valuables or treasures). Above him was the judge who was competent in both traditional law and poetry, with an honour price of 10 *sets*. The highest grade was the 'judge of three languages', who was competent in traditional law, poetry and canon law and had an honour-price of 15 *sets*. The grading of judges is not found elsewhere, and may have been peculiar to the *Nemed* school. Each *tuaithe* seems to have an official judge, the *brithem tuaithe*, who was presumably appointed by the king.[5]

Liam Breatnach suggests that there were three periods covering a continuous legal tradition from the Old Irish period (c600-900AD), through the Middle Irish period (c900-1200), to the Classical Modern Irish period (c1200-1650). The end of this tradition coincided with the demise of the Gaellic aristocracy and the social system that supported it.[6]

The *Brehon* Laws governed a society that was essentially federal, not feudal. At the time eastern Europe was almost totally feudal. Because the Irish were federal their political system had not evolved with any strong centralised form of government, nor a system of universal law. It was into such a country that, over a period of centuries, wave upon wave of English armies came until, by sheer weight of numbers, the Irish were subdued.

The centralised code of English law imposed on them after the first invasion in 1169 did not take root until the 16th century, when the English applied their military screws more tightly. If there had been in Ireland a despotic monarchy, a feudal civilisation that ground down the people and exalted the nobles, it is probable that the English would have been driven out. But the Irish national genius was in harmony with a concept of freedom and humanity, which a mammon-ridden world has never known elsewhere, and through the centuries it fought obstinately for its own concept of the proper order of things.[7]

The 1603 Treaty of Melifont marked the official end of the prevailing federal clan system, and the Disarming Act of 1695 marked the temporary end of the Irish power of military resistance. The way was then open to attempt to conquer the Irish mind as well, with the Penal Laws being used as the chief instrument for this enterprise. It should be noted that during all this period, until well into the 16th century, the *Brehon* Laws held sway in the countryside and provincial towns. It was only on the eastern seaboard and especially around Dublin (within the Pale) that English law was observed to any degree prior to this. That eventually three centuries later the English left Ireland – except for Ulster – is now a matter of history. But by that time centralised government and a centralised code of law were well implanted.

Social Structure

In order to understand the breadth, width and wisdom of the *Brehon* Laws, it is important to have some knowledge of the social structure of ancient Ireland. It is clear that they were in universal use until the English conquest (and indeed used in parts of Ireland for many centuries later), and pertained to every facet of Irish life.

> Six cows are the fine for breaking a tribesman's two front teeth; 12 heifers for maiming a homeless man.
> For pulling off the hairs of a virgin bishop the fine is one yearling heifer for every 20 hairs.[8]

Our main information on the economic basis of early Irish society comes from the law texts. They describe a self-sufficient mixed farming economy based on the rearing of cattle, sheep and pigs and on the growing of cereals. The economic system was sustained on the inter-relationship of lord and client: the lord advanced a fief of stock or land to his clients and in return received rent and services. Sufficient wealth was generated to sustain not only a hierarchy of lords and kings, but also various professional men, of whom the most important are poets, judges, smiths, physicians and wrights (skilled workers).[9]

It was primarily a rural society. Built-up townships were few and far between, and usually constructed around a monastery. There must have also been trading settlements on the coasts, particularly in the south and east. The wisdom-text *Tecosca Cormaic* includes 'ships putting into port' as one of the signs of a good king. Their cargo would have included wine, fine cloth and various other luxury items. There is also evidence of the import of British horses. Little is known about exports from Ireland at the time of the law texts.[10]

Irish society generally could be divided into six classes: the kings of various grades, the professional classes, the *flaiths*, who constituted a type of nobility, freemen possessing property, freemen possessing no property (or very little), non-free classes. Progress could be made between the ranks depending on wealth accrued and qualifications.

So Irish society was hierarchical and class-based; egalitarianism was not a feature. The laws reflected this and an offence against a person of high rank carried a greater penalty than one against a commoner. While in later times Roman law and canon law would uphold equality before the law, native Irish law did not.

The whole social structure from a legal viewpoint was built upon a person's honour-price, or *log n-enech* (literally, the 'price of his face'). This had to be paid for any major offence committed against him eg murder, satire, serious injury, refusal of hospitality, theft, violation of his protection. A person's capacity to perform most legal acts was linked to his honour-price. Someone could not make a contract for an amount greater than his honour-price, nor could he go surety beyond this amount. Likewise his oaths and evidence were only given a weight commensurate with his honour-price.[11]

There were three levels to Irish social structure: the *fine*, the *sept* and the *tuath* (*clann*). The smallest organism – political and social – next to the immediate family was the fine (pronounced 'finna'). It was more than a family, but it was in the family that it took its origin. It closely corresponded to our notion of extended family or whanau since in the course of time the term came to be applied to a group of kindred families, or to a joint family group of four generations.

Originally the family had its allotted portion of land, but as children and grandchildren arrived at maturity and became heads of families themselves, or at least at an age where they could inherit and possess property and share in responsibilities, the original land became divided and subdivided among them. This aggregate of individuals, freemen born, members of the same clan, deriving their descent from the same ancestor, bound together by ties of kinship and interest and possessing a common portion of land, made up the corporate body called the *fine*. At its head stood the *flaithe-fine*. He was the paterfamilias, the representative of the *fine*. He was to sue and be sued in its name, to guard its interests and defend its rights.[12]

The kin-group or *fine* is the group most referred to in the law texts. The members are all descendants through the male line of the same great-grandfather. A kin-group possesses considerable legal power over its members. Each kin-group had its own kin-land (*fintiu*) for which every legally competent adult male in the group had some degree of responsibility. No-one could sell his share of the kin-land against the wishes of the rest of the kin.[13]

The kin-group had social responsibilities in relation to its members. It was also liable for the fines and debts of its members, so if an offender absconded, his kin became liable. If payment was not forthcoming the plaintiff could claim cattle from a kinsman of the offender, using a special form of distraint. The head of the kin was known as the *agae fine* or *cenn fine*. He was chosen – presumably by election among the kin-members – on the basis of his superior wealth, rank and good sense. He spoke for his kin on public occasions, such as an assembly or court of law, and gave pledges on behalf of his kin to ensure the fulfilment of any responsibility that any kin-members may have towards the king, Church or poets.[14]

The next level of social structure was the *sept*, which has no English equivalent but is similar to the Maori hapu. The *sept* was an intermediate organism between the *fine* and the clan. It consisted of a number of *fines*, as the clan consisted of a number of *septs*. It was one of the divisions of the clan assigned a specific part of the territory, and over it and this district a *flaithe* was supposed to preside. No rule is stated as to the number of persons or *fines* that might be a *sept*. The right of the *sept* to undisturbed possession of its assigned portion of the territory was greater than that of the fine, was subject only to that of the clan, and was very rarely interfered with.[15]

At the next level existed the *tuath* or *clann* (clan). Each clan was a distinct group and tried to be self-sufficient and self-contained. A clan had the land as its property. After the clan in degree of importance came the *sept*, where one existed, and then the *fine*. The individual was left little to do but fill the position assigned to him or her and conform to the system.[16]

The clan built small monasteries and schools, endowing them with lands, stock and other necessities. As a rule it dedicated every first-born son to the Church and it retained to itself the right of succession to all posts, clerical and lay, so long as it possessed qualified people. The clan had its bishop or abbot with episcopal faculties and territorial jurisdiction.

Tuath, Cinel and *Clann* were synonyms meaning a small tribe or nation descended from a common ancestor. A king and clan being able, subject to certain limitations, to adopt new members or families, or amalgamate with another clan, the theory of common origin was not rigidly adhered to. Kinship with the clan was an essential qualification for holding any office or property. The rules of kinship largely determined status with its correlative rights and obligations, supplied the place of contracts and of laws affecting the ownership, disposition and devolution of property, constituting the clan an organic, self-contained entity, a political, social and mutual insurance co-partnership.

The solidarity of the clan was its most important and all-pervading characteristic. According to the traditional view the entire territory occupied by a clan was the common and absolute property of that clan, a portion being set apart for the maintenance of the king. Warriors, statesmen, *brehons, ollamhs*, physicians, poets and even eminent workers in the more important arts were also rewarded with free lands. Rank, with the accompanying privileges, jurisdiction and responsibility, was based upon a qualification of kinship and of property held by a family for a specified number of generations, together with certain concurrent conditions, and it could be lost by loss of property, crime, cowardice or other disgraceful conduct. A portion of land called the *cumbal senorba* was devoted to the support of widows, orphans and old childless people.[17]

The law texts indicate that the basic territorial unit was the tuath, conveniently translated 'tribe' or 'petty kingdom'. On the evidence of genealogies and other sources, it is calculated that there were probably 150 kings in Ireland at any given date between the fifth and 12th centuries. Each of these kings would have ruled over his own *tuath* (and many others would also have been overlords of the *tuatha* of other kings). Any estimate of the total population of Ireland at this period is of course highly speculative, but a figure of something under half a million has been proposed. On this basis the average *tuath* could be reckoned to have contained about 3000 men, women and children.

According to one law text, no *tuath* can be regarded as a proper *tuath* unless it has an ecclesiastical scholar, a churchman, a poet and a king. The life of a *tuath* centred on its king: all the freemen owed him their direct loyalty and paid him a special tax. At any time the king could summon them to a *slogad* or 'hosting' to repel invaders or attack a neighbouring *tuath*. He also convened the *oenach*, a regular assembly for political, social and perhaps commercial purposes.[18]

Each clan had two local assemblies of its own for the transaction of ordinary business. One was called the *cuirmtig*, and was open to all clansmen who paid tribute (a type of tax for the wellbeing of the common good). The other was called the *dal*, and appears to have been open only to the heads of *septs*, although it may have included heads of *fines* as well. The *dal* was a type of second chamber or upper house where decisions made at the *cuirmtig* were ratified or otherwise. Each clan also had a further assembly called a *tocomra*, at which the king or chief was elected.

Of local assemblies, the *oenach* appears to have been the most important. *Oenach* is a word meaning a fair, and in effect once the assembly came together, what amounted to a cattle fair sprang up alongside. In time the *oenach* was also taken advantage of for holding a high court of justice to hear appeals, Church synods, a place for musical, poetry and bardic contests, weapon displays, athletics, horse racing and dancing. In time these supplementary activities overshadowed the original ides of a local assembly where decisions were made.

In ancient times there were two national assemblies, which brought people together from all over the country. The most important was the Feis of Tara, held every three years, which was an assembly of the leading men of the land. It was restricted to leaders – kings, *flaiths*, warriors, *brehons*, chiefs, poets, leading bards. The Feis of Tara died out in the sixth century. Another celebrated national assembly was held annually for many centuries at Tailltenn on the Blackwater in Meath. It was a general assembly of the people and was not restricted to those of rank and distinction. Its purpose was social and political, and laws were debated and enacted. This assembly lasted into the reign of King Roderick O'Connor, and was last held in 1168AD.

Up until this time the country was governed essentially by a small aristocratic ruling class, the principal titleholder being a king. Next to the kings were nobles or princes of varying grades. A wealthy person could in time aspire to become a noble if he accrued enough wealth. Theoretically even peasants could aspire to the highest office.

In practice the most important social distinctions seem to have been between those who were *nemed* (privileged) and those who were not *nemed*; and between those who were *soer* (free) and those who were *doer* (unfree). The chief categories of *nemed* in society were king, lord (*flaithe*), cleric and poet. Some texts include the physician, judge, blacksmith, coppersmith, harpist, carpenter and other craftsmen as a lower appendage of the *nemed* class. But it is clear they do not enjoy full *nemed* privileges.

Ranking below the *nemed* was the non-*nemed* freeman, who probably made up the majority of the adult male population at this period. He had an honour-price in his own right and could take independent legal action. He attended the assembly and thereby played a part, however small, in decisions affecting the *tuath*. The law texts distinguish two main categories of non-*nemed* freemen: the *ocaire* and the *boaire*, who can roughly be equated respectively with the 'small farmer' and the 'strong farmer' of 20th-century Ireland.[19]

The most important *nemed* person in a *tuath* is the king. But there could be ranking even among kings, with some acquiring dominance over other *tuatha*, receiving military assistance from them in times of war.

However, as Kelly points out, the King of Ireland who figures so prominently in the sagas, is rarely mentioned in the law texts. He says that though the idea of a kingship of all Ireland had already gained currency by the seventh century, no Irish king ever made it a reality and most law texts do not even provide for such a possibility.[20]

Under ancient Irish law the land did not belong to the king or the chief or the landlord, but to the tribe. The lowest of the free-tribesmen had as much an inalienable right to their share as had the chief himself.

One of the important things spelt out in the *Brehon* Laws was that the poor, the aged, the orphans and the widowed were to be provided for within their clan.

There were detailed instructions as to how they were to be looked after. For example, law decreed that the sick were to have ample ventilation and to be provided with fresh water. Detailed regulations were spelt out governing care for the aged:

> When you become old your family must provide you with one oatcake a day, plus a container of sour milk.
>
> They must bathe you every 20th night and wash your head every Saturday.
>
> Seventeen sticks of firewood is the allotment for keeping you warm.[21]

Free clansmen, who formed a type of middle class, provided for their care. This was paid to the clan's *flaithe* or chief to oversee their wellbeing. Such tributes were often paid for in kind and one farmer would make a speciality of breeding one particular class of stock, another a different class. The *flaithe* took up the tributes from the different farmers at different seasons of the year, thus maintaining a supply for those in need. The *flaithe* was kept informed of stock levels within the *sept*. The *flaithe* was also bound to provide bulls and stallions for the use of the *sept*. These were very useful functions, and they by no means exhausted the duties which by law the *flaithe* was bound to discharge.[22]

Senchas Mar

In the 19th century two famous Irish scholars, Professors Eugene O'Curry and John O'Donovan, transcribed some ancient texts of *Brehon* Law into 17 volumes. Their study reveals not just dry and dusty ancient law texts but:

> ...thousands of details. Details that described ancient life in the days when the Irish still lived in mud huts and small ringed settlements, and paid their bills in cows and bacon, handsome gold brooches and ordinary wooden bowls: the brewer testing a grain of malt against his tooth to guard against bitterness in the ale; farmers lugging sides of beef to the chieftain to pay their quarterly rent; a pregnant wife who craves a morsel of food; mischievous boys shouting at pigs... the Irish laws serve as a repository of primitive customs, some dating back 3000 years and most gathered by Celtic wanderers from various members of the far-flung Indo-European family.[23]

Much of the law has been lost in the mists of antiquity and much more was destroyed by the English colonists. Under the infamous Penal Laws imposed by England, it was very risky to be caught with any Irish manuscript. Subsequent to these translations many other laws and manuscripts have been found that add to those of these two scholars.

At the beginning of the written tradition belong four important texts, the first three in Old Irish. They were the most famous of them, the *Senchas Mar*, the *Bretha Nemed Toisech*, written in Munster in the second quarter of the eighth century, and the *Cain Fuithirbe*, an earlier Munster text completed sometime between 678 and 683AD. The *Collectio Cannonum Hibernensis* was the fourth text, written in Latin in the eighth century.[24]

The *Senchas Mar* contained some of the most important traditions, customs and laws. It is regarded as the greatest work on traditional Irish law, both civil and criminal. It contains much of the law existing before the advent of St Patrick, who had a marked influence on much of *Brehon* Law. The *Senchas Mar* also included a very important section on the Law of Distress, which assumed such an important role in Irish legal history. Other volumes covered ancient laws on hostage sureties, the law of fosterage, of tenure of stock, of social connections. There were tracts on taking possession of land, tenancy, the rights to water, divisions of land, social ranks, laws relating to poets and their verse, to the Church, chiefs, pledges and other contracts.

Noted scholar D. A. Binchy suggests that another group of ancient law texts also existed. He calls them the *Nemed* (holy or privileged) Collection. They contain many duties and rights of artists, poets and bards and seem to have emanated from the Munster area. There is also evidence to suggest that there were other law sources as well, and Kelly makes reference to them.[25]

Within the *Senchas Mar* there is a special treatise called the Book of Aicill. It is taken up primarily with what we now call criminal law. It comprises principally the opinions of two eminent leaders, both men of law. The first was King Cormac mac Airt (otherwise called Cormac ua Cuinn), King of All Ireland, who ruled from 227 to 266AD. He was a great reformer of national institutions in his time, including the historic Feis of Tara. A patron of literature, art and industry, he wrote (or had written) several works on law, history and other important subjects.

The second author of the Book of Aicill was Cennfaeladh, who lived in the seventh century. He was a soldier and a lawyer. He appears to have rewritten the whole work and undoubtedly modernised it, bringing it into harmony with the requirements of Christianity, which by this time had become the principal religion of Ireland. His re-editing of King Cormac mac Airt's seminal work in essence constituted a new, revised and enlarged second edition of the work.

These law traditions are all built on a philosophy of restorative justice. Reconciliation, reparation and healing, along with mercy and forgiveness, are the hallmarks of their practical application.

Irish Criminal Law

It appears that in ancient Ireland almost any crime could be dealt with by way of a fine, which seems unusual in a race known for its fighting traditions. The law texts present a fine as a possibility in practically every case, even if in many instances it was impossible for the accused to pay on his or her own. This is where the strength of the fine came into play. In spite of the absence of a state system of law enforcement in pre-Norman Ireland, it is likely that in most cases the prestige of the law and of the judge's office – combined with the system of pledges and sureties – would have ensured that the fines imposed by judges in court were actually paid.[26]

In later times there was a set procedure for the perusal of law cases. Kelly's research reveals eight stages that were followed before a decision was reached.[27] Many correspond to current law practice in modern Western jurisdictions. One could assume that such detailed procedures developed under the guidance of ecclesiastical law and were used more often for serious rather than minor cases.

There were basically three levels of advocacy. One, called a 'fettering advocate', was competent in enforcing the decisions made on behalf of the court. This one had a role that appears to be a cross between our bailiffs and police. A second role was that of 'court advocate', who pleaded a case on his own behalf. The third role was that of an 'advocate whom judgment encounters', who played a role not unlike a court lawyer today.

The practising lawyers, then, both judges and advocates, were distinguished not only according to their competence in the law, but also according to the societal and political divisions of early Christian Ireland. Judges were appointed either by church or lay authorities, and advocates acted for both laymen and ecclesiastics. Advocates were distinguished according to the status of the people they acted for, while judges were distinguished according to the political importance of the king or monastery that appointed them.[28]

On the surface there also seems to have been no hard and fast line drawn between civil and criminal offences in the *Brehon* Laws. However, in practice there were some subtle but real distinctions. In civil cases the defendant often had the right to choose the judge, whereas usually in criminal cases the *brehon* was first approached, often at the instigation of the victim.

It is of profound significance to note that a restorative rather than a retributive philosophy prevailed. The laws discouraged revenge and retaliation and permitted capital punishment only as a last resort. They contained elaborate provision for dealing with crime, but the standpoint from which it was regarded and treated was essentially different from ours. The state, for all its elaborate structure, did not assume jurisdiction in relation to any crimes except political ones, such as treason or the disturbance of a large assembly.[29]

In the case of a crime committed by an individual, the *fine* and the *sept* were liable. People against whom the crimes had been committed were left to sue for redress by summoning the offender to appear before a *brehon*, who heard the case and assessed the amount of fine that should be imposed. The *brehon* had the traditional laws and standards to guide his judgment. If the defendant did not pay immediately, a levy of distress could be placed on his goods.

There were no prisons and there were hardly any public servants who could correctly be called police or detectives. The people were their own police. Their activity was sharpened by the knowledge that a *sept* had to pay for a secret crime committed in its territory, unless the crime had been committed by an outsider. This liability continued as long as the criminal lived, whether his crime was against person or property.

If the crime was purely personal the *sept* was no longer liable, for the crime died with the criminal. But if it was against property, the *sept* remained liable. Every clan and clansman had a direct interest in the suppression and prevention of crime.[30]

The strong bonding within the community, helped by a law seen to be fair and equitable towards all, meant that it was in everyone's interests to maintain and support it. The only way someone could escape the consequences of criminal behaviour was to flee. But to flee was to leave all personal property behind, which meant the *fine* or the *sept* would have to bear responsibility for the penalty. To escape was to become an outcast and to live as a fugitive.

Reparation was the usual method of penalty. There were several levels at which fines operated. The *brehon*'s role was to give judgment on the penalties. Fines could be paid in differing forms and combinations of them. There were varying currencies – ounces of silver, *sets* (treasures), cattle and *cumals* (literally a female slave, but more often 'a unit of value') being the most common. Cattle were most often used as payment, the basic unit being a milk cow accompanied by her calf.

> For stealing your pigs or your sheep,
> for stripping your herb garden,
> for wearing down your hatchet or wood-axe,
> you may take your neighbour's milk cows to the public animal pound for three days.
> If he does not want his cows taken to the pound for his crimes or his bad debts,
> he may give his son as security instead.[31]

The severest fine was the *eiric* or *eric*, a fine for murder or manslaughter. The actual amounts varied with the circumstances; for the wealthy it was far more severe than for the poor. The level of intent and malice was also a major factor. A murderer would usually pay at least twice the amount assessed for manslaughter, but it could be much more.

Honour-price as mentioned earlier was another form of fine and was determined by status. The same law that arranged the different ranks of society and fixed their respective rights and privileges and liabilities also fixed the honour-price. For criminal offences or breach of contract this honour-price was forfeited in part or in total. The whole of the honour-price would be forfeited for a murder, with reparation going partly to the injured family and partly to the king.

In the case of certain particularly vile crimes, the criminal was expelled from the clan and from the territory, even though the fine had been recovered. An habitual criminal might also be expelled, and by expelling him and lodging a security against his future misdeeds his relatives could free themselves from responsibility. A person so expelled became an outlaw, with no status or right whatever, no legal capacity and no protection from the law. And anyone who gave him food or shelter became liable for his crimes.[32]

Fines were accompanied by other less specific penalties. Along with the fine went the shame of offending, a sense of public humiliation, a loss of status that could include the disqualification from holding public office, from suing others, from acting as a juror, and from inheriting land. These penalties could be short term or longer.

The principles governing the severity of an offence and penalty to be imposed were guided by four factors: the damage done, the status of the injured person, the status of the offender, the accompanying circumstances.

So, for example, a man of high rank was always fined more than a man of low rank in a like case. A property offence against a poor person would be punished more severely than if it was committed against a person of wealth. An assault against a highly ranked person was more severely punished than a similar offence against a peasant.

For large fines, the penalty could be paid in varying currency: several cows, some silver and some food could constitute the full payment. For assaults, the system ran the same way. A fine of two cows was considered heavy for a blow that did not draw blood. It was up to the *brehon* to decide.

Sanctuary

Another feature of importance contained in the *Brehon* Laws was that of sanctuary. The *maighin digona* was the area house of every clansman and within this area the owner and his family were inviolable. Rank determined the size of the sanctuary around a home. For a low-class person it was quite a small clearing; for someone of high rank it could be an area stretching up to 1000 paces. For chiefs, bishops and nobles it could be that area measured by the distance one could hear the sound of a bell, or the crow of a rooster. The owner of the *maighin digona* was empowered to extend protection to a fleeing stranger, but such sanctuary needed the owner's consent.

Murder

In the case of murder, Irish law sought compensation rather than the death sentence. This same practice of seeking reparation instead of the death penalty was also carried out by the ancient Greeks, the Gauls, the Franks, the Swedes, the Danes, the Germans and the Saxons.

It seems two main types of fine were normally paid to the victim's kin. The first was the fixed penalty for homicide, which amounted to seven *cumals* for every freeman irrespective of rank. The other main fine was based on the honour-price of the victim's kin and was distributed among both his paternal and maternal kin. If the victim was of high rank it could become a very expensive business, to which kinsmen were expected to contribute.[33]

Where the *eric* could not be paid or there were special circumstances, the family of the victim could kill an offender. But there was no state execution. There are varying opinions as to how often a retaliatory execution was carried out; it would seem to have been a relatively rare occurrence.

The *Brehon* Laws give various qualifications as guidelines for dealing with murder:

> The fine for killing a bond-person held as security for a loan (or for killing a slave) is 21 cows;
> for killing a free farmer of Erin the fine is 42 cows.
> For killing a noble the fine for homicide is paid, plus an additional amount determined by his rank in society.
> Fines are doubled for malice aforethought.[34]

There is ample evidence that Irish opinion was generally against the death penalty. There are several passages to the effect that no-one was put to death as long as the *eric* was obtained, and that an assailant should not be put to death if he was known or could be arrested. For high treason hanging was a possibility, and on occasion a murderer could be put into an open boat and exposed to the possibility of death at sea.

Conclusion

The philosophy of restorative justice upon which the *Brehon* Laws were based covered all criminal offending, including murder. Retaliation and retribution based on vengeance were not a part of that philosophy. The whole aim was to restore to wellbeing the victim and the community, and there is evidence of real flexibility in the way the laws were framed so as to make sure that happened.

Retribution and vengeance only came with the colonisation of Ireland by the English and the imposition of English law, which eventually saw the *Brehon* Laws disappear from the penal code of Ireland. One suspects, however, that they have not altogether disappeared from the deepest subconscious of the Irish people.

Footnotes

1. Mary Dowling Daley, *Irish Laws*, Appletree Press, Belfast, 1989, p46
2. Ibid, p29
3. Ibid, p50
4. *Encyclopaedia Britannica*, Vol. 4, Encyclopaedia Britannica Ltd, London, 1959, p85

5. Fergus Kelly, *A Guide to Early Irish Law*, Dublin Institute for Advanced Studies, Dublin, 1988, 1991, p51
6. Liam Breatnach, 'Lawyers in Early Ireland', article in *Brehons, Sergeants, and Attorneys*, ed Daire Hogan and W. N. Osborough, Irish Academic Press, Dublin, 1990, p2
7. P. S. O'Hegarty, *The Indestructible Nation*, Maunsell and Co Ltd, Dublin, 1918, p48
8. Daley, op cit, p25
9. Kelly, op cit, p3
10. Ibid, p6
11. Ibid, p8
12. Monsignor D'Alton, *History of Ireland*, Vol. 1, Gresham Publishing Co Ltd, London, 1925, p25
13. Kelly, op cit, p12
14. Ibid, pp13-14
15. Laurence Ginnell, *The Brehon Laws*, T. Fisher Unwin, London, 1894, pp107-09
16. *Encyclopaedia Britannica*, p85
17. *The Course of Irish History*, ed T. W. Moody and F. X. Martin, Mercier Press, Cork, 1967, p45
18. Kelly, op cit, p319
19. Kelly, op cit, pp9-10
20. Ibid, p17
21. Daley, op cit, p59
22. *Encyclopaedia Britannica*, op cit, p86
23. Daley, op cit, p4
24. Breatnach, op cit, p2
25. Kelly, op cit, p246
26. Ibid, p214
27. Ibid, p191
28. Breatnach, op cit, p13
29. Ginnell, op cit, pp123-24
30. Ibid, pp185-86
31. Daley, op cit, p48
32. Ginnell, op cit, p191
33. Kelly, op cit, p126
34. Daley, op cit, p47

CHAPTER ELEVEN

God's Way: Biblical Justice

Scripture has a bad name when it comes to dealing with criminal justice. What person in the street, when asked what scripture has to say about crime, will not immediately think of the quote 'an eye for an eye, a tooth for a tooth'? Or quote one or other of the Ten Commandments?

That such quotes are usually taken out of context and misunderstood as a result seems to escape notice. Indeed, one might go as far as to say that the underpinning of Western law and the justification for our horrendous prison system can to a large extent be attributable to what Christians have perceived to be God's view of such matters as found in scripture.

In a study such as this, it is important to include a chapter on biblical justice because of the Christian influence on the development of a codified law in Western history and its influence on the penal system. To ignore these influences because of the secular nature of the age would be to remain blind to an influence of major significance.

In this chapter I will seek to look at the misquotes used to justify our current system, at the true nature of biblical justice, and the implications for the future if a biblical vision was enacted.

What Does Scripture Say?

The Bible appears to have much to say about crime and punishment. Naturally it deals with what flows from violations of law, and in particular with what flows from violations of its most sacred law, the Torah, which contains the commandments of God. But all law was not of equal status in biblical times. Consequently, how one dealt with offenders varied depending on a wide variety of circumstances.

There was no centralised code of law or criminal justice system such as we have now. That is something that developed in Western civilisation, and it really only started to take root in a centralised way from the 13th century. Such law is really quite a late development.

So when Jesus is accused of breaking the law on the Sabbath, rather than being arrested and charged, he merely has an argument with his accusers about the ruling itself and the nature of law, and he is left to move on.

A Jewish understanding of Hebrew law has often been quite different from a Western Christian understanding of the same law. For example, Martin Buber, the famous Jewish scholar, in his German translation of the scriptures, translates 'an eye for an eye and a tooth for a tooth' as 'an eye for the value of an eye, a tooth for the value of a tooth'.

As scripture scholar Herman Bianchi points out, there is no historical evidence that one would lose an eye as a punishment for assaulting and damaging the eye of another. The eye and the tooth notions are symbolic. (Incidentally, that particular phrase occurs only three times in the whole of scripture.[1]) The concept of *lex talionis*, the law of proportionality, simply says that you should never claim more than the value of what is damaged. If property worth 100 gold coins is stolen, then you cannot claim 200 coins in return. If you took more than what was just, then you in turn could be punished.

The emphasis was usually on restitution and restoration, not vengeance and punishment.[2] Restitution was seen as a way of setting things right. If property was stolen, then the property should be returned; if damage was done to someone's house or field, then the person responsible for the damage should repair it.[3]

Later in the New Testament, Christ specifically rejects this notion when he says quite emphatically: 'You have heard it said "an eye for an eye". But I tell you, do good to those who harm you.'[4]

The focus on crime in biblical times was not so much on individuals as on the community. Corporate responsibility was central to the Hebrew understanding of crime.

First (Old) Testament understanding renounced any scapegoating that claimed that crime was only the responsibility of a few evil individuals within the society. When the law was broken, there was corporate responsibility. Violence and breach of law pointed to a crisis in the very fabric of the society.

It is from this understanding that the prophets are able to warn that the entire nation is doomed because some widows have been mistreated or because the hungry have not been allowed to glean the fields. Not only all the people but the land itself is caught up in sin and all its consequences, for the meadows lie barren and the mountains quake and the trees bear no fruit. For Israel, the fullest response to crime was not the isolated punishment of an individual law-breaker, but the repentance of the entire nation.[5]

Herman Bianchi has pointed out that in the West we have translated the Ten Commandments as imperatives, thus losing something of their meaning in their original context. In Martin Buber's Hebrew text, the verbs express future tense, not imperatives. The Law of Moses begins with an introduction that contains a promise. Translated, it has God saying: 'I am the Lord your God. When you follow my indications, my Law, my wise ways, I will bring you freedom and life.'

> Thus the commandments are better understood as meaning: 'When you follow my wise indications, you will not steal any more, you will not kill, you will not commit adultery.' The scriptures go on to show that when the Jewish people did follow God's law they were blessed, and when they went astray, they were not. In modern terms we too can have a blessed society, when we try to break down the bureaucracies that have taken everything from us, when we give neighbourhoods another chance to live as neighbourhoods, then we won't steal any more, we won't kill any more. It is a promise. It is the promised land.[6]

The central feature of biblical law is a constant calling forth of the people to a future promise. The emphasis is on the future health and wellbeing of the community, and not on the immediate transgressions of the law. The covenant agreed to by Moses and the people with Yahweh always emphasises this future direction. It also helps explain why rabbis are constantly in debate about the meaning of the law. In some English translations it is not as clearcut and imperative in its practice as it might sometimes appear.

How then did the West come to see God as a punishing High Court judge-type figure who hovers over our everyday activities like an eye-in-the-sky policeman? This clearly is not the emphasis of the scriptures. We have done that it seems by largely misinterpreting the actual meaning of some key passages of scripture, and by failing to recognise the context within which they were written.

There are several key words in scripture that indicate the presence of justice in a much fuller sense than what we usually understand. Justice is part of the very essence of God, as can be seen from reading the psalms and the prophets, especially Isaiah, Jeremiah, Micah and Amos, and from reflecting on the Gospels. As theologian Kevin O'Reilly says:

> In the Bible God is called the just one. What is this justice of God? According to the Old Testament authors, the justice of God is not the quality whereby God rewards the good and punishes the wicked. God is just when he intervenes in the lives of the underprivileged, especially orphans and widows, to save them from the injustices of men (Deuteronomy 10/18). God is just when he defends the cause of the innocent. God is just when he establishes those who have been exploited by wicked men. God is just when he saves the poor.[7]

A key word for justice is *t'sedeka*, which Buber translates as 'to bring the truth, to be truthful, to speak the truth'. Justice, then, is very much related to a way of life, a personal commitment of lifestyle, not just an academic theory. A person who lives *t'sedeka* seeks to live justly and to bring justice eventually to all.[8] Another key word is *t'shuvah*, which means 'a halt' so that things can turn around. It contains the notion of conversion and repentance. A person who stops drinking alcohol because of problems, practises *t'shuvah*. Bianchi argues that the modern law must allow the opportunity for *t'shuvah*, a turnaround, to be accomplished.[9]

Hesed is an important word and reflects the love that contains justice as its motivating force. *Mishpat* reflects the social expression of God's justice in the relationship of God with the people, and the people with one another.

Wayne Northey gives us some hints on how to interpret what, at first sight, appear to be retributive passages in scripture:

- Judaic law is much broader and deeper than Western state law. It is primarily theological and conveys, as indicated, all the dimensions of the relationship between God and humanity. It was not simply narrowly concerned with legal or criminal data.
- The law codes were really in fact only quasi-legal. The primary purpose of the law was to create a people of God who would adhere to God's will. The concern was thus much more religious than criminal, or even civil.
- Some of the language seen to be most legally orientated was actually homiletical, exhorting God's people to holiness. The writing was often as if the Israelites were living according to God's law. (cf Exodus 23/22-4).
- Some of the references to prohibitions and punishments are more descriptive than prescriptive – as much describing an actual event as a warning, indicating it should or should not happen again. (cf Leviticus 20/27, Numbers 15/36).
- It is probable that a ritualistic form of expiation or atonement in the temple, rather than an applied punishment, accompanied the redress of crimes or sins in the bulk of cases. (cf Numbers 16, Leviticus 4, Leviticus 6/1-7). Otherwise, compensation was the norm, not so much seen as a punitive measure but as a means of making peace come to all concerned.[10]

As scripture scholar Virginia Mackey concludes, in their scripture and tradition, Jews have urged caution in judgment, have shown reluctance to punish, and have exhibited the desire to make atonement, restitution or reconciliation after conflicts. This is their interpretation of 'making right', 'making peace', or 'achieving *shalom*'. The predominant theology is one of restoration.

Perry Yoder, a distinguished biblical studies professor, says that while retributive justice is found in the First Testament, it is often in the context of shalom justice, whereby the motive for it being meted out is setting things right.[12]

Shalom and Covenant

The two most central concepts of biblical law and justice relate to *shalom* and covenant. Howard Zehr points out that *shalom* is not just a peripheral theme of scripture but a basic core belief from which God's vision and plan for creation and the development of the human family flow. Hence notions of salvation, atonement, forgiveness and justice have their roots in *shalom*.[13]

In English *shalom* is usually translated to mean peace, but that is a very inadequate translation. Perry Yoder describes three basic dimensions to its meaning. They are physical wellbeing, including adequate food, clothing, shelter and wealth; a right relationship between and among people; and the acquisition of virtue, especially honesty and moral integrity. The absence of *shalom* means the absence of one or other of these features.[14]

There is a flow-on of this concept in the New Testament where Christ's life and teachings and eventually his death and resurrection transform relationships between and among people, thus inaugurating the Reign of God, the New Creation, wherein *shalom* – justice, peace, righteousness – are lived by believers.

The other major concept that has a direct relationship with law and justice is that of covenant. A covenant is a binding agreement between parties. There were several in the scriptures, starting with God and creation in Genesis. Then there was the one with Abraham, Sarah and the newly created People of God, followed by the one with God and Moses representing the people on Mount Sinai when the Ten Commandments were given.

The culminating covenant came with Jesus and the whole of humanity at the Last Supper. This was enacted through the suffering and death of Jesus on the cross at Calvary and through the resurrection, and subsequently ritualised at the celebration of the Eucharist or Mass. This new covenant opened up for humanity a new way of viewing things, of relating, of recognising the dignity of each person within the context of their community.

Tragically over the centuries the Church has often been a far from benign influence on the development of just social structures, including the criminal justice system prevalent in the West. However, this does not exclude its potential to yet fulfil something of the vision of which the ancient prophets dreamed and for which Jesus died.

In his seminal book on restorative justice, *Changing Lenses*, Howard Zehr says that biblical justice seeks to make things right, and this often means liberation for the unequal. Thus biblical justice shows a clear partiality towards those who are oppressed and impoverished. It is clearly on the side of the poor, recognising their needs and disadvantages. Biblical justice is open-eyed, with hands outstretched to those in need.

He goes on to say that since biblical justice seeks to make things better, justice is not designed to maintain the status quo. Indeed, its intent is to shake up the status quo, to improve, to move towards *shalom*. The move towards *shalom* is not necessarily good news for everyone. In fact it is downright bad news for the oppressor. It also stands in contrast to that justice which, by working to maintain order, works in fact to maintain the present order, the status quo, even when it is unjust.

The test of justice in the biblical view is not whether the right rules are applied in the right way. Justice is tested by the outcome. The tree is tested by its fruit. It is the substance, not the procedure, that defines justice. And how should things come out? The litmus test is how the poor and oppressed are affected.[15]

In biblical times such justice was enacted on an everyday basis in Jewish settlements. Citizens went to the city gates to seek justice from the judges or elders who presided there for this purpose. The whole focus for this 'court' setting was to find a solution for the aggrieved person. As Karl Barth points out, the judge was not primarily the one who rewarded some (distributive justice). He was the one who created order and restored what had been destroyed.

Restoration, then, was the keynote, not retribution. The words in Hebrew for 'paying back' and 'recompense', *shillum* and *shillem*, have the same root words as *shalom*. Restoring *shalom* was what such courts were all about. Helping people re-establish their covenant with God and one another was at the heart of this justice. When punishment was meted out, and on occasion this included execution, it was always seen as a necessary element to the restoration of the covenant and the re-establishment of *shalom*.

As Zehr says, biblical law was intended as a means, not an end in itself. The best law was unwritten law, and it was the spirit, not the letter, of the law that mattered. This was the original focus of the Torah, but in time it became rigidified. It was this legalism, this rigidity, that Christ so objected to. This perspective also helps to explain why so often the spirit rather than the letter of the law seemed to be carried out in the First Testament. As Christ points out in his comments about the Sabbath, law was made for people, not people for the law. The intent was that 'wise indications' be internalised, that the thrust of the law be followed.[16]

The New Testament and Justice

In the New Testament Jesus clearly states that justice should be based on principles of forgiveness and reconciliation; that retaliation plays no part. He forgave the Genasene maniac, the prostitute, the adulteress, the tax gatherer who was an extortionist, the robber. He charged us both to place distinctions between wrongdoers and the virtuous, but to see ourselves as all in the same camp – brothers and sisters with varying strengths and weaknesses. He rejected any notion of just deserts in the vineyard workers parable (Matthew 20/1-16), and in the story of the prodigal son and loving parent (Luke 15/11-32).

In the story of the rich man and Lazarus (Luke 16/19-31), Jesus explicitly teaches that the poor man has rights and the rich man is obliged out of a sense of justice, not charity, to share what he has from his table. Here Luke draws on Leviticus 25/35, which spells out the obligations of the rich to the poor. The rich man fails to recognise that though he may well have come by his wealth by perfectly legal means, in justice he still owes part of his wealth to Lazarus, who has nothing. He fails and is condemned.

Here Jesus explicitly expounds the nature of justice in terms of sharing with the needy, the poor, the vulnerable. Lazarus and the rich man can only ever meet and be reconciled as brothers through the sharing of the riches. Reconciliation, then, is at the heart of the New Testament understanding of justice. Or, as biblical scholar Ronald Craygrill says, reconciliation among humans is the identifying mark of God's new creation.[17]

Swiss theologian Siegfried Meurer has an interesting reflection on that other very important parable on justice, the vineyard owner and the day labourers, in Matthew 20. In this parable not only are those who wish to question God's right to give to all equally sent away, but so are those who understand justice and goodness to stand in contradiction. Justice must serve life and its sustenance.[18]

Meurer further states that the one who punishes must grant the one punished the possibility of making amends. He concludes that punishment seen as retaliation, whether by the individual or by society, is rejected, for it (retaliation) alone is the reserve of God. Likewise, the state is not allowed to exercise retaliation. He also speaks of the contrast between the Jewish and subsequent Christian understandings of justice, and that of the Roman Empire. The former is restorative emphasising reconciliation with the neighbour, the latter retributive, emphasising the maintenance of order at all cost through the maintenance of law.

Imprisonment in the New Testament
Imprisonment is condemned by New Testament teachings where it represents a power of death that is separate from and opposed to God. Death is also present in other forms, including illness, hunger, injustice and opulence. The proclamation of liberty to captives does not relate simply to a notion of spiritual freedom. Such an interpretation helps make sense of the miraculous nature of the deliverance of the apostles from prison in two instances, Acts 5 and 12. As Griffith says, the releases are an assertion of divine authority over the state and over the fallen principalities and powers. Deliverance is also life-affirming in that it is a renunciation of that death with which imprisonment is biblically identified.[19]

In a reference to the Matthew 25 injunction that Christians should visit the imprisoned, Griffith says that the word used, *episkeptomai*, does not merely mean to visit in our modern sense but to spend time with people and establish relationships and personal contact. The same verb is used to refer to the divine activity of caring for, redeeming and freeing. As such it is a prelude to the reintegration of the prisoner into the community as a full member, restoring that person with a place and full rights.[20]

Sanctuary
A final word on justice at the time of Jesus concerns the notion of sanctuary. It is a

further illustration that Jewish law valued life over property, and valued people over punishment. Several mentions are made in the ancient scriptures to cities of refuge (Deuteronomy 4/41-3, 19/1-3, Numbers 35/6-34). Daniel Vanness, in his book *Crime and Its Victims*, says that both Israel and its neighbours recognised the right of a person needing protection from revenge to go to the altar in the temple, where the person was to be kept from harm until the matter could be decided through formal judicial process (Exodus 21/12-14). But the altar might be far away, and the wrongly accused person might be caught before reaching the protection of the sanctuary. So the law provided for six cities of refuge, which were to be centrally located and reached by well-built roads, so that someone suspected of murder could get to protection easily.

People were more important than punishment and, as a result, procedural safeguards were built into the law so that the rights of the offender could be protected while the case was being considered by the judicial authorities.[21]

Sanctuary is a tradition that is not only scriptural but has a civic tradition with a rich and moving history. The concept of sanctuary was so compelling that it was recognised in Roman law, medieval common law and English common law. In the 1600s every church in England could be a sanctuary. During the 17th century the whole of the North American continent was seen as a sanctuary from the political and religious persecutions in Europe.

Two of the most heroic periods of the tradition occurred during the 1850s in the United States and during World War II in Europe. After the passage of the Fugitive Slave Act (1850), which made it illegal to harbour or assist a slave in gaining freedom, some northern churches became stations on the underground railroad in defiance of federal law. More recently many convents, churches and monasteries hid Jews fleeing the Nazis during World War II in defiance of law prohibiting such practices.[22]

Sanctuary has also been used extensively by political and religious refugees who break immigration laws to enter a country. Most recently, sanctuary has been provided by hundreds of church groups of all denominations in the United States in their efforts to help Central American refugees escape torture and death at home. The refugees, mainly from El Salvador and Guatemala, have fled the 'death squads' and the military and police apparatus (mainly trained in the US) that have sought to suppress any social change destined to free the people from poverty, malnutrition, illiteracy and hopelessness.[23]

At the US borders they have been met by tough immigration policies and either detained in refugee camps or sent immediately back to their native countries. For thousands, this has proved to be a death sentence. From the early 1980s many parish churches in the US opened their doors to these fleeing refugees by providing personnel and transport to bypass the border posts and enter the US illegally. More than 70,000 US citizens have actively participated in breaking US immigration law in order to provide sanctuary.[24]

Such law-breaking forms part of the morality of those who seek to provide true justice from a biblical perspective. Like Jesus dealing with accusations of breaking the Sabbath, they simply argue that law is there to serve the wellbeing of the community, and not the rich and powerful elite who benefit from and wish to maintain the status quo in Central America.

Like the Ploughshares activists in the nuclear arms context, they argue that justice and freedom as understood in the sacred scriptures cannot be hindered or contravened by legislation. In a hierarchy of law, those that preserve life are the most important, and immigration laws and laws of property are those that become secondary. They illustrate this by arguing that people are morally allowed to smash their way into burning houses to rescue children even though they damage property on entering, which is against the law.

They pose the question, who would not have attempted to smash open the doors of railway wagons carrying Jews to concentration camps and death because the law says that property damage is illegal? For such people, the law only has true validity when it leads to true justice.

Sanctuaries have been used down through the ages primarily by both those who have committed crimes, including serious crimes, and by refugees escaping oppression. The sanctuary remains inviolable while they negotiate an agreement. Because they offer safety, hope and healing from terror, punishment and fear, sanctuaries are symbols of restorative justice.

Conclusion

Unlike our modern Western system, which looks to the past, biblical justice always looked to the future. It always held up before the people a view of what might be if they remained true to the covenant and sought *shalom*. As Zehr says, biblical justice was an active progressive force seeking to transform the present order into one that was more just. In so doing, it sought in particular to protect the weak, the vulnerable and the poor.

It contained an overall thrust and many constitutive elements that would be of immense benefit to any modern society. Any society could learn from a re-examination of its history, philosophy and practice.[25]

Footnotes

1. Exodus 21/23-25; Leviticus 24/19-20; Deuteronomy 19/21
2. Herman Bianchi, *New Perspectives on Crime and Justice*, MCC Office of Criminal Justice, Elkhart, Indiana, 1984, p3
3. Lee Griffith, *Alternatives to Calling the Police: Some Biblical and Historical Perspectives*, paper presented at the Christian as Victim Conference, 1982, Kansas City, Missouri, p3

4. Matthew 5/38-42
5. Griffith, op cit, pp3-4
6. Bianchi, op cit, p6
7. Kevin O'Reilly, *Towards a Christian View*, Prison Chaplains' Association, New Zealand, 1982, p3
8. Bianchi, op cit, p3
9. Ibid, p4
10. Wayne Northey, *Justice in Peacemaking: A Biblical Theology of Peacemaking in Response to Criminal Conflict*, MCC US Office of Criminal Justice, Ontario, May 1992, p16
11. Virginia Mackay, *Punishment in the Scripture and the Tradition of Judaism, Christianity and Islam*, National Inter-Religious Taskforce on Criminal Justice, New York, 1982, p2.
12. Perry Yoder, *Shalom: the Bible's Word for Salvation, Justice and Peace*, Faith and Life Press, Newton, Kansas, 1987, p130
13. Howard Zehr, *Changing Lenses*, Herald Press, Scottdale, Pennsylvania, 1990, p133
14. Yoder, op cit, p130
15. Zehr, op cit, pp139-40
16. Ibid, p144
17. Ronald S. Craybrill, *Repairing the Breach: Ministering in Community Conflict*, Herald Press, Scottdale, Pennsylvania, 1981, p12
18. Siegfried Meurer, *Das Recht im Dienst der Versonnung und des Riedens*, Theologischer Verlag, Zurich, 1972
19. Griffith, op cit, p5
20. Ibid, p5
21. Daniel Vanness, *Crime and Its Victims*, Inter-Varsity Press, Leicester, 1986, pp116-17
22. Renny Golden and Michael McConnell, *Sanctuary – the New Underground Railway*, Orbis Books, Maryknoll, NY, 1986, p15
23. Ibid, p2
24. Ibid, p3
25. Zehr, op cit, p146

CHAPTER TWELVE

Sentencing Circles: New Hope For Canada

Okimaw Ohci Healing Lodge - the name means Hills of Thunder - is a collection of brightly painted wood-framed buildings set on a hillside near Maple Creek, a farm town in south-western Saskatchewan. Warden Norma Green has a background in social work, not corrections, and is addressed as 'Kikawaw', Cree for 'Our Mother'. Prison staff, most of them Indian, dine with residents in the mess and sometimes privately in the inmates' townhouse-style living units.

The point, said Green, is not only to connect prisoners with their heritage but to impress on them their responsibility for their crimes and their place in the Indian community.

Okimaw Ohci Healing Lodge is North America's first prison exclusively built for Indian inmates and a centrepiece of Canada's venture into separate justice programmes for Native people.

Those most familiar with the effort, including non-Indian judges and prosecutors, are increasingly optimistic that for many Native offenders these alternative procedures are more effective and less expensive than established courts and prisons. They point to studies that show as much as an 80 percent reduction in repeat offences among Indian defendants dealt with by Native justice programmes rather than the courts.[1]

The question of whether or not aboriginals in Canada can obtain a measure of justice from the dominant criminal justice system is a debatable and pressing issue. Much of the evidence suggests not.

The Canadian criminal justice system has failed the aboriginal peoples of Canada: First Nation, Inuit and Metis people, on-reserve and off-reserve, urban and rural in all territorial and governmental jurisdictions. The principal reason for this crushing failure is the fundamentally different world views of aboriginal and non-aboriginal people with respect to such elemental issues as the substantive content of justice and the process of achieving justice.[2]

This ringing indictment of the Canadian criminal justice system came not from a group of rioting prisoners on a Montreal prison rooftop, nor from a radical First Nation spokesperson. It came in the conclusion of a report of the Royal Commission on Aboriginal Peoples, set up by the Canadian government, and presented to the Governor-General in Council in February 1996.

Recent figures show that there are 783,980 aboriginals in Canada, 212,650 Metis and 49,255 Inuit people, constituting 6 percent of Canada's population. But they are clearly discriminated against at every level of life, consequently topping practically every social distress indicator. The Royal Commission report spelled this out in graphic detail:

- Aboriginal people are over-represented in the criminal justice system, most dramatically and significantly in provincial and territorial prisons and federal penitentiaries.
- Over-representation of aboriginal people in the criminal justice system is a product of both high levels of crime among aboriginal people and systemic discrimination.
- High levels of aboriginal crime, like other symptoms of social disorder, such as suicide and substance abuse, are linked to the historical and contemporary experiences of colonialism, which has systematically undermined the social, cultural and economic framework of indigenous peoples, including their distinctive forms of justice.
- Responding to and redressing the historical and contemporary roots of aboriginal crime and social disorder require the healing of relationships both internally among aboriginal people and externally among aboriginal and non-aboriginal people.
- At the heart of a new relationship between aboriginal and non-aboriginal people must be recognition of aboriginal people's inherent right of self-government. This right encompasses the authority to establish aboriginal justice systems that respect and reflect aboriginal concepts and processes of justice.[3]

As in similar countries when the colonising power had imposed a foreign criminal justice structure on the indigenous people, the First Nation peoples of Canada show all the symptoms of oppression. Huge disparities between the dominant culture and various First Nation peoples exist in health, housing, employment, education, addiction levels and crime and imprisonment rates. Aboriginal people are the recipients of the worst features of each.

This was not the first indictment of the Canadian criminal justice system. Five years previously, the Aboriginal Justice Inquiry of Manitoba had reached the same conclusion.

In almost every aspect of our legal system, the treatment of our aboriginal people is tragic. We marvel at the degree to which aboriginal people have endured, and continue to endure, what the justice system is doing to them. However, they have paid the price of high rates of alcoholism, crime and family abuse.[4]

That commission, which travelled 18,000 kilometres visiting 36 aboriginal communities, seven cities and five prisons through 123 days of hearings, found aboriginal people generally lived in appalling social conditions. It found their social structures nearly non-existent, their self-esteem smashed, their hope dwindling in the face of the constant onslaught of structural and personal discrimination.

Through their research in Manitoba they found a picture of incredible human suffering. Most aboriginals lived in poverty, unemployment ranged in varying communities from 60-90 percent, suicide was double the national average. It also discovered that half of the aboriginal people were involved in the criminal justice system one way or another, that 60 percent of young offenders in prison were aboriginal, as were 70 percent of women inmates.

The commissioners agreed that much of this had been caused by the destruction over succeeding generations of the distinctive aboriginal traditions and cultural practices. As one submission stated, 'If only the white people had left us out on the land the way we always were, this would never have happened.'

The Manitoba Commission left a haunting challenge to all Canadians of good will.

> Canada's treatment of its first citizens has been an international disgrace. To fail to take every step to redress this lingering injustice will continue to bring suffering and tragedy to aboriginal people, and to blacken our country's name throughout the world.[5]

Their frustrations were succinctly expressed by Chief Louis Stevenson addressing the Manitoba Inquiry:

> It is these substandard living conditions, unfair and unequal opportunities, unequal education, chronic unemployment, and inadequate housing that generate the frustration and anger which leads to offences and criminal activity.[6]

Eminent Cree lawyer Mary Ellen Turpel, herself no stranger to poverty and discrimination, told the National Round Table on Aboriginal Justice:

> I would suggest that when we carefully take apart aboriginal experiences and perspectives on the criminal justice system or for that matter any other 'issue' – a tangled and over-arching web gets spun. From economic and social disempowerment to problems in the criminal justice system, aboriginal people's issues are seemingly indivisible. One crosses over to another in an interconnected and almost continuous fashion. Alcoholism in aboriginal communities is connected to unemployment. Unemployment is connected to the denial of hunting, trapping and gathering economic practices. The loss of hunting and trapping is connected to the dispossession of land and the impact of major development projects. Dispossession of land is in turn connected to loss of cultural and spiritual identity and is a manifestation of bureaucratic control over all aspects of life. This oppressive web can be seen as one of disempowerment of communities and individual Aboriginal citizens.[7]

Already aboriginal Canadians are imprisoned at an incredibly high rate compared to other Canadians. The Canadian Bar Association in its submission to the Royal Commission on Aboriginal Peoples stated:

Government figures which reflect different definitions of 'Native' and which probably underestimate the number of prisoners who consider themselves Native show that almost 10 percent of the federal penitentiary is Native (including about 13 percent of the federal women's prisoner population) compared to about 2 percent of the population nationally. In the west and northern parts of Canada where there are relatively high concentrations of Native communities, the over-representation is more dramatic. In the Prairie region, Natives make up about 5 percent of the total population but 32 percent of the penitentiary population, and in the Pacific region Native prisoners constitute about 12 percent of the penitentiary population while less than 5 percent of the region's general population is of Native ancestry.

Bad as this situation is in the federal system, in a number of western provincial correctional systems it is even worse. In British Columbia and Alberta, Native people, representing 3-5 percent of the province's population, constitute 16 percent and 17 percent of the admissions to prison. In Manitoba and Saskatchewan, Native people, representing 6-7 percent of the population, constitute 47 percent and 60 percent of prison admissions.[8]

Traditional Aboriginal Justice

That indigenous peoples the world over had fully integrated, holistic, deeply spiritual social systems and detailed systems of justice is now taken for granted by educated people.

> From the sophisticated, socially stratified and economically diversified civilisations which thrived on the Pacific Coast, to the migratory-hunting and more egalitarian Algonian and the Iroquoian agriculturalist tribes of the Eastern Woodlands, to the Inuit who managed to subsist in the extremely harsh Arctic climate, aboriginal societies exhibited a rich kaleidoscope in cultural, linguistic and sociopolitical organisation.[9]

The Manitoba report also makes this clear:

> Aboriginal peoples have always had governments, laws and some means of resolving disputes within their communities. North American Aboriginal societies were dynamic cultures that adapted constantly to meet changing circumstances... They never surrendered their original right to govern themselves in accordance with their customs and cultures.[10]

Sociologist Marianne O. Nielsen writes of the nine general characteristics of Native traditional justice. The two most important are, firstly, 'justice was not a separate institution but an integral part of the socialisation process and the social, religious, economic and organisational functioning of the group'. In most instances, wrongdoers were 'counselled'by elders, their wrongdoing explained and encouragement and future direction for the future given. Secondly, 'traditional justice was based mainly on preserving the welfare and harmony of the group, meaning that the interests of the individual were often of secondary importance'.[11]

This principle of the common good being of paramount importance is a fundamental characteristic of many other indigenous cultures, including the Maori of Aotearoa, the ancient Hebrews of the Bible and the Celts.

Other ancillary features of traditional justice included:

- The principle that conformity to the norms of the group was more important than punishment. The group always sought 'a balance'between the individual and the collective. Maintaining the balance was important.
- Justice was flexible and often depended on the context as to whether an offence or an imbalance had been created.
- Sanctions where applied were immediate and designed to further the wellbeing of the groups.
- Justice was based on informal control mechanisms when dealing with more minor transgressions, but by more formal means involving elders when dealing with serious offences.
- Reparation and reconciliation were key elements in regaining the balance. A person who injured another might have to care for the victim's family for a period. The elders would in time bring a 'sentencing circle'together to get resolution to a more serious offence.
- Positive reinforcement and affirmation were very much a part of this 'restoring the balance' process. The focus wasn't always on the negative effects of the offence. Praise and gifts could be given to encourage healing, reparation and reconciliation, and the 'redressing of the balance'.[12]

Aboriginal lawyer Mary Ellen Turpel suggests that in proposing an aboriginal criminal justice system for Canada there should be a number of aspects different from the current criminal justice system:

- The notion of arriving at truth through adversarial combat or argument conflicts with aboriginal traditions of avoiding confrontation and maintaining emotional restraint. Aboriginal people are reluctant to criticise even an adversary publicly, and are often perceived as a result to be surly or uncooperative.
- There is no understanding of 'guilt' nor 'intent' in aboriginal tradition. Instead there is an emphasis on taking personal responsibility and notions of shame.
- There is a deep distrust of professionals – lawyers, judges, social workers – among most aboriginals. (The Cherokee are an exception to this.) In the dominant society these people are respected because of their training. In aboriginal society, respect is given to people with life experience, faithfulness to aboriginal culture and traditions, competence in language, and commitment to the community. For example, judges seek a win/lose result. Aboriginal elders want instead to seek a better balance of life for the offender and the community and traditionally focus more on that aspect rather than the offending incident.
- A jury of strangers is an alien concept. Traditionally, aboriginal people are

'judged' by their own people who know them, their families and their situations well.

- The notion of impartiality is not important to Aboriginal people. They are best 'restored' or 're-balanced' by those who know them best.
- Punishment resulting in imprisonment or fines paid to the state is totally alien. Restoring sound harmony, healing wounds, maintaining the balance of the whole community and the individuals involved are the primary aims of aboriginal justice. The victim and the victim's family sit in the middle of this justice equation.[13]

Shame obviously played an important part in these processes. Rupert Ross, Crown attorney, believes that we often forget, or fail to recognise, that an aboriginal person who offends his own tiny community and is taken to court (or before council, which may be more intimidating still), very frequently feels degrees of personal shame and of fear about losing his community's welcome, which in themselves stand as significant deterrents to repeated misbehaviour. They know that their acts will be remembered by all and be subject of comment by all for long into the future.

He suspects that we also forget the degree to which the misbehaviour of one person brings shame upon the whole family. The very fact that they must bear the shame adds to the regret and discomfort of the individual who caused it all. The offender knows that wherever family members go they will be gossiped about.[14]

Restorative Justice and Sentencing Circles

The First Nation peoples of Canada have a long experience of restorative justice practices. Like all indigenous cultures, they always sought as the primary aim of their justice system to repair the damage of the offence and start the healing processes for both victim and offender. In recent times there has been a revival of the processes of restorative justice taking the form of the traditional Sentencing Circles.

Sentencing Circles are now quite common in some communities in Canada. This initiative has come from aboriginal communities, springing up originally in the Yukon and Northwest Territories. Key personnel here have included judges Barry Stuart and Heino Lillies in the Yukon, where both Sentencing Circles and Elders' Panels are held. The latter consists of the judge sitting with elders on a panel when deciding cases. Similar initiatives are under way in Ontario, British Columbia, Quebec, Manitoba and Saskatchewan.

> The frightened aboriginal boy stood in the middle of the circle looking at the 15 elders holding hands around him. In turn, each elder spoke with the teenager about why he continued to drink and breach the probation imposed on him for breaking into and trashing a teacher's home. 'They told him how much they

loved him and that they weren't being mean when they were talking to him and how he was giving the clan a bad name by getting into trouble,' recalls Georgina Sidney of Teslin, a community 180 kilometres south-east of Whitehorse, Yukon. In Teslin, Natives are re-introducing traditional tribal justice.

'When we were finished he went around hugging everyone. He was just crying. It just had an effect on him.' Sidney, a member of Teslin's tribal justice committee, is convinced Native people can do a better job of dealing with family violence, civil law and minor crimes than the current justice system. 'The way we approach it is to help them out rather than kick them while they're down,' she says.

The boy, who faced possible imprisonment for breaching the provisions of his probation, is instead working on a trapline in the bush with his uncle – a discipline mutually agreed on by the courts.[15]

This example of the use of the Sentencing Circle is one of many such instances being developed by First Nation peoples and other Canadians as they grapple with the one-law-for-all legacy of colonisation.

In the Big Trout Lake District in the 1920s and 1930s these Circles were commonplace. Social order was maintained through their use. In the summer community, the leaders met in these Circles to review what had happened in the winter groups and to maintain order in the summer settlement. Circles were made up of representatives of the smaller winter groups along with the leaders of the summer community and the spiritual leaders.

They would call a Circle to discuss the cases. The chief would bring the person who had been reported into the Circle and would say to him, 'What do you say? Is it true you did this thing?' The person being asked would usually reply, 'Yes, it is true.' And at that time the chief would usually start talking to him. After the chief had finished talking to him, the others would follow. The spiritual leader would be the last person to talk to the person. The process worked when it was applied.[16]

While sadly it has fallen into disuse in the Big Trout Lake District, it is a process being used more and more elsewhere. The Community Holistic Healing Circle (CHCH) deals with cases of sexual abuse in the northern Manitoba First Nation of Hollow Water, and in the surrounding Metis communities of Manigotagan, Aghaming and Seymourville. It has worked exceedingly well for 10 years in these areas and in particular in Hollow Water, a small 600-person community to the east of Lake Winnipeg. One particular case involving widespread sexual abuse illustrates the depth, the beauty and possibilities of the process, and the positive results experienced by the participants and the wider community.

Berma Bushie, co-ordinator of CHCH, reports.

About 10 years ago, after five years of research, 24 people representing most families in the community decided to change the way they were. There had been two or three generations of sexual abuse. 'We couldn't pass on this horror to the next generation.' This was just a surface problem. Along with alcoholism, suicides and violence, the abuse was linked with massive unemployment and loss of the traditional way of life. 'It has not been pleasant to deal with as your community turns on you.' Denial is still there. However, the programme has reduced the incidence of abuse from approximately 80 percent to about 30 percent, partly through its educative effort in the community. Only two of the 48 worked with have reoffended in the 10 years they have been operating.

Existing systems, including the criminal justice system which required them to give evidence in court, had not been protecting the children. By contrast, 'children felt safe to talk when they knew that the abuser wouldn't be sent away'. They always believe the children. Why should they lie when they are in such a dependent position?

There are two teams, one working with the victim, one with the offender. They deal only with victims aged 0-18 years, and only with first offenders. When the offenders are confronted, the workers talk about the help that can be given (from elders, psychologists etc) and the success of prior cases, using other victimisers as a resource. (They prefer the word victimisers instead of offenders on the grounds that all those accused are themselves victims.) They are told that if they want to take part they must acknowledge their responsibility and agree to a psychological assessment. Most have denial mechanisms but 90 percent admit their offending when they know they will be helped. The alternative to the programme is to be handed over to the police.

Nearly all admit the abuse at the first intervention and without using the five days offered to think it over. Once admitted, they make a statement to the police and (to protect the child) have to plead guilty in court. A four-month adjournment is obtained and monthly reports are made to the court. The victimiser is placed on bail with special conditions that he has no alcohol and does not associate with the victim.

During the adjournment period, four types of Circles are held. This is because all affected groups must be worked with and also the process must be handled in stages. You would never put a victim and offender together at the first stage because of the power imbalance. The first Circle is with the workers and the victimiser, getting him/her to acknowledge in detail what has been done and its implications. This Circle may need to be repeated more than once. The second Circle is with the victimiser and his/her family, so the family can see that the victim is not to blame. The third Circle involves the victim and victimiser being brought together to begin repairing the damage, especially the guilt and shame always felt by the victim. And the final Circle involves the victim meeting with the community so the restoration process to a place of respect can begin.

Then the official Circle is convened. A pre-sentence report is prepared for the court. The court comes to the community and is set up in a circular fashion with chairs all round. Those attending include victim and victimiser and their families and support groups, as well as Crown and defence lawyers. Former clients may also attend and political leadership is also invited.

An eagle feather, signifying honesty and 'speaking from the heart,' travels round the circle four times, each person holding it while speaking. The first time, each states why they are there. On the second, each speaks directly to the victim, to absolve them of guilt and blame, and applaud them for their courage in making disclosure. The third time, each speaks to the offender, so they can understand that these crimes affect families and communities. The fourth time, we give recommendations to the judge. We don't believe in jails and never recommend them. They are horrible places, no healing. Our people only come out with anger, rage and fear. So far our recommendations have always been accepted by Judge Murray Sinclair, who hears our cases. We do a lot of lobbying with the prosecutor and others for the acceptance of our recommendations. We ask the court to accept the fact that we have a system that works. Each case is taken back to the community for review every six months.[17]

The Hollow Water experience has seven spiritual values underpinning its philosophy, according to Bushie's co-worker, Marcel. They are respect, kindness, sharing, honesty, caring, strength and humility. They see a sacred relationship with nature, people being totally dependant on creation and on the practice of these principles for their survival. As outlined earlier, it is necessary to bring balance back into the community and into individuals. These teachings of the elders are seen as being true for all people.

Reflecting on the Hollow Water experience, Rupert Ross, Crown attorney, nominates three distinct features that differentiate aboriginal and non-aboriginal justice systems.

The first is that the decision-making influence is dispersed among many people as part of the search for consensus. The second is that aboriginal women are primary participants at every stage of the process. The third feature is that the people involved, whether the offender, the victim or the families affected, can be neither understood nor assisted as long as they are seen as isolated individuals. Instead people must be seen as participants in a large net of relationships. This is intimately connected to aboriginal world views, in which the philosophy of inter-relationship forms people's understanding of who they are and their responsibilities to each other, their ancestors and the generations yet to come. An important part of the strength of this philosophy is that behaviour that is characterised as criminal - and in particular the behaviour that is most disruptive and destructive in aboriginal communities (and aboriginal people see family and sexual assault as part of this) is itself intertwined in a larger net of the destructive historical experiences of aboriginal people.[18]

The Saskatchewan people also practise restorative justice. In a Television New Zealand *Assignment* programme screened in May 1996, a man of mixed race, Rodney Obej'on, who had a previous criminal record of 28 convictions, was charged with attempting to run down a police officer, using his vehicle as a weapon.

A Sentencing Circle was held, attended by Judge Bria Hucular, the offender, the victim, the prosecutor and elders of his people. Circle members addressed

Rodney. The prosecutor sought 12 months' imprisonment. A man from Alcoholic Anonymous spoke of the alcohol addiction that Rodney had and what he could do about it. Elders warned him of the dangers he'd face if he kept up his current behaviour patterns.

Rodney addressed the Circle. He apologised for his actions and said that the last time he'd been in prison he'd wanted to commit suicide. Judge Hucular decided there would be no point in further imprisonment, and accepted a package from the group that included alcohol treatment.

Robert Whiteman was another offender interviewed on the same programme. He had robbed a woman, Faye Tamosiunis, at a service station. Robert had followed the same course as Rodney. He apologised for his actions, offered to repay the money stolen, to undergo counselling for his gambling addiction and, instead of imprisonment, accepted several months of home confinement with an electronic monitoring bracelet as his companion. He and Faye are now good friends. 'I know deep down Faye has forgiven me. That's a big burden off my shoulders.'[19]

Up until February 1996, more than 100 Circles had been held in Saskatchewan, and only two cases had been appealed. Justice Bayda of the Saskatchewan Court of Appeal, in response to a plea from the Crown for guidelines for Sentencing Circles, set out two mandatory criteria.

1) The willingness of the offender; and
2) The existence of a community willing to participate.

He stated that having reviewed all the relevant criteria, the judge must answer the question, 'Is a fit sentence for this accused who has committed this offence better arrived at by using a restorative justice approach or the ordinary justice approach?[20]

But restorative justice is not a process restricted to aboriginal communities or First Nation peoples. Already models are being introduced into the traditional court system. One such case grabbed international attention through an award-winning radio documentary about it. *Kevin's Sentence* reflects a tragedy repeated the world over, wherever young people, cars and alcohol mix in a deadly cocktail.

It was a tragedy waiting to happen. In the small hours of the morning three teenage youths headed home in their car from a night out socialising and drinking at a pub. The driver, 19-year-old Kevin Hollinski, started skylarking with a carload of girls, playing chase at high speed. Suddenly, he lost control, his car spun a full 360 degrees, smashed against two poles snapping them off, and ploughed into a tree where it came to rest. His two companions, lifelong friends Joey and Andrew, lay in the wreckage, critically injured. Returning to consciousness, Kevin briefly had his hand shaken by his dying friend Joey, before he crawled to safety. Minutes later Andrew and Joey were dead, their necks broken by the impact.

Hours later, Kevin was charged with dangerous driving, causing the death of two passengers. Bailed to appear in court later, he was facing a probable jail term of 18-24 months. There appeared to be few mitigating circumstances.

However, his lawyer, Ed Greenspan, and the families of the dead youths thought otherwise. Asking the obvious question as to what good could be served by a prison term, they invited the judge in the Ontario Court of Justice to consider applying restorative principles rather than merely retributive ones. Joey's mother, Cindy, spoke of the high esteem in which they held Kevin, of his great love for her son, and what a loving, caring and kind young man he was. Andrew's father, Dale, told the court how when Andrew had had an eye transplant, it was Kevin who had driven him everywhere whenever he was needed. Prosecuting Sergeant Lloyd Graham wasn't impressed and thought a jail term as a deterrence was necessary. Kevin's lawyer described deterrence as 'a false god of our judicial system', and suggested the court not apply harsh rules indiscriminately.

The judge agreed. Moved almost to tears by the obvious remorse of Kevin and by the forgiving and compassionate testimony of the two parents, the judge sentenced Kevin to 750 hours of community service, 200 of which were to be used in going around talking to high-school students of the dangers of drinking and driving. Some time later the Crown appealed, but three judges of the Ontario Appeal Court took only 45 minutes to reject it.

Sergeant Graham, Cindy and Dale joined Kevin in his talks with the students. Within 12 months he had addressed 14 high schools and 8300 students on the dangers of drinking and driving. The smashed car became exhibit A in their joint effort, with all four addressing the forums. The thousands listened in awe to the testimonies. More than 1000 high schools have now seen the video of their presentation. It was the reluctant believer Sergeant Graham who had the last word. 'Here's a case where we actually won one. I think he deterred a greater percentage of those 8300 than anything else could.'[21]

In a submission to the Royal Commission, the Aboriginal Affairs Directorate, Department of Justice, Ottawa, commented:

> As we see it, the Sentencing Circle plays two primary purposes. 1) It promotes the community healing process by providing a forum for the community to address the parties of the victimisation at the time of sentencing. 2) It allows the court to hear directly from the people most affected by the pain of victimisation. In the past the Crown and the defence have attempted to portray this information. We believe it is now time for the court to hear from the victim, the family of the victim, the victimiser, the family of the victimiser, and the community-at-large.[22]

The Royal Commission, while obviously enthusiastic about the potential of Sentencing Circles, advises caution in relation to the presumption that all elders might be eligible to part of the Sentencing Circles when indeed many themselves may well be victims earlier in life of sexual violence and remain unhealed. Such people need to go through the healing process themselves first. They also make a strong point that sexism flowing from patriarchy forms a strong feature in many aboriginal communities, and women need to be given a much greater say in restorative processes.[23] They also believe that:

> Sentencing Circles and Elders' Panels have a useful but limited role. They provide a good example of how the current system can be made significantly more responsible to aboriginal concerns without a radical restructuring of the process. It must be noted that determinations of guilt and innocence are still made by the court in these cases, and the bases for making these determinations remain the standard ones of the non-aboriginal justice system. As well, the actual sentencing decision is the judge's. The judge is under no obligations to follow the suggestions of the Elders' Panel or the Sentencing Circle. Sentencing guidelines set down by courts of appeal and maximum sentences enshrined in the criminal code take precedence over any suggestions from the community.[24]

Self Determination

The issue of an aboriginal justice system is part of the wider issue of aboriginal self-determination. The Aboriginal Justice Inquiry of Manitoba concluded that Native communities should run their own criminal and legal systems. It suggested that tribal justice be constitutionally protected and guaranteed.

The Royal Commission on Aboriginal Peoples is also clear that the establishment of aboriginal justice systems is tied to the development of aboriginal self-determination and self-governance.

> We have already stated that at the core of a new relationship between aboriginal and non-aboriginal people must be recognition of aboriginal people's right of self-government. It is our conclusion that this right must encompass the authority to establish aboriginal justice systems.[25]

They concluded that 'the pursuit of justice is an integral part of the pursuit of self-government'.[26] The Law Reform Commission of Canada holds the same view and has endorsed the right of aboriginal peoples to establish their own justice system.[27] So does Article 33 of the United Nations Draft Declaration on the Rights of Indigenous Peoples:

> Indigenous peoples have the right to promote, develop and maintain their institutional structures and their distinctive judicial customs, traditions, procedures and practices, in accordance with internationally recognised human rights standards.[28]

Conclusion

A momentum is gathering among indigenous peoples worldwide demanding self-determination. Restorative justice is an inherent part of that process. It is cutting boundaries and challenging dominant cultures to think again about criminal justice. Sentencing Circles are an important part of the Canadian demands for better justice. Their philosophy, values, principles and praxis are a gift and a challenge to the dominant culture, sagging under the weight of an expensive, discriminatory, largely negative retributive system. If restorative justice practices in Canada bring a better form of justice to all, then Canada could be poised to make a paradigm leap in its criminal justice processes.

Footnotes

1. *Globe and Mail*, Ottawa, May 1996
2. *Royal Commission on Aboriginal Peoples, Bridging the Cultural Divide, A Report on Aboriginal Peoples and Criminal Justice in Canada*, Ministry of Supply and Services, Canada, February 1996
3. Ibid
4. A. C. Hamilton and C. M. Sinclair, Report of the Aboriginal Justice Inquiry of Manitoba, *The Justice System and Aboriginal Peoples*, Queen's Printer, Winnipeg, Manitoba, August 1991.
5. Ibid, p674
6. R. A. Silverman and Marianne O. Neilsen, Aboriginal Peoples and Canadian Criminal Justice, Butterworths, Toronto and Vancouver, 1992, p55
7. Mary Ellen Terpel, 'On the Question of Adapting the Canadian Criminal Justice System for Aboriginal Peoples — Don't Fence Me In', 1993 paper prepared for the National Round Table on Aboriginal Justice Issues for the Royal Commission on Aboriginal Peoples, p166
8. Royal Commission, op cit, pp29-30
9. Daiva Stasiulis and Nira Yuval-Davis, editors, *Sage Series on Race and Ethnic Relations*, Vol. II, 1995, Sage Publications, London
10. Manitoba Inquiry, op cit, p22
11. Silverman and Neilsen, op cit, p244
12. Ibid, pp244-47
13 Terpel, op cit, pp174-78
14. Ibid, p152
15. Silverman and Neilsen, op cit, p207
16. Royal Commission, op cit, pp23-24
17. F. W. M. McElrea, 'Rape — Ten Years' Progress?', address to Inter-Disciplinary Conference, Wellington, New Zealand, 29 March 1996, quoting an interview with Berma Bushie, Community Holistic Circle Healing, Hollow Water First Nation, Manitoba.
18. Royal Commission, op cit, p69
19. TVNZ, *Assignment*, 30 May 1996
20. Royal Commission, op cit, p112
21. CBC Radio, *Kevin's Sentence*, replayed RNZ National Radio, 7 July 1996
22. Royal Commission, op cit, p166
23. Ibid, p113
24. Ibid, p113
25. Ibid, p54
26. Ibid, p65
27. Ibid, p57
28. Ibid, p76

CHAPTER THIRTEEN

African Justice:
Compensating, Healing, Reconciling

> In traditional African society, legal proceedings are community affairs aimed at reconciling the parties and restoring harmonious relations within the community.
>
> *M. S. W. Bapela[1]*

It is not without misgivings that I, a New Zealander, living not in Africa but in the South Pacific, should try to write about traditional African judicial processes. That I have been a reasonably frequent visitor to Africa since 1975 does not fully redeem the situation. However, that I have been encouraged by African friends to write, have sought the best advice, and done conscientious research, does, I believe, qualify me to broach the subject with caution and, I hope, accuracy.

Like all indigenous peoples, the hundreds of tribal groupings and peoples of Africa have an oral tradition of history, beliefs and stories passed from generation to generation. Their social customs too were passed on. These were woven from countless generations of experience, formed by trial and error, guided by their values and beliefs. Fine books and learned papers were not written. Customs were simply practised, and everyone understood them.

In their intellectual system, as expressed in language and material symbol, ritual and law, there is a great similarity between Nguni, Sotho, Venda and Tsonga. Details varied in grammar and vocabulary, in the rules of marriage and rituals celebrated, but the framework was constant. People thought in categories of kinship; they assumed the dependence of the living upon their dead ancestors, who might be propitiated by prayer and sacrifice, and who were angered by quarrelling among their descendants; they assumed the existence of chiefs and some relationships between the health of the chief and the fertility and wellbeing of his people; they assumed the rule of law and thought the primary function of a chief was to settle disputes and achieve reconciliation between conflicting parties; they assumed a moral order intrinsic in the universe.[2]

As the evil vestiges of apartheid are swept away and openness and free exchange of information again enter South African society, the positive nature of much of traditional African life is becoming more apparent to the wider community. The positive features of extended family life and tribal identity, of the cultural dimensions of dance and social interaction, of having a close identity with the land, of following a philosophy of restorative justice, will become more widely appreciated.

In particular, the positive qualities of the traditional African justice philosophy and processes will be an important new discovery for the wider society as it seeks new ways of limiting crime and social disorder by allowing for apology, compensation, healing and eventual reconciliation.

What may not be known is that such processes have always been carried on to a degree even through the worst years of apartheid and, while undoubtedly affected by retributive central justice policies, have continued to be an effective means of maintaining social order in villages and townships across the nation.

Long before the advent of white man's law in Africa, a sophisticated set of judicial processes saw to it that justice was enacted. While the style was similar from one area to another, the details of the process varied from place to place. Depending on the tradition or the tribe, justice could be effected in a variety of ways. Social stratification played a major part in how hearings were conducted, and how resolution was reached. For example, it was a much more serious matter for a person to assault a king than it was to assault a slave. Such law processes were only part of an intricately woven mat of interdependent parts which formed the spirit and practice of tribal life. All these dimensions of life came together to form an holistic framework that guaranteed the continual progress of the tribe and maintained its life-giving belief structures.

Different religions brought varying influences to bear. The Muslim influence brought a different inculturation to Christianity, and the old religions continued to have a heavy influence on procedures. The innate wisdom and knowledge of the interconnectedness of all living beings had a significant effect on crime and violation of laws.

Some societies had matriarchal lines of leadership, others patriarchal and warrior threads. Some societies had a class of slaves whose rights were minimal; others did not. Some tribes were settled and rarely moved far except for grazing or seeking water in times of drought. Others were nomadic, resting occasionally for lengthy periods in the same place before moving slowly on.

Sometimes all power was invested in the chief, sometimes in a council of elders, and sometimes with the overall community. Whatever the form, the restoration of harmony within families and tribes was always the aim, and punishment of the culprit of secondary importance.

As far as the administration of justice was concerned, in traditional African society every man was his own lawyer, and his neighbour's too, in the sense that

170

litigation involved whole communities, and all the local men could and did take part in forensic debate. Women did not ordinarily participate in court cases other than as witnesses, but among the men there was little division of functions. The concept of professional judges acting according to formalised rules as part of a specialised and aloof administration was quite foreign to African jurisprudence, as was the notion of men hiring themselves out on the basis of their talent to plead. When pre-judicial attempts to resolve disputes failed, the arguments could be pressed to judgment before the chief, whose word was law; but the chief invariably acted as spokesman for his councillors, who in turn sought to uphold and reinforce the established norms of the tribe. In this context the good chief was reckoned not by the terror he could inspire or the magnanimity he could display, but by his skill in articulating the sense of justice (just-ness) of a relatively homogeneous community, which involved his applying universally accepted rules and precedents to particular disputes in a manifestly appropriate way. His authority derived not from his control of armed force or from his place in a learned bureaucracy, but from his position as leader and representative of the community.[3]

The protection of the innocent and the restoration of balance were the main focus of law enforcement, rather than the punishment of the guilty. The traditonal unit of African society was the group, not the individual. When a crime was committed it was more important to have the victim's family compensated than to have the villain or culprit punished.

> The purpose of the court is not to discover and apply a rigid law. Its function is to try to provide a compromise which will as far as possible be acceptable to the parties and will be regarded by the community generally as the right decision. The aim is restore an equilibrium that has been disturbed or to provide compensation for a wrong that has been committed.[4]

Legal proceedings were community affairs in which a central aim was to reconcile the disputing parties and to restore harmonious relationships within the community. Precedents were not required although the application of law in previous situations might, in difficult cases, act as a guideline. There were few rules regarding the admissibility and relevance of evidence. Character testimony and previous convictions were commonly used in the decision-making process and there were no hard and fast rules regarding the burden of proof. The accused was typically not asked to plead and all persons were recognised as competent to give evidence. Legal process aimed at restoring the community equilibrium through restitution, reconciliation and compensation.[5]

A central feature of African legal systems was a concern to shame the offender, and then to reincorporate him or her once that initial expression of community repugnance had been demonstrated. Traditional African courts tended to avoid as far as possible the segregation of the offender or marginalisation of him or her into a sub-community of similar social rejects.[6]

It should be noted in passing that the supernatural always played a part in African understanding of justice. Violation of tribal law often entailed a violation of the 'balance of nature', which had to be reconnected.

For example, the Karimojong of Uganda had a supernatural level of awareness which made for the provision of guides and sanctions of a universally accepted moral order. Traditionally they had no police or army, and ultimately it was the elders who guarded and imposed the rules.

> Whether individually or collectively, Karimojong consider obedience and respect for elders to bring good fortune through their beneficence; and equally, disobedience and disrespect to bring individual punishment and suffering, or collective calamity. The attributed ability of elders to intercede with deity on the community's (or individual's) behalf, or to refuse to do so in time of need, or positively to curse, provides a graduated range of supernatural sanctions with which to back their decisions.
>
> Cursing by elders is the major punitive sanction, applied in varying degrees of doom, just as good behaviour is rewarded by appropriate blessings. Mild cursing may cause barrenness in wives or cattle, failure of crops, early death. More serious forms of curse, collectively expressed, may dramatically generalise such woes. Offending Karimojong are, it appears, deeply and immediately concerned to avert the wrath of retribution. They must plead or pray for remission.
>
> The moral basis is repeatedly emphasised by the meaning which Karimojong attach to this pleading before elders. Every form of pleading takes place within the structure of Karimojong belief, and 'connotes someone struggling with a force greater than himself that may only be removed at its behest rather than his own'. So an offender's remission depends upon forgiveness by the powers that underpin society. But this comes only when the forces of good are enabled by appropriate individual action and voluntary acceptance to overcome the forces of evil.[7]

Witchcraft and sorcery are other elements very real to indigenous traditional cultures. One can only touch on them and acknowledge their existence here.

Witchcraft stands for evil in the sense that it strikes at men and women who fail in their social duties and who, in so doing, open the gate to evil. In another light it operates as a belief restraining evil, or punishing anyone who harbours evil, with troubles that we should usually regard as mere misfortune. Either way, to see witchcraft as an extraneous and arbitrary element is to misread the nature of this civilisation. Having supposed good in the form of a given moral order, Africans have been obliged to suppose evil in whatever undermines it. God without the devil is what no people have yet been able to imagine.[8]

Traditionally, witchcraft was held to be responsible for most of the bad things that happened. This is a very widespread and traditional feature of the African view of life and death. Sometimes a judicial hearing was able to deal to offending in a restorative way. Other times, because of the effect of witchcraft on the lives of the families, such families would have to deal to their problems. Thus, as Davidson points out, 'When the law could not do the job for you, you could turn to the spirits.'[9]

Flexibility was a keynote of the Ibo system of justice. They had a very relaxed way of dealing with judicial procedures.

> A man might attempt to settle with the individual who had aggrieved him. If this failed he could appeal to a respected elder to intervene or call members of the two families together. He could also appeal to the ward or village elders. There were no set rules as to where he should begin his appeal for redress but he could appeal against the decision of the families to the ward elders and finally to the *ama-ala* of the village.[10]

For the Nguni, that general grouping of tribes linked by language that includes the Xhosa, a higher fine was levied for murder, assault, seduction or adultery if the injured party was of a chief's lineage. For the Xhosa, traditional law and order were very conciliatory. Survivors from the ship *Stavenisse*, wrecked in 1686, reported that:

> Revenge has little or no sway among them, as they are obliged to submit their disputes to the king, who, after hearing the parties, gives sentence on the spot, to which all parties submit without a murmur; but should the matter in dispute be of great importance, and when he cannot rely upon his own judgment, he refers the parties to an older king in his neighbourhood. When a father beats his son so as to draw blood, and complaint is made to the king, he must pay the king a cow as a fine.[11]

Already, then, every man was regarded as a 'shield of the chief' and any assault on him was treated as an assault on the chief himself. The fine went to the chief and not the kinsman or the injured, as it did among many other African people. Cases were tried at the chief's court and every adult man had the right to attend and speak. Disputes were tried publicly. A chief could traditionally himself be tried and fined by his own privy council.[12]

Records of the 18th and 19th centuries among the Xhosa and Mpondo, and also in the 18th century in Natal, depict a society in which disputes were settled in court, trade regulated, and the power of the chief himself bridled.[13]

The Sotho were distinguished from their neighbours in the 1800s by the fact that most of them lived in large settlements. Each large settlement was a capital in which an independent chief lived with many of his followers, and each was surrounded by cattle-posts where stock were kept.

The political unit was a chiefdom, the office of which was hereditary, passing from father to senior son. The chief presided over his own court, and there was no other higher court to which someone could appeal. All the chiefs saw themselves as holding equal rank. None of the Sotho chieftains was a military kingdom in which authority was maintained by force. Order was secured rather through negotiation and compromise.[14]

The Tswana, like the Nguni, were characterised by a great development of law and a respect for the courts. The *kgotla* (which means both a courtyard and a court of law) was the centre, physically and metaphorically, of every capital. The first travellers found both the chief in Dithakong and the regent in Kaditshwene sitting in the *kgotla* with counsellors, settling disputes. And not only did every capital have its *kgotla*; every lineage that occupied a section of the capital had its own central courtyard – its *kgotla* – and there disputes between members of a lineage were either settled by arbitration, or sent on to the chief's court.[15]

> All the courts were concerned with reconciling the disputants and their families, rather than enforcing a legal code, but a distinction existed between the Tswana chiefdoms and that of the Lobedu. Among the Tswana (as among the Nguni) certain offences – murder, assault, witchcraft and slander – were treated as attacks on the chief, who represented the state, and the fine in such cases went to the chief; but among the Lobedu even murder and assault were treated as offences against the kinsmen of the injured party, and only witchcraft was clearly an offence against the state. The chief was beneath the law and among Rolong and Kgatla could be tried by his own counsellors.[16]

Mediation was the key to problem-solving among the herding tribes, especially the Khoikhoi (Hottentots). Disputes were heard before all the men of the camp assembled under the leadership of the senior kinsmen of the clan (extended family). For serious offences between members of different clans the chief of the horde (group of clans), sitting with the heads of the clans, heard the case. Compensation was the aim but a person could be sentenced to death for something as serious as murder.

> The institution of chieftainship thus emerged with the herders in South Africa, if we take arbitration in dispute and the enforcement of a decision by a court of some sort as the mark of chieftainship. The custodian of a hunting band did not settle disputes; the senior kinsman of the senior lineage in a Nama horde did so, but his authority was limited. He could not interfere in disputes between members of the same clan, which were settled by the head of the clan without appeal to the chief of the horde, and he could not control a blood feud between two of his clans. The authority of a Khoikhoi chief was thus considerably less than that of any Nguni or Sotho chief.[17]

Nomadic tribes such as the !Kung had their own way of maintaining law and order and administering justice. The leadership rights over water and vegetable foods rested with the custodian, who passed the hereditary office on to his son (or failing a son, to a daughter). There was no chief with power to adjudicate in disputes and enforce judgments.

> The whole band, however, is concerned to reconcile quarrelling members, for the loss of a hunter means a serious loss in food and, if weapons are used, the smallest scratch may mean death, since the poison with which arrows are smeared is deadly.[18]

Modern South Africa

The restorative philosophy of African traditional justice has a lot to offer modern South Africa. As was seen from the earlier chapter on the effects of the current retributive philosophy which has focused almost exclusively on punishment, most of it through brutal and violent means, it is time South Africans woke up to the traditions of the majority and sought less primitive but maybe more effective non-violent ways of criminal justice process.

Karen Van Eden, a Bachelor of Social Science honours student at the University of Cape Town during 1995, carried out research among the people of the Eastern Cape.

She found that within the Thembu community of the Eastern Cape, when a child has offended against an adult member of a community, the parents would be expected to accompany the child to apologise to the offended person. If property has been damaged or stolen, negotiations take place between the parents of the child and the offended family in order to decide how to correct the problem. In situations where the two families are unable to reach agreement, the case is taken to a higher authority within the community.[19]

Chief Holomisa, chairperson of the Congress of Traditional Leaders of South Africa, explains the sophisticated and complex legal processes that are followed:

> If the offence has been committed against a member of the same family then the parents or the guardians of the offending child will reprimand the child, and if it has to do with another family then the heads of the two families come together and they find a way of rehabilitating or disciplining that child. But if it is an offence of such magnitude that it requires the attention of a higher authority then the sub-headman of the given locality has to deal with it. He has to preside over the case. The sub-headman is someone who is responsible for the families or homesteads living in a particular locality. He is usually [from] the most senior of the families that live in that particular area. But if it is an offence of a more serious nature that requires someone higher than a sub-headman then it is referred to the headman ... If a matter calls for another higher authority the case goes to what is known as the chief.[20]

Another example occurred in Engcobo in the Eastern Cape in June 1995 when a young man accused of making a schoolgirl pregnant appealed to a chief's court in the hope of avoiding a fine. Payment of a fine to the girl's father would compensate for the loss in *labola* due to her pregnancy. In this respect the problem was really a matter between the two families.

> The hearing was held in a room that resembled a schoolroom, and at one end sat three people, namely the chief, the headman and a scribe. Benches surrounded them in the form of a semi-circle on which sat the complainant, the accused and their respective families. Behind them were chairs for anyone else in the community who wished to attend. Everyone present was given an opportunity to be heard if they had something to contribute.

175

A lot of time was spent questioning the people who had seen the young couple together during the time when the girl got pregnant, as the young man denied that he was responsible.

The proceedings took about an hour, after which the chief, the headman, the scribe and two other people of importance in the community left the room to confer. After some time they returned to present judgment. The young boy was found guilty. As a result, the father of the boy was required to pay a fine of six cows: five to the family of the young girl and one to the court. In closing, the chief asked those present if there were any objections. There were none.[21]

This process, rather than dividing and alienating opposing parties, as tends to happen under modern Western law processes, allows the families to bond.

In the case concerning the young girl's pregnancy, the father of the accused was required to pay the fine of six cows, but this did not mean that the son did not have to take responsibility. The onus is on the son to eventually 'pay back' the cows by, for example, working for his father. This ensures that the son is bonded to the father over a long period of time. This concept could be viewed as 'asymmetrical reciprocity', whereby the father carries the punishment until the son is able to reciprocate at a later stage.[22]

Another illustration of the healing and reconciling approach of traditional African justice occurred in a village near Cofimvaba in the Eastern Cape.

There was once a quarrel in this area between the youth of two different regions. Now what actually happened was we engaged in a fight and some of us were injured. The elders discovered it and we were taken to the headman's place. We were warned not to fight again and some people whose possessions were taken had to be returned. And we were told not to be seen fighting anywhere in the village again.[23]

Through this approach these youth were educated by a caring community. They were encouraged to take responsibility for their actions by having to face the disapproval of the community. They were required to repair the damage by returning belongings they had taken, calling a truce and apologising to the community. In this way they were actively involved in the restorative justice process – a process that taught them the values of responsibility, respect, caring and knowledge. The youth involved in the fight went on to form a choir group as a diversion, which brought the two opposing groups together in common interest.

Van Eden also makes the point that restorative processes such as the above help to empower the participants and the community. She quotes American researchers who, like her, believe that much crime occurs because of alienation from meaningful participation in the processes of life:

The evolution of [Western] culture has placed young people in a powerless situation in which they have no meaningful role in society. Persons without a sense of autonomy come to see themselves as pawns in a world where others control their destiny. Children who lack a sense of power over their own behaviour

176

and their environment are developmental casualities whose disorders are variously labelled as learned helplessness, absence of an internal locus of control, and lack of intrinsic motivation. Such young persons are scarred by alienation and school failure, and often seek alternative sources of power through chemicals or membership in a youth counterculture. While some children are deprived of autonomy, others are pushed towards premature independence.[24]

People's Courts

As township life grew during the apartheid years, so the maintenance of law and order fell more and more into the hands of townspeople. The security and police apparatus of central government proved to be an inadequate and often inappropriate forum of social control. Alternative forms of administering justice, based on traditional African ideas but adapted to multi-tribal, urban townships, took a hold.

During the 1980s other courts were also established and widely used at times. 'People's Courts' were largely characterised by a recognised formal or informal structure, which held regular meetings in townships in order to address problems that were of both a civil and criminal nature, with the aim of re-establishing and maintaining inter-personal harmony among community members.[25]

These replaced the much earlier Bantu Commissioners' Courts, established in 1927, which dealt primarily with such minor matters as breaches of pass laws and liquor regulations. These courts tended to be offender-centred rather than community-centred. They also replaced the *Makgotla*, which had operated mainly in the Transvaal and were very unpopular. They differed too from what were known as 'kangaroo' courts, which operated irregularly and generally under the command of youth or gangs.

> First, they were local in terms of personnel, of problems, of authority, in procedures and in accountability. Second, they demonstrated a clear commitment to mediation, reparation and restoration of the communal equilibrium. Although coercion is clearly a key resource in communal problem solving, it is not an end in itself. Third, they celebrate diversity. Different 'histories of struggle' are viewed as justifying different ordering processes. Divergences in ethnic traditions, in the composition of township communities – sometimes riven by the factors of traditional culture, of property, of gender and especially of age – ensured no direct replication of ordering processes.
>
> Finally, and perhaps most crucially, there is no neat division between the policing of the streets and the decision-making in the People's Courts. Nor in a judicial context is a distinction made between civil and criminal matters. There is a high degree of vertical and lateral integration. Anglo-Saxon concepts of the divisions of functions have not the same clarity – or relevance – within township ordering.[26]

Since the legalisation of the African National Congress in 1990, People's Courts have evolved into widely used community courts. They place a great emphasis on community participation. The general functioning of community courts involves court 'hearings', which take place regularly during times suitable for community members to attend, for example in evenings or over weekends, and in the language most suitable to those participating. Those presiding are democratically elected community members who then form part of a street committee, and jurisdiction is restricted to domestic and interpersonal disputes as well as petty crime and rights violations.[27]

Sipho Citabatwa, secretary of Guguletu's NY141 Street Committee, explains that the aim of the hearing is to determine:

> ...how we can solve the very problem that [the offender] has made so that he or she must understand that we are not dealing with the issue because he or she is a criminal. We are dealing with the issue because he or she is a part of the community. He or she is needed in the community. He or she can be an asset to that community. But now we are trying to turn him or her back to what is right so that he or she can be a good father or mother. We are building these youth so that as the times go on when they are old enough we can rely on them and have a good leadership.
>
> One needs to understand the social environment of that person and deal with him or her accordingly. You cannot heal a wound not knowing what causes that wound. So if you can know what causes that wound and you start with the actual causing factor then you can try and destroy it.[28]

If consensus cannot be reached at a street committee level, the problem is taken to the area committee of SANCO (the South African National Civic Organisation) to be resolved. This is a senior supervisory body.

Sipho Citabatwa further explains that where the offender has committed a crime and guilt has been established, the community members participating, the victims and the offender are consulted with regard to appropriate action. This is the same restorative approach that characterises family group conferencing in New Zealand:

> [The street committee] wants property to be returned or, for example, the window to be fixed. We don't actually punish the wrongdoer, we educate the wrongdoer. Like, taking him or her to projects which are existing in the township like the brick factory at the end of Guguletu section three. Like going at Uluntu Centre ...That person would go and clean those places maybe for three months.[29]

Conclusion

The restorative philosophy is alive and well among the indigenous African populations of Africa. It is nowhere better illustrated than in South Africa where, after 400 years of generally repressive and often brutal colonisation, it continues to operate both in a pre-colonial form in rural areas such as among the Thembu in the Eastern Cape, and in adapted forms of community courts in the townships.[30]

The examples of Inkundla and the community courts illustrate the positive

178

influence that restorative justice has on community-building. They serve as a reminder of the interdependence of life. In the rural areas of the former Transkei, every adult is responsible for the upbringing of a child. If a child has been disobedient, it is up to the adult(s) concerned to report the matter to the relevant people, and together they will work out a solution. In the townships, the community courts rely on all members of the community to keep the peace and to find solutions when it has been disturbed.[31]

The restorative tradition has much to offer the new post-apartheid South Africa. Its healing, reconciling, compensating philosophy is rooted deeply within the traditions of the vast majority of its peoples. The Roman-Dutch-English law heritage, while retaining real strengths in the protection of the innocent, has a fatal flaw in its almost total focus on retribution and punishment. The violent application of the latter through imprisonment, floggings and execution has for 400 years been a blot on civilisation as a whole, and not just South Africa.

A parallel restorative system based on personal and collective responsibility, recognition of and empowerment for victims, and an overall aim of repairing damage done and healing the effects of crime, can only offer hope to all involved.

Footnotes

1. M. S. W. Bapela, 'The People's Courts in a Customary Law Perspective', Unpublished paper, Institute of Foreign and Comparative Law, UNISA, 1987
2. Monica Wilson, 'The Sotho, Venda and Tsonga', from *A History of South Africa to 1870*, edited by Monica Wilson and Leonard Thompson, 1969, 1982, Croom Helm, London and Canberra
3. Albie Sachs, *Justice in South Africa*, Chatto Heinemann for Sussex University Press, London, 1973
4. R. S. Suttner, 'Towards Judicial and Legal Integration in South Africa', *South African Law Journal*, LXXXV, 1968
5. Mike Brogden and Clifford Shearing, *Policing for a New South Africa*, Routledge, London, 1993
6. Basil Davidson, *The Africans*, Longmans Green and Co, London and Harlow, 1969
8. Ibid
9. Ibid
10. Ibid
11. Wilson, op cit
12. Ibid
13. Ibid
14. Ibid
15. Ibid
16. Ibid
17. Ibid
18. Ibid
19. Karen Van Eden, 'What Can Indigenous African Customs Teach Contemporary Juvenile Justice?', unpublished paper, Institute of Criminology, University of Cape Town, 1995.
20. Chief Holomisa interviewed by Karen Van Eden at Parliament, 14 June 1995
21. Don Pinnock, Institute of Criminology, University of Cape Town, interviewed by Karen Van Eden, 2 October 1995
22. R. M. Kessing, *Cultural Anthropology – A Contemporary Perspective*, Holt, Rhinehart, Winston, New York, 1976
23. Van Eden, op cit
24. Ibid
25. L. K. Brendtro, M. Brokenleg and S. Van Brockern, *Reclaiming Youth at Risk – Our Hope for the Future*, Bloomington, Indiana 1990

26. Brogden and Shearing, op cit
27. Van Eden, op cit
28. Sipho Citabatwa interviewed by Karen Van Eden in Guguletu, 14 July 1995
29. D. Nina, 'Popular Justice in a New South Africa: from People's Courts to Community Courts in Alexandra', occasional paper, Centre for Applied Legal Studies, Johannesburg, 1992
30. Citabatwa, op cit
31. Van Eden, op cit

CHAPTER FOURTEEN

Restorative Justice: A Parallel System

There are many cases involving crime where justice could be much better served if only the mindsets of the parties involved were more open. Court hearings are just one way of seeking justice. Other ways include more use of diversion, victim-offender facilitation and restorative justice conferencing.

Recently in the District Court in Christchurch, a case was called involving a defended hearing in which a taxi driver had been charged with assault. The case took two hours to complete. In essence the charge related to queue-hopping at the airport and whether the defendant had pushed or hit the complainant. At the end of the hearing the judge found the case proven. He decided that because the man had already been suspended for nearly five months from work (at a cost to him and his family of five months' income) and would lose his taxi licence if convicted, he would discharge him under Section 19 of the Criminal Justice Act, and order $200 court costs. The complainant and his two witnesses left the court grumbling at the perceived 'light' penalty, while the defendant appeared upset that his story wasn't believed.

Was this process the best way to seek justice in this instance? I believe not. It was good practice under the present parameters. But let's briefly examine what happened. No fewer than 11 people were tied up for a morning – the judge, the stenographer, the registrar, the complainant, the defendant, four witnesses and two police. It cost the taxpayer several thousand dollars, including Income Support payments for five months. None of the key players went away happy. There was no reconciliation, no acceptance of the result, no peace.

A much more productive and cheaper way could have been found using restorative justice processes. Following a model similar to that now used universally in youth justice cases, the various interested parties including the victim and the offender could have met with a facilitator. Provided both agreed and the offender acknowledged responsibility for the incident, a round-table meeting could have been held in conducive surroundings. It might have been held on the airport site, resulted in apology, forgiveness, reconciliation, some compensation and a continuation of work for all. The case could have been resolved within days, instead of taking five months. Which system makes greater sense? The answer is clear, I suggest, to anyone with an open mind.

Recently the police charged a University of Canterbury cleaner with the theft of 22 envelopes valued at $2. Since the cleaner pleaded not guilty, there was a defended hearing. This lasted the best part of two days and cost taxpayers more than $3000. All this so that 'justice' might be done. When it's all over, each envelope was worth more than $150!

And was justice done? Of course not. Whatever other component parts justice has, common sense should be one. There was no common sense here. This was retributive justice in its most ridiculous form.

In this case, university authorities had already effected justice by meeting with the cleaner and dealing with the matter internally. They adopted a restorative approach and the result was a satisfactory outcome to all. Justice was actually achieved. But not for the long arm of the state.

It is time to take seriously the appalling results of nearly 200 years of a failed criminal justice system which is fixated on vengeance and punishment and employs an ever-expanding system of imprisonment. It is time too to set aside the mindset of the colonial master and look to the sound elements within most indigenous traditions which, with adaptation, could supply a much better form of criminal justice. Quite simply, there are better ways of doing things.

There is a dingy, run-down housing estate in Walstall in England where community organisations are working with the West Midlands Police in setting up a motor project. Young people in the area are given old cars to repair and when they are fixed the youngsters can race them against each other. The whole estate is involved and it costs practically nothing.

In England it costs aproximately £20,000 a year to keep a person in prison. Spending some of that money on projects such as the motor project protects cars and people. It gives the young people some direction and fulfilment, and most no longer end up in prison.[1]

There is a tremendous amount of emotional baggage to any discussions on issues of law and order, crime, prisons, harsher penalties, habilitation centres and safer communities. Many of us have been victims of crime. The law, the police and the government often seem to be impotent in dealing with rising amounts of criminal behaviour in the community. Fear begets more fear.

Many claim that the law is unjust anyway, that it is tilted to favour the rich and powerful while prosecuting the poor unfairly. It is generally accepted that imprisonment makes people worse rather than better. All the various policies tried over the years within the retributive penal system have failed dismally. The straight, hard-labour, bread-and-water routine so popular in the early part of this century brutalised inmates, turning many into incorrigible recidivists. The medical model of corrections, prevalent in the 1960s and 1970s, whereby everything was seen in terms of therapeutic needs, also failed.

The unit-management style currently in vogue will ultimately be seen as a failure too. Programmes are useful in prisons, but the negative framework of punishment in which they are conducted nearly always negates the possibility of substantial positive change. Just as you cannot cure an alcoholic in a brewery, so you cannot reform inmates in a prison.

You cannot punish and reconcile at the same time. Contradictory objectives can only lead to stalemate or total paralysis. This is not a problem of opinion or ideology. It is simply a question of logic.

The case-management system, which the Justice Department in New Zealand applied as its major response to the 1989 Prison Systems Review (Roper Report), seeks to reconcile the contradictory objectives of reform within a punishing environment. Justice Roper said you couldn't have both together. It would not work. He was right. While a reforming approach does have some positive effects within the prison system, it does not succeed in its aim of changing the basic orientation of the vast majority of inmates. Case management has simply become a better system of control of inmates. It has also allowed the Department of Corrections to continue to expand its empire and its burgeoning budget, and maintain its power base.

A Parallel System

Restorative justice is a philosophy that embraces a wide range of human emotions, including healing, mediation, compassion, forgiveness, mercy, reconciliation as well as sanction when appropriate. It also recognises a world view that says we are all interconnected and that what we do, be it for good or evil, has an impact on others. Restorative justice offers a process whereby those affected by criminal behaviour, be they victims, offenders, the families involved or the wider community, all have a part in resolving the issues that flow from the offending.

Under restorative justice, victims and offenders assume central roles and the state takes a back seat. The process does not focus on vengeance and punishment but seeks to heal both the community and the individuals involved. This is done by a process that puts the notion of reparation, not punishment, at the centre.

In simple terms, while retributive justice asks first 'how do we punish this offender?', restorative justice asks 'how do we repair the damage of this offending?' They provide two distinctly different starting points, embracing two different philosophies.

Under a philosophy of restorative justice, crime is no longer defined as an attack on the state but rather as an offence by one person against another. It is based on a recognition of the humanity of both offender and victim. The goal of the restorative process is to heal the wounds of every person affected by the offence, including the victim and the offender. Options are explored that focus on repairing the damage.

The main process takes place at a community group conference (CGC), chaired by a facilitator, to which victims and offenders and appropriate support people are invited. The three key components of the restorative justice equation are the offender, the victim and the community. Obviously a willingness to co-operate is central to the concept. To be involved in any useful way, the offender must acknowledge responsibility for the crime committed and express honest regret. The full implications of the offence need to be spelt out and confronted. The offender needs also to face the causes of the offending and, where possible, make restitution. Concrete evidence of more appropriate behaviour in the future is also required.

Victims need to examine their feelings and take full advantage of any support network that will facilitate healing. Victims are helped to see that their own victimisation is only intensified by feelings of retributive action against the offender. Where appropriate they become involved in the process of restorative justice with the offender and the community.

The community's role is to create the conditions most favourable to the restoration of both offender and victim. It aids the healing process by providing mediators, judges and the like. Provided there is co-operation, the parties reach agreement about repairing the damage where possible. Obviously in some cases like murder or rape it is not, although healing, forgiveness and reconciliation are still possible after a period. Besides whatever reparation is possible, the offenders may be required to work in the local community for a set period, perform periodic detention or even go to prison. The important thing is that no-one gets shut out of the process. Everyone gets heard.

All those involved get a chance to put a human face on the crime. They have a chance to begin a process of healing. They become empowered again. The offenders get to take responsibility for their criminal behaviour. Each of these processes produces an added dividend for family life and the wider community. There will be less alienation, stronger bonding among family members, a greater degree of personal and social empowerment.

It is important to note that not all victims are going to necessarily welcome a community group conference. Many will be very wary. This will especially be true for many child and female victims of violence and/or sexual attacks. Such conferences must at all costs seek to prevent victims from becoming doubly victimised. A major issue here is that of power imbalance between the victim and the offender. This should not be underestimated. Such cases underline the need for skilful, well-trained facilitators. It should be noted also that secondary victims – family and friends – may fruitfully participate in such a conference without the primary victim's presence. Given the effect of such crimes and the amount of grief and pain they cause, it can be argued that community group conferences are more needed in these instances than for many other crimes.

In a controlled facilitated process the offenders meet the victims at a CGC and have to face up to what they have done. They hear of the victims' anger and anxiety, and the victims hear the offenders' explanation. There may be mitigating circumstances; there may not. The offender may apologise, may express a genuine wish to change. Provided there is co-operation, the parties reach agreement about repairing the damage.

It would be silly to claim that all the damage can be repaired immediately – sometimes it never can be. Certainly in murder and rape cases it can't. But at least those involved get the chance to put a human face on the crime and begin the process of healing. They become empowered again. The offenders get to take some responsibility for their criminal behaviour.

The idea of incorporating compensation, reconciliation, healing and forgiveness into criminal law is more than merely corrective. Such elements reflect a whole fresh way of approaching criminal offending in the community. They present a vision of improving life right throughout the community, and of making justice more accessible, effective and fair.

Restorative justice involves a shift from state power to community power. It should be remembered that it is only in recent centuries that the state has come to play such a prominent role in citizens' lives. Prior to that the community retained most power within its local confines.

Ranjini Rebera, a Sri Lankan-born Christian feminist, identifies three images of power: *power over*, *power to* and *power with*. *Power over* reflects the typical authoritarian model of the traditional court: the judge in an all-powerful position, everyone else in varying positions determined by relationship to that position. *Power to* can be seen as a source of energy or the ability to create.

Power with reflects the new relationship found with restorative justice. Here members of families work collectively to create a momentum that leads to positive change and growth for them all. This type of power transforms and is available even to the most vulnerable members of the family. No longer are people purely recipients of authoritative directives from on high. Within the restorative structures they become responsible for what will happen or not happen.[2]

Advantages of Restorative Justice
The restorative process offers tremendous advantages over the retributive system. Five stand out:
1. Restorative Justice is Indigenous
In countries such as Australia, South Africa, New Zealand, Canada and Ireland,

which are all seeking to shape new independent identities and discard the worst effects of either oppression or colonial history, the reshaping of the processes of law is an essential dimension and sign of a developing maturity and sense of identity. There is certainly no logical reason – except vested interest – why the best elements of the indigenous traditions of many lands could not be applied to criminal offending. They have much to teach Western countries. Such wisdom and practices would leave us all the richer.

Sentencing Circles, the tradition of the First Nation peoples, having successfully in recent years completed a period of trial under modern conditions, could be adopted more extensively in Canada. The same restorative philosophy could be applied much more widely south of the border among the various nations of Native Americans.

Right throughout Africa, Central and Latin America and in Asia, indigenous cultures survive and offer ways forward for criminal justice processes. In Australia, where Aboriginal peoples are the subject of widespread attention by the police – an Aborigine is 27 times more likely to be imprisoned than a white Australian – traditional justice practices could be expanded among Aboriginal communities, and given full recognition and status by the government and state authorities.

Maori traditionally operate a system of justice based on the overall good of the community and the desire to restore its wellbeing. A restorative model of justice could be a bridge to partially meeting demands from some quarters for a separate Maori system of criminal justice. Such a process would not fulfil the guarantee of te tino rangatiratanga (absolute authority) contained in article 2 of the Treaty of Waitangi. Nor would it provide the protection of te ritenga Maori guaranteed in article 4, which is part of the oral tradition of the treaty. This tradition allows for the protection of religious freedom and customary law and formed part of the discussion held before the treaty was signed. The power to make law and exercise authority through Maori legal institutions would still not rest with Maori.

But if the current retributive system could adopt the philosophy and praxis of restorative justice, then there would be no essential difference between the philosophy and aims of the system operating and those of traditional Maori justice, be the setting in a courtroom, a marae or a church hall. Different systems, different procedures and different styles would reflect different cultures. But there would be one philosophy, one aim, one praxis.

2. Restorative Justice Places Victims at the Centre of the Justice Equation

Under the current retributive system victims are shoved either right outside or stuck on the periphery. How much of the punitive wave of anger that sweeps the country after a particularly nasty crime flows from the unresolved anger, grief, hurt and pain of the victims of crime? We all initially feel like stringing up a thief who has taken our car or burgled our home. But our emotions settle with time and we all know that such a lashing-out would probably do as much damage as the original crime and would not solve anything.

The experience of our youth justice system offers us some positive insights. Given the opportunity, it is amazing how contrite and shamed so many young people become after meeting their victims at a family group conference called under the Children, Young Persons and Their Families Act. It is also noticeable how forgiving, gracious and helpful so many of the victims are towards the offenders once they have been able to put a human face and history on the crime.

Anne Hayden, network co-ordinator for the Te Oritenga Restorative Justice group, says that victims need validation of their experience. They need recognition of their trauma and the opportunity to express it.

> While on the one hand I do not tell them what to ask for at a community group conference, I do raise the possibility with them that it is often helpful to think about what they would consider satisfactory outcomes. They might have questions they would like to ask directly of the offender. Similarly, emotions they have experienced and may still experience are more healthily dealt with if they are directed at the source of the original injury or trauma, the offender. I emphasise that it is okay to cry, or to verbally express anger. It is important to appreciate that each person harmed by crime has temporarily lost power or control over themselves or their loved ones, possessions, or property for at least the duration of the crime. More often than not this powerlessness remains with them in varying degrees for an undefined length of time ranging from one hour to many decades. The powerlessness can manifest itself in lost autonomy, confidence or safely participating in previously habitual activities.

Howard Zehr also writes of the needs of victims to speak their feelings, to receive restitution, to experience justice. They need answers to questions that plague them such as who was at fault; so often victims blame themselves. But above all else, victims need the experience of forgiveness.

I am not suggesting that forgiveness comes easily, but it is a process of letting go. Victims need to be able to let go of the crime experience so that while it will always – must always – be part of them, it will no longer dominate their lives. Without that, closure is difficult and the wound may fester for years.[3]

In the current retributive system victims so often find themselves mere footnotes in the process of justice. The offender has taken power from them and the criminal law system also denies them power. Re-empowering victims enables them to be healed.

Many years of prison ministry have shown me how little remorse there is among inmates simply because they never have to meet their victims and see the devastation they have caused. This hardening of the arteries of emotion and repression of shame and grief are the principal causes of recidivism and in so many committing even greater crimes upon release. Prison guarantees re-offending and offers victims nothing.

3. Restorative Justice Offers Healing To All Involved

I often draw people's attention to the case of Father Michael Lapsley, the New Zealand-born Anglican priest who was a victim of a South African state security letter-bomb. It blew off both of his hands, he lost an eye and had horrendous internal injuries, which still plague him today. If anyone had reason to feel embittered he did. But he is a brilliant model for those who seek to deal with the effects of crime in their lives and the need for victims to work towards forgiveness.

> After the bombing, I was as helpless as a newborn baby for three months. There was literally nothing I could do for myself. But I also said to myself that my struggle now is a struggle to get well, a struggle to return, a struggle to live my life fully, as joyfully, as completely as possible, and that would be my victory. I also realised that if I was filled with hatred, bitterness, self-pity, desire for revenge, that they would have failed to kill my body but would have killed my soul, and I would be a permanent victim. Today I would say that I see myself not simply as a survivor, but I am a victor over evil and hatred and death that apartheid represented, a sign of the triumph of good.
>
> When it comes to forgiveness, I would say this. Forgiveness does not come cheaply. In South Africa, we sometimes try to make it something glib, cheap and easy. Forgiveness is about confession, about remorse, about amendment of life, about reparation. That is why I believe in restorative justice, not retributive justice. If someone says to me, 'I am sorry I did that and I want to make some sort of amends,' I would say, "Of course, I forgive you".[4]

Archbishop Desmond Tutu, who chaired the Truth and Reconciliation Commission and heard literally thousands of testimonies from victims and offenders, speaks eloquently about forgiveness as an essential component of healing.

> I have been bowled over by the incredible humility one has experienced from the victims, both black and white, who have suffered as much as they have. By rights they should have been hate-ridden by lust for revenge. They have exhilarated me by how ready they are to forgive. I have come to see that yes, of course, you have to have an acknowledgment by the wrongdoer that they have done something that was very wrong, that they owe to us confession so that the victim, the survivor, be enabled, be willing to forgive.
>
> But I have come to believe fervently that forgiveness is not just a spiritual and ethereal thing unrelated to the real world, the harsh world out there. I have come to believe very fervently that without forgiveness, there is no future.[5]

The dictionary defines forgiveness as a process of ceasing to feel resentment against another. It would appear to include the idea of giving up one's natural impulse to strike back and exact revenge. It is often a very difficult thing to accomplish, particularly in a culture that is staunch and macho in its philosophy. 'Don't get mad, get even' is symptomatic of the philosophy of our modern consumer culture. It reflects the philosophy of revenge.

For victims of crime, forgiveness is letting go of the power that the offence and the offender have over them, while not condoning or excusing that person. It means no longer letting the offence and the offender dominate. Without this experience of forgiveness, without this closure, the wound festers and takes over our lives. It, and the offender, are in control. Real forgiveness allows one to move from victim to survivor.[6]

Offenders are not only punished by the criminal justice system, but severely damaged as well. They don't have to face up to their offending, so they don't grow in responsibility. Offenders are not really held accountable, despite rhetoric to the contrary. Judges often talk about accountability, but what they usually mean is that when you do something wrong, you must take your punishment. Genuine accountability means, first, that when you offend, you need to understand and take responsibility for what you did. Offenders need to be encouraged to understand the real human consequences of their actions.

But accountability has a second component as well: offenders need to be encouraged to take responsibility for making things right, for righting the wrong.[7]

Just as victims need an experience of forgiveness, so do offenders. How else can they put the past behind them and positively confront the future? The retributive criminal philosophy provides little encouragement and virtually no room for an offender to confess, repent, change direction, turn life around, admit responsibility and make things right. The justice system simply encourages anger, rationalisation, denial of guilt and responsibility, feelings of powerlessness and dehumanisation. As with victims, the wounds just fester and grow.[8]

It is interesting to note that in Japan, which has a very low imprisonment rate of 37 per 100,000, forgiveness is a central part of the criminal justice philosophy. Letters of apology from the offenders to their victims are frequently followed by letters from the victim to the police asking that criminal proceedings be dismissed.[9]

Forgiveness is not something that the victim does for the benefit of the offender. It is the process of the victim letting go of the rage and pain of the injustice so that he or she can resume living freed from the power of the criminal violation. We encounter injustice daily in our homes, our places of work and in the affairs of nations. We can ill afford to respond to the grievances, large or small, in ways that are likely to escalate conflict and perpetuate cycles of violence. In many situations it is precisely the quest for justice as retribution that prevents many grievances from ever being channelled into forums that can bring resolution and redress. Limiting justice to retribution turns interpersonal disputes into tit-for-tat feuds, and border skirmishes into fully fledged wars.[10]

4. Restorative Justice Places Responsibility for Crime in the Hands of Those Who Commit It

Restorative justice brings a dimension of community responsibility into being. It recognises that we all form part of the one human family and that we have responsibilities towards one another. To focus always on the individual as if we always exist outside a grouping at work, at home, in the community, in a sports club – wherever – is to focus too narrowly. It is one of the great weaknesses of the Western judicial system.

Sheeting home responsibility for criminal behaviour to the individual in the context of family and friends usually brings massive shame and regret to offenders. How often have I sat in jail and talked to burglars who had done 20, or 30 or 80 burglaries, and still have no comprehension of the damage done in people's lives? To them it is simply property stolen to feed their families, their drug habits, or their greed. It is the same with most other offenders. Only a tiny percentage ever face the reality of what they have done.

Their general approach towards a system that treats them like schoolchildren is that once their punishment is done, there is no more need to worry. 'I've done my time' becomes their catchcry. They have had their 'just deserts', says the state. They have paid their debt to society. There is clearly no room for either victims or positive change in such a scenario.

5. Restorative Results Are Better For All

Victims consistently report their appreciation of having had the opportunity to tell their stories and to confront offenders with their sense of injury, anger and outrage. Responses by offenders show more frequent acknowledgment of guilt, deeper appreciation for the consequences of their wrongdoing and a greater sense of remorse. The statistics from carefully monitored evaluations of a variety of programmes evidence the extraordinary success of victim-offender mediation and the validity of the claims of its proponents.[11]

In research conducted in 1996 into the impact on victims of family group conferencing, Allison Morris and Gabrielle Maxwell from the Institute of Criminology, Victoria University of Wellington, found:

> Our research showed that, when victims were involved, many found this a positive process. About 60 percent of the victims interviewed described the family group conference they attended as helpful, positive and rewarding. Generally, they said that they were effectively involved in the process and felt better as a result of participating. Victims also commented on two other specific benefits for them. First, it provided them with a voice in determining appropriate outcomes. Second, they were able to meet the offender and the offender's family face to face so they could assess their attitude, understand more why the offence had occurred and assess the likelihood of it recurring.[12]

The British Home Office reviewed all of the victim-offender programmes in Britain. It found that, as in the US, victims express extremely high levels of satisfaction both in terms of the fairness of the process and the opportunity to participate. Through mediated contracts victims received higher levels of compensation than as a result of mandatory orders. Lower rates of recidivism reflected improvements in offender behaviour.

Probably the best model to reflect upon is the process of the Children, Young Persons and Their Families Act, which has been tremendously successful in New Zealand. Since the act came into force in 1989, using a restorative philosophy and the family group conference as its principle mechanism, the number of young offenders appearing before the courts has dropped from 13,000 cases a year to 1800. Clearly the rate of young people undergoing custodial sentences has also shown a dramatic reduction. Restorative conferencing among the young is obviously having some success.

New Zealand's principal Youth Court judge, Michael Brown, says the primary objectives of a criminal justice system must include healing the breach of social harmony and social relationships, putting right the wrong, and making reparation rather than concentrating on punishment. The ability of the victim to have input at the family group conference is, or ought to be, one of the most significant virtues of the youth justice procedures. On the basis of our experience to date, we can expect to be amazed at the generosity of spirit of many victims and (to the surprise of the professionals participating) the absence of retributive demands and vindictiveness. Victims' responses are in direct contrast to the hysterical, media-generated responses to which we are so often exposed.[13]

The New Zealand police are equally enthusiastic. Senior Sergeant Laurie Gabites of Police National Headquarters, Wellington, sees the act as law that has offered the community more benefits than many other pieces of legislation. It has offered benefits for both victims and offenders. It has offered offenders a chance to participate in the decision-making. It has offered help and support for victims and given them a chance to play a part in the justice system that has probably never been equalled anywhere else in the world.

It has also involved families in a way that has seen them making decisions about breaches of the law by way of consensus. He believes the law deserves closer examination as a blueprint for legislation to be applied to adults.[14]

Gabrielle Maxwell studied the act in its first three years of operation.

> We looked at nearly 700 young offenders. We looked at over 200 cases which went to a family group conference and 70 cases that appeared in the Youth Court. I want to celebrate some of the successes we saw at that time. I want to allay some of the myths there are about the problems with the FGCs and I also want to identify some of the weaknesses, bearing in mind that this was 1990 and 1991, just a year after the act got under way and I think we need time to learn

how to operate a new system. In fact in some ways I want to stress how extraordinary these successes are in such a revolutionary endeavour.[15]

Criminology Professor Allison Morris writes: There are a number of clear advantages in restorative justice: offenders can be held accountable, victims can be heard, victims may feel better as a result of the process, and outcomes which more fully address victims' and offenders needs or interests can be reached. Importantly, many of the defects arising from current examples of restorative justice relate to bad practice rather than to fundamental flaws in its underlying properties.

In addition, there are advantages in restorative justice to the State. Family group conferencing in the youth justice system, for example, has resulted in fewer court appearances – a reduction by almost two thirds between 1987 and 1996 – and fewer custodial sentences – a reduction by more than 50% between 1987 and 1996. And, contrary to public and media perceptions, juvenile crime is not escalating out of control. Though it has increased, the rate of increase over the last ten years is smaller than for adults. The fastest growing crime population has been the over 30s: an increase of 155% compared with an increase of 24% in juvenile crime!

But the most important question is, 'does restorative justice reduce reconviction'? There are some encouraging data here from some pilot restorative justice projects but the follow up period was very short. Gabrielle Maxwell and I, on the other hand, have been involved in trying to track a sample of young offenders who took part in family group conferences in 1990–91. We found that about three-quarters were not convicted within a year, around a third were conviction free after six years and that around a third were persistently reconvicted after six years.

Is this better or worse than the previous youth justice system or than the adult system? It is impossible to say with confidence – there are no comparable data. A recent study by Psychological Services in the Department of Corrections showed that the reconviction rates after five years of offenders aged 14 to 17 who received adult sanctions were between 85% and 90%. Clearly, against this, the conferencing sample did quite well, but this is not really an appropriate comparison because of differences between the two samples in terms of severity of offence or persistence of offending. It does show, however, that conventional penal sanctions have minimal effect and it is difficult to imagine that conferencing could do any worse than this.[16]

Praise for the act comes from Australia too. Criminologist John Braithwaite, of the Australian National University, Canberra, writes that reforms to the New Zealand juvenile justice system since 1989 have had the effect of bringing shame and personal and family accountability for wrongdoing back into the justice process.

He says if the young offender's football coach is a person looked upon with respect, then he could be invited to the FGC. Braithwaite has attended a conference with 30 members of the community in the room. Conservative politicians who say they want to strengthen the family and do something for victims as the forgotten people in the criminal process should support this process, Braithwaite says.[17]

New Zealand's Future: Restorative Justice for Adults

Things have been moving in New Zealand towards restorative justice for adults for some years, and facilitation groups have been established in many parts of the country. In Timaru, for example, Project Turnaround, an official government pilot programme, has been operating very successfully for two years and has dealt with with more than 200 cases. Fewer than 10 percent of contracts agreed to at restorative conferences fail to be completed and result in the offender returning to court. Both imprisonment and re-offending rates have dropped dramatically in that time. In 1993 under the old regime, 116 people went to prison from South Canterbury. In 1997 only 30 were jailed. Crime has gone down in the region in practically every year since this form of sentencing was introduced. For example, in 1997 crime levels dropped 7 percent regionally while the national crime level continued to rise.

In Auckland more than 70 cases of adult restorative justice were held in 1998 involving community group conferences. Nearly all contracts were accepted by the court and completed by the offenders. One or two high-profile ones were not.

A sampling of those cases includes:

- A man charged with dangerous driving causing death. There were 15 present at the CGC, which took three hours. After apologies and explanations from the defendant and responses from the victim's family, the CGC recommended a $6000 donation go to an education fund in memory of the deceased, and that the defendant do some community work.
- A woman charged with threatening to kill, possession of a firearm and forgery of a prescription. She expressed deep regret and explained the reasons for her actions. There were seven present at the two-hour conference, which recommended psychiatric, drug and alcohol assessment, attendance at an anger-management programme and extensive counselling.
- A man charged with assault with intent to injure. There were eight present for the CGC. After apology and explanations, the conference recommended alcohol counselling, an anti-violence programme and community work.
- Two young men charged with the aggravated robbery of a dairy with a toy pistol. The offenders showed deep remorse. They apologised to the 12 people present at the CGC, offered to do community work and pay some compensation. The CGC, which lasted more than two hours, accepted a probation officer's recommendation of a two-year suspended prison sentence.
- A club manager charged with theft as a servant. He apologised to club officials in a CGC and agreed to repay the $6500 stolen in instalments. The police later withdrew the charge.

- A man charged with common assault. He agreed at his CGC to recommendations that he do an anger-management programme, pay $500 towards new dentures for the victim, attend alcohol abuse counselling and write a letter of apology to his victim, who was not present. Seven attended his conference.
- A man charged with assault with intent to commit grievous bodily harm. The offender apologised to his victim at his CGC, at which five were present. The conference recommended he do an anger-management programme, write a letter of apology, do 50 hours of night classes for School Certificate English and maths, go to race relations classes at the local polytech, and that he and his partner (his victim) attend marriage couple counselling.
- A man charged with aggravated robbery, attempted kidnapping, threatening to kill and assault with a weapon attended a CGC with 10 others. He showed genuine remorse, and listened intently to the victims as they expressed their outrage at what had happened. The conference recommended that given the likelihood of a prison sentence, he should develop work skills, do anger management, get some education and seek psychological counselling while in prison. He later received 18 months' imprisonment, a substantial reduction because of his remorse and willingness to change.
- A grandfather charged with indecent assault and doing an indecent act attended a CGC with 10 others. After apology and explanation, many tears and much anger, the conference recommended counselling and therapy, that he do the SAFE programme for sexual offenders, be given some form of periodic detention and a suspended prison term. Later the judge agreed with the non-custodial recommendations, but noted that 15 months' imprisonment would have been the alternative, had the man not shown remorse and a desire to change.
- A woman charged with fraud by using a document to obtain pecuniary advantage attended a CGC. She apologised for her behaviour and showed genuine remorse. She accepted the recommendations of the conference that she write a letter of apology, repay $1500 at $50 per week, and perform 80 hours of community service.
- A young man charged with three counts of theft attended a CGC. He apologised to his victim and agreed he had let down everyone who had tried to help him. The conference recommended reparation of $100, 40 hours of community work, that he seek out a drug programme and get himself physically fit.
- A young man charged with excess alcohol, causing death and injury and driving while disqualified came to a CGC attended by nine people, including the dead person's parents. He offered an apology and showed remorse. The conference acknowledged that imprisonment was likely but, even in the face of this, the offender agreed to write full letters of apology to all affected, do a drug and alcohol programme, attend an alternatives to violence programme, continue study for his trade certificate and, at their invitation, to continue to correspond with the deceased's parents. He later received 18 months' imprisonment.

Some dimensions of restorative justice already have widespread support in New Zealand. In early 1994 a *Listener*/Heylen poll found that in response to the statement 'offenders should meet with their victims and where possible try to put things right', 55 percent agreed or agreed strongly, while a further 20 percent were either neutral or didn't know. Only a quarter disagreed. In response to a further statement that we should 'place more emphasis on probation where offenders may be supervised in the community', 62 percent agreed or agreed strongly, a further 20 percent were either neutral or didn't know, and only 18 percent disagreed.

It would appear that, contrary to radio talkback wisdom, there is a reasonable foundation in the wider community prepared to accept a structural move away from imprisonment towards more positive, restorative, non-custodial options in New Zealand.

In November 1997 the New Zealand Cabinet accepted a proposal recommending four pilot restorative justice processes be set up to last a period of three years, and sought $7.2 million to fund them. About 1200 cases were expected to be dealt with in this time. The money was not forthcoming from the 1998 Budget but should be available in the future. These pilots would be in addition to any existing schemes, such as Project Turnaround.

In July 1998 the Court of Appeal in New Zealand heard its first case involving restorative justice. The court made it clear in its judgment, R v. Clotworthy (CA114/98), that it believed restorative justice principles were already in place in New Zealand law. The judges found for the Crown in this particular case on charges which involved wounding with intent and aggravated assault. However, in their judgment they said:

> We would not wish this judgment to be seen as expressing any general opposition to the concept of restorative justice (essentially the policies behind sections 11 and 12 of the Criminal Justice Act). Those policies must, however, be balanced against other sentencing policies, particularly in this case those inherent in section 5, dealing with cases of serious violence. Which aspect should predominate will depend on an assessment of where the balance should lie in a particular case. Even if the balance is found, as in this case, to lie in favour of section 5 policies, the restorative aspects can have, as here, a significant impact on the length of the term of imprisonment which the court is directed to impose. They find their place in the ultimate outcome that way.

Conclusion

Many people said in years past that the youth justice system was beyond reform. Our history of Social Welfare homes, borstals, detention centres, youth prisons and corrective training was one of failure, yet because they were such a part of an entrenched retributive and punishing philosophy, little could be done to change the situation. It was all a part of our English retributive heritage, and the radical shift needed to really make any substantial difference would never happen. History has shown such sceptics to be wrong.

Restorative justice is a philosophy that offers us a chance to practise the qualities that make people great – true justice based on apology, compassion, healing, mercy, reconciliation, forgiveness and, where appropriate, sanction. It offers the processes whereby those affected by criminal behaviour – be they victims, offenders, the families involved or the wider community – all can have a part in resolving the issues that flow from the offending.

We need a quality of criminal justice that recognises the immense value that these virtues bring to the quality of life and acknowledges the centrality of and need to enhance and protect the common good. No-one is saying 'be soft on crime'. Rather the plea is to take this tougher option and utilise all the great human qualities that reflect a power that can and does change human behaviour for the better.

Now is the time for a radical shift to a parallel system of criminal justice involving restorative justice processes. These include conferencing, victim-offender facilitation and more diversion.

History is teaching us every day that if we continue to operate a criminal justice system oriented principally towards punishment based on vengeance, and continue to ignore the opportunities that restorative justice offers, we will continue to reap its bitter harvest of high crime rates, fear and insecurity. The time for change is now if we are to bequeath the 21st century a criminal justice system worthy of its name.

Footnotes

1. Vivien Stern, Cantor Lecture, 'Crime, Policy and the Role of Punishment', London, *RAS Journal*, October 1993
2. *The Tablet* (NZ), 16 January 1994
3. Howard Zehr, *IARCA* Journal, March 1991, pp6-8
4. Rev. Michael Lapsley, S.S.M., *Submission to the Commission for Truth and Reconciliation*, Kimberley, South Africa, 10 June 1996.
5. Archbishop Desmond Tutu, Interview with Linda Skates, Radio New Zealand, 7 June 1998
6. Howard Zehr, *Changing Lenses*, Herald Press, Scottdale, Pennsylvania, 1990
7. Ibid
8. Ibid
9. John Haley, paper from *Restorative Justice on Trial*, ed Heinz Messmer and Hans-Uwe Otto, NATO Scientific Series, Kluwer Academic Publishers, London, 1992, p105
10. Dean Peacey, ibid, p557
11. John Haley, *Crime and Justice Network Newsletter*, Mennonite Central Committee, Akron, Pennsylvania, September 1991
12. Allison Morris and Gabrielle Maxwell, article in *Criminology Aotearoa/New Zealand*, September 1996, No. 6
13. M. J. A. Brown, Viewpoint, *NZ Listener*, 25 September 1993
14. L. Gabites, New Zealand Law Conference transcript, 4 March 1993
15. Gabrielle Maxwell, ibid
16. Allison Morris and Warren Young, *Reforming Criminal Justice*, September 1998
17. John Braithwaite, *The Youth Court in New Zealand A New Model of Justice*, Legal Research Foundation, No. 34, 1993

Glossary

Maori

Aotearoa	traditional name for New Zealand believed given by Maori explorer Kupe, now in general use as an alternative name
aroha	love
hara	crime, offence
hapu	sub-tribe
hui	gathering, meeting
iwi	tribe, people
karakia	prayers
kaumatua	elder
kawanatanga	government
kei te pai	all right, OK, good
kuia	woman elder, old wise woman
mana	personal standing, prestige, influence, power
Maori	name given to the indigenous people of Aotearoa/New Zealand
marae	meeting ground
marama	light, daylight
matuatanga	parenting role
mea tuhonohono	bringing harmony, togetherness
muru	rob, plunder, confiscate
Ngai Tahu	major tribe in the South island
Ngati Kahu	North Island tribe
Ngati Porou	major tribe on the East Coast, North Island
Ngati Te Rangi	tribe on the west coast, North Island
Ngati Ranginui	tribe on the west coast, North Island
Nga Puhi	major tribe in Northland
Pakeha	name given by Maori to those of European descent
pakeke	adult, difficult
putao	widow

rangatira	chief, elder
ritenga Maori	Maori custom
rongopai	Gospel
runanga	council of elders
Tainui	major North Island tribe
taha wairua	spiritual matters
tangata	person, people
tangi	funeral, tears, weeping
taniko	embroided border
taonga	treasures
tapu	sacred, forbidden, of the gods
taua muru	raiding party
tikana Maori	Maori customs, rules
tikana o nga hara	criminal code
tino rangatiratanga	sovereignty
tipuna	ancestors
tohunga	expert, specialist, priest
Te Wai Pounamu	South Island
utu	price, revenge
whaikorero	make a speech
whanau	family, including extended family
whakama	shame
whakapapa	geneology, ancestry
whare	house
wharenui	meeting house
wharerunanga	assembly house
whare tangata	sacred personhood

Samoan

'aiga	extended family
ali'i	a high-ranking chief tracing genealogy back to the gods
aumaga	a group of untitled men
fa'a Samoa	Samoan lifestyle and traditions
fono	village council of chiefs
'ie toga	fine mat
ifoga	practice of humbling oneself to compensate for an injury
malae	marae, meeting area
mamalu	dignity
mana	influence, power, prestige
Mata'afa	titled chief

198

matai	a chief
nu'u	district, field
Papalangi	European
tulafale	an orator or a lower-ranking chief with special duties

Aboriginal

janarumi	council of discussion or talk (Jaraldi)
kopara	debt settling, a ritualised response after a birth, death or marriage to restore the accepted spiritual balance
magarada or *manejag*	a gathering involving combat to settle a grievance (Arnhem Land)
moity	family grouping
mulgree	law of Creation
naduni	sickness (Jaraldi)
nathagura	fire ritual (Waranuna)
nildjara	pointing bone (Jaraldi)

Irish

agae fine or *cenn fine*	head of a wide extended family
aigre	a Brehon, an advocate or barrister
breitheamh	a judge
brithem	a Brehon, a judge, an arbitrator
boaire	a big farmer
clann (tuath)	clan, small tribe, petty kingdom
cuirmtig	a regional assembly open to all clansmen
cumal	a unit of value; also a female slave
cumbal senorba	a portion of land set aside for the support of widows, orphans and childless elderly couples
dal	assembly open to heads of septs and possibly fines
doer	unfree
drui (druid)	priest, prophet, teacher
eiric or *eric*	a fine for murder or manslaughter
feis	festival
fine	family or extended family
fintiu	land owned by the family
flaithe	a chief of a family or a group of families
flaithe-fine	the male head of the extended family
log n-enech	honour-price, or literally 'the price of his face'
maighin digona	a sanctuary around a house
nemed	a privileged person, sacred, holy

ocaire	a small farmer
oenach	a regular assembly for political, social or commercial transactions. It could also be a fair or community gathering
sept	members of related extended families. Similar to a Maori hapu.
set	a treasure, something of value
slogad	playing host
soer	free
tocomra	a special assembly at which a chief or king might be elected
tuaithe	an area or territory
tuath (pl. tuatha)	common term for a clan, small tribe, petty kingdom

Hebrew

hesed	love/justice
mispat	justice, right relationships
shalom	peace, harmony, wholeness
shillem	recompense
shillum	paying back
t'sedeka	justice, seeking truth
t'shuvah	a halt, a turnabout